THE
ANDREW MURRAY
DAILY READER

BOOKS BY ANDREW MURRAY

Abiding in Christ
Absolute Surrender
The Andrew Murray Daily Reader
The Believer's Daily Renewal
Believing Prayer
The Blood of Christ
Divine Healing
The Fullness of the Spirit
Humility
A Life of Obedience
Living a Prayerful Life
The Ministry of Intercessory Prayer
The Path to Holiness
Teach Me to Pray

THE
ANDREW MURRAY
DAILY READER

IN TODAY'S LANGUAGE

Edited by
Jeanne Hedrick
and
Nancy Renich

BETHANYHOUSE
Minneapolis, Minnesota

ABOUT
ANDREW MURRAY

MENTION THE NAME Andrew Murray and certain thoughts immediately spring to mind: consecration and wholehearted surrender to God; the all-sufficiency of Christ; the necessity of dying to self and yielding to the Holy Spirit; the joy of faith and intimate relationship with Him. These messages, which have gone around the world and changed countless lives, came from a man who was both ordinary and extraordinary.

Born in 1828 of missionary parents serving in South Africa, Andrew was blessed with a rich spiritual heritage, keen intellect, and a happy, playful disposition. His godly father played an important role in the spiritual development of Andrew and his ten siblings. He sent Andrew and his older brother John to Aberdeen, Scotland, for schooling when Andrew was ten years old. There they lived with their uncle. A devout Christian minister himself, their uncle often entertained prominent evangelists and preachers in his home. This proved to be a great spiritual advantage to the Murray boys and eventually they both decided (with some encouragement from their father) to pursue the ministry for their vocation.

In 1845 they began theological studies in Holland, at the University of Utrecht. Unfortunately rationalism and formalism were taking root in the churches there and theological studies at the university were often marked with controversy. Andrew and John managed to keep their orthodox faith, even to thrive, in that environment by seeking out the company of likeminded students.

During his years of study in Holland Andrew experienced a true spiritual conversion—an encounter that gave him great assurance in his relationship with the Lord. In a letter to his father you can sense his excitement: "And equal, I am sure, will be your delight when I tell you . . . that your son has been born again."

In 1848 Andrew and John were both ordained by the denomination of their parents: the Dutch Reformed Church. At twenty, Andrew was the youngest candidate ever ordained by that church body. Both returned to South Africa to become pastors. Andrew's church was in the frontier town of Bloemfontein. Set in the wilderness, his parish covered some 50,000 square miles. While sparsely populated with people, it had an abundance of wild creatures including ostriches, wild pigs, leopards, wolves, wild dogs, and even lions! In spite of his youth Andrew quickly won the hearts of the Dutch colonists by his hard work and ardent care for their families.

Andrew became afflicted with severe pain in his arms and hands at a young age. The doctors could find no cure, and the problem stayed with him throughout his life. But in March of 1855 he found a delightful distraction from his health problems. While staying in the home of a godly layman named Rutherfoord, he met their daughter Emma. It must have been "love at first sight" because the normally sensible pastor proposed marriage to her within a few weeks' time. She did not immediately accept but did agree to write to him. Eventually he won her heart and they were married in July 1856.

Although seven years younger than Andrew, Emma was a wonderful companion to him. She was very accomplished in music, literature, and the arts. She was intelligent and widely read, proving herself capable of managing their large household extremely well. Even more important, Emma was a godly woman who loved people; this made her well suited to the ministries of hospitality and pastoral care that she assumed. She was especially helpful with Andrew's writing, taking his dictations when he could not write himself because of his pain. Together they raised four sons and four daughters.

In 1860 they moved to Worcester to take a new congregation. When revival suddenly broke out in his church (later called the Great Revival of 1860) Andrew was skeptical at first, fearing it was nothing more than emotionalism. But when he was convinced that it was indeed a work of God's Spirit he became an important catalyst for bringing revival to other places as well.

Respect for Andrew Murray continued to grow within his denomination, and in 1864 he became joint pastor for the large Dutch Reformed church in Cape Town. Here he found many expressions for ministry in addition to pastoring, including social work for the poor, establishing schools, and serving on international church councils. In time Andrew's exhausting schedule added to his already weakened health. So when he was offered a call to a much smaller congregation in 1871 he accepted it. From that small parsonage in Wellington Andrew Murray's ministry spread around the world as he began to set to paper his spiritual insights. His ideas concerning deeper life, church renewal, and revival flowed from him like a river, producing many books that were eventually translated into several languages.

In 1882 Emma and Andrew took a trip to Europe to try to find some relief for a new malady that was afflicting him—severe and extended laryngitis. While in London he met a pastor who encouraged Andrew to seek divine healing for the condition. So they checked into a healing center and shortly thereafter his throat was instantly and permanently healed. There was a big change in him when they returned home. His daughter Emmie wrote: "More and more was developed that wonderful and beautiful humility which could never be put on, but could only be the work of the indwelling Spirit. It was felt immediately by all who came into contact with him."

Emma died of a stroke at the age of seventy in January 1905. Andrew retired from the pastorate the following year but continued to write, speak, and travel as he felt able to do so. Then on January 18, 1917, Andrew passed into the presence of the Lord. He was eighty-eight years old. On the day before he died he said to those in the house, "We have such a great and glorious God we ought to be always rejoicing in Him." As he had lived, so he died—with words of praise for His Redeemer.

The rich legacy of Andrew Murray's life continues to bless people even today. His ageless insights into the kingdom of God encourage us to pursue a deeper life of fellowship and fruitful ministry with our King. May you enjoy the benefits of all he learned at the feet of Jesus!

ABIDE AS CHRIST ABIDES IN THE FATHER

CHRIST TAUGHT His disciples that to abide in Him was to abide in His love. The hour of His suffering is near, and He cannot speak much more to them. No doubt they have many questions to ask Him about His love and their abiding in Him. He anticipates and meets their wishes, and gives them His *own life* as the best expression of His command.

> *"As the Father loved Me,*
> *I also have loved you;*
> *abide in My love. . . .*
> *You will abide in My love,*
> *just as I . . . abide*
> *in His love."*
> JOHN 15:9–10 (NKJV)

In His life of humiliation on earth He tasted the blessing and strength of knowing himself to be the object of an infinite love, and He dwelt in it all through His days; from His own example He invites you to learn that in this the secret of your rest and joy can be found. You are one with Him: Yield yourself now to be loved by Him; let your eyes and heart open up to the love that shines and presses in on you on every side.

The believer who studies this life of Christ as the pattern and the promise of what his life can be learns to understand how the verse "Without Me you can do nothing" (John 15:5 NKJV) is the forerunner of "I can do all things through Christ who strengthens me" (Philippians 4:13 NKJV). Dependence, subjection, and self-sacrifice are for the Christian as they were for Christ: the blessed path of life. Just as Christ lived through and in the Father, even so the believer lives through and in Christ.

Christ was the revelation of the Father on earth. He could be His revelation because the Father loved Him, and He lived in that love. *Believers are the revelation of Christ on earth.* They can only be this when there is perfect unity. We are His representatives, His revelation to the world that Christ loves us with an infinite love that gives itself and all it has.

Abiding in Christ

Be Filled With the Spirit

OTHER WORDS concerning the Holy Spirit are found in Acts 2:4: "They were all filled with the Holy Spirit" (NKJV) and Ephesians 5:18: "Be filled with the Spirit." The one text is a narrative, telling us what actually happened. The other is a command, telling us what we should be. If there is any doubt about its being a command, we find it linked to another in the first part of the passage in Ephesians: "Do not get drunk on wine. . . . Instead . . ."

If I were to ask you if you obeyed the command not to be drunk with wine, you would no doubt answer, "Of course, as a believer, I obey that command." But what of the other: "Be filled with the Spirit"? Have you obeyed it as well? Does your life manifest the presence of the Holy Spirit? If not, are you willing to take the command to heart and say, "By God's help I will obey. I will not rest until I am filled with the Spirit"?

Now the question comes, What is needed in order to be filled with the Spirit? To find the answer we must allow God to search our lives. We might ask ourselves, "Am I in the condition in which God can fill me with His Spirit?" Some of you may be able to honestly answer, "Thank God, I am ready." If you can say this, you may realize that you have been kept back from this full blessing by lack of knowledge, prejudice, unbelief, or a wrong idea about what being filled with the Spirit is.

Being filled with the Spirit is simply this: The whole personality is yielded to His power. When the soul is yielded to the Holy Spirit, God himself will fill it.

Absolute Surrender

THE MORNING HOUR

FROM THE EARLIEST ages God's servants have thought of the morning as the time especially suited for the worship of God. It is still regarded by most Christians both as a duty and a privilege to devote some portion of the beginning of the day to seeking seclusion and fellowship with God.

In the morning, O LORD,
you hear my voice; in the
morning I lay my requests
before you and wait
in expectation.
PSALM 5:3

In speaking of the extreme importance of this daily time of quiet prayer and meditation on God's Word, someone has said: "Next to receiving Christ as Savior and claiming the baptism of the Holy Spirit, we know of no act attended with larger good to ourselves or others than the formation of an indisputable resolution to keep the watch and spend the first half hour of the day alone with God." At first glance such a statement may appear too strong. The act of receiving Christ as our Savior is one of such infinite consequence for eternity, and the step of claiming the Holy Spirit is one that is so revolutionary in the Christian life, that such a simple thing as the determination to keep the morning watch hardly appears important enough to be placed alongside them. If, however, we remember how impossible it is to live our life in Christ as our Savior from sin or to maintain a walk in the leading and power of the Holy Spirit without daily, close fellowship with God, we will see the truth of the statement.

The true practice of Christianity strives toward having the character of Christ so formed in us that in our most common activities His temper and disposition will be displayed. Do not be disturbed if the goal appears too high to attain or occupies too much of your time in the hour of private prayer. The time you give it will be richly rewarded.

The Believer's Daily Renewal

Cleansed by the Blood to Serve the Living God

But now in Christ Jesus you who once were far away have been brought near through the blood of Christ.
EPHESIANS 2:13

ONE OF THE MOST glorious blessings made possible for us by the power of the blood is that of drawing near to the throne, into the very presence of God. The precious blood of Christ has opened the way for the believer into God's presence; and fellowship with Him is a deep spiritual reality.

He who knows the full power of the blood is brought so near that he lives in the immediate presence of God and in the enjoyment of the unspeakable blessings attached to it. Here the child of God has the assurance of God's love; he experiences and enjoys it. God himself imparts it. As God's child, he makes known to the Father, with perfect freedom, his thoughts and wishes. In this relationship with God he possesses all that he needs; he lacks no good thing. His soul is kept in perfect rest and peace because God is with him. God's eye is ever upon him, guiding him. In fellowship with God he is able to hear the softest whispers of the Holy Spirit. He learns to understand the slightest sign of his Father's will and to follow it. His strength continually increases, for God is his strength and God is ever with him.

Fellowship with God exercises a wonderful influence on our life and character. The presence of God fills us with humility, holy fear, and circumspection. We live as in the presence of a king. Beholding the image of God, we are changed into the same image. Dwelling with the Holy One makes us holy.

May this high privilege awaken your desire for relationship with God, to dwell in sweet fellowship with Him and He with you. May it become impossible for you to be satisfied with anything less. This is the true Christian life.

The Blood of Christ

THE MOST WONDERFUL promises in all of Scripture are those regarding answers to prayer. To many such promises have raised the question, How can I ever attain the faith that knows that it receives all it asks?

It is this very question our Lord would answer today. When He gave the above promise to His disciples, He first pointed out where faith in the answer to prayer comes from and where it finds its strength: "Have faith in God."

The power to believe a promise depends entirely on our faith in the one who promises. It is only when we enjoy

*"Have faith in God,"
Jesus answered. "I tell
you the truth, if anyone
says to this mountain,
'Go, throw yourself into
the sea,' and does not
doubt in his heart but
believes that what he says
will happen, it will be
done for him. . . .
Whatever you ask for in
prayer, believe that you
have received it, and it
will be yours."*
MARK 11:22–24

a personal loving relationship with God himself that our whole being is opened up to the mighty influence of His holy presence and the capacity will be developed in us for believing that He gives whatever we ask.

The connection between faith in God and faith in His promises will become clear when we think about what faith really is. It is often compared to the hand or the mouth by which we take and appropriate what is offered to us. Faith is also the ear by which we hear what is promised, the eye by which we see what is offered. I must *hear* the person who gives the promise—the very tone of his voice gives me courage to believe. I must *see* him—in the light of his eye and his countenance, all fear passes away. The value of the promise depends on the one giving the promise; my knowledge of his character and dependability creates faith in his promise. In the case of God our Father, there can be no doubt as to His character and power to hear and answer and provide.

Believing Prayer

Devotional Life and Commitment

"But you, when you pray, go into your room, and when you have shut your door, pray to your Father who is in the secret place; and your Father who sees in secret will reward you openly."
Matthew 6:6 (NKJV)

WE USE THE WORD *devotion* in two senses: first, with regard to prayer in our public and private devotional times; and, second, with regard to the spirit of devotion, or commitment (devotedness) to God, which is to be the mark of our daily life. We have these two thoughts in our text. If in our private devotions we truly meet our Father who sees in secret, He has promised us the open reward of grace to live our life to His glory— the entire and continual commitment of our whole personality to His will. The act of commitment in private devotion secures the power for that spirit of commitment that is to extend through our daily life to His glory.

An outstanding passage concerning this principle of commitment to God is found in Leviticus 27:28: "Nevertheless no devoted offering that a man may devote to the Lord of all that he has, both man and beast, or the field of his possession, shall be sold or redeemed; every devoted offering is most holy to the Lord" (NKJV). The story of Achan (Joshua 6:17–18) is a solemn commentary on how this principle works out: "Now the city shall be doomed by the Lord to destruction, it and all who are in it. . . . And you, by all means abstain from the accursed things, lest you become accursed when you take of the accursed things, and make the camp of Israel a curse, and trouble it" (NKJV). *Accursed* means "devoted" or "committed" to God for destruction. The punishment, first on Israel in its defeat and then on Achan, gave a somber illustration of the serious meaning of devotion or commitment in God's sight. Commitment is the whole-hearted and irrevocable surrendering to God of what may never be taken back again. The person or thing is "most holy to the Lord."

The Believer's Call to Commitment

According to the Measure of Faith

Then Jesus said to the centurion, "Go! It will be done just as you believed it would." And his servant was healed at that very hour.
Matthew 8:13

THIS PASSAGE of Scripture brings before us one of the principal laws of the kingdom of heaven. In order to understand God's ways with His people and our relationship with the Lord, it is necessary to understand this law thoroughly and not to deviate from it. Not only does God give or withhold His grace according to the faith or unbelief of each but it is also granted in greater or lesser measure in proportion to the faith that receives it. Faith in God is nothing less than the full opening of the heart to receive everything from God. Man can receive divine grace only according to his faith. This applies as much to divine healing as to any other grace of God.

We have already remarked that to the same degree that the church has allowed itself to become worldly, her faith in divine healing has diminished until it has virtually disappeared. Believers do not seem to be aware that they may ask God for the healing of their sickness and thereby be sanctified and fitted for His service. They have come to seek only submission to His will and to regard sickness as a means to be separate from the world. In such conditions, the Lord gives them what they ask. He would have been ready to give them more, to grant them healing in answer to the prayer of faith, but they lacked the faith to receive it.

"It will be done just as you believed it would." We commend, then, to every suffering one who is looking for healing, and seeks to know Jesus as his divine healer, not to allow himself to be hindered by his unbelief, not to doubt the promises of God, but to be strong in faith, giving glory to God. As with all your heart you trust in the living God, you will be abundantly blessed. Do not doubt it.

Divine Healing

EVERYTHING MUST BE SACRIFICED FOR IT

When he has done this, then the Son himself will be made subject to him who put everything under him, so that God may be all in all.
1 CORINTHIANS 15:28

IT LIES IN THE very being and nature of God that He must be all. From Him and through Him and to Him are all things.

Sin consists in nothing but this, that man determined to be something and would not allow God to be everything; and the redemption of Jesus has no other aim than that God should again become everything in our heart and life. Christ himself showed in His life on earth what it means to be nothing and to allow God to be everything.

The *all* of God is what we must seek. There should be no use of our time, no word on our lips, no motivation of our heart, no satisfying of the needs of our physical life that is not the expression of the will, the glory, and the power of God. God must not be merely *something* to us or even *a lot,* but *all.*

Even as believers we often make it our first aim to find out who we are, what we desire, what pleases us and makes us happy. Then we bring in God in the second place to secure this happiness. We do not discern that God must have us at His disposal even in the most trivial details of our life to manifest His divine glory in us. We are not aware that this entire filling with the will and operation of God would also prove to be our highest happiness. We do not know that the very same Christ, who once lived upon the earth as the obedient, lowly servant of God, is prepared to abide and work in like manner in our heart and life now.

Take Christ afresh today as the one who has given His life that God may be all, and yield your life for this supreme end. God will fill you to overflowing with His Holy Spirit.

The Fullness of the Spirit

HUMILITY AND DEATH TO SELF

HUMILITY IS THE BLOSSOM of which death to self is the perfect fruit. Jesus humbled himself unto death and

He humbled himself and became obedient to death.
PHILIPPIANS 2:8

opened the path in which we too must walk. Humility must lead us to die to self: so we prove how wholly we have given ourselves up to it and to God; so alone we are freed from our fallen nature and find the path that leads to life in God, to that full birth of the new nature, of which humility is the breath and the joy.

Humility means giving up self, taking the place of perfect nothingness before God. Jesus humbled himself and became obedient unto death. In death He gave the highest and perfect proof of having given up His will to the will of God.

If you would enter into full fellowship with Christ in His death, and know the full deliverance from self, humble yourself. This is your duty. Place yourself before God in your helplessness; consent to the fact that you are powerless to slay yourself; give yourself in patient and trustful surrender to God. Accept every humiliation; look upon every person who tries or troubles you as a means of grace to humble you. God will see such acceptance as proof that your whole heart desires it. It is the path of humility that leads to the full and perfect experience of our death with Christ.

True humility will manifest itself in daily life. The one who has it will take the form of a servant. Claim in faith the death and the life of Jesus as your own. Enter into rest from self and its work—the rest of God. Every morning remind yourself afresh of your emptiness so that the life of Jesus may be manifested in you. The souls that enter into *His* humiliation will find *in Him* the power to see and count self as dead and, as those who have learned and received of Him, to walk with all lowliness and meekness, forbearing one another in love.

Humility

A PROPER KNOWLEDGE OF WHAT SIN IS

But God demonstrates his own love for us in this: While we were still sinners, Christ died for us.
ROMANS 5:8

TO UNDERSTAND GRACE and to understand Christ aright, we must understand what sin is. How can we come to this understanding? Through the light of God and His Word.

Come with me to the beginning of the Bible. We see man created by God after His image and pronounced by his Creator to be very good. Then sin entered. It was rebellion against God. Adam and Eve were driven out of the Garden and brought, along with untold millions, under the curse and utter ruin.

When we visit Mount Calvary we see the hatred and enmity with which the world cast out and crucified the Son of God. Here sin reached its climax. Christ was made sin and became a curse as the only way to destroy the power of sin. In the agony of Gethsemane, when He prayed that He might be spared the terrible cup, and in excruciating pain on the cross with its deep darkness and desertion by the Father, we get a faint glimpse of the curse and the indescribable suffering sin brings. If anything can cause us to hate and detest sin, it is seeing Christ on that bitter cross.

Remember that you are a child of God. Sometimes you commit sin: you allow it to fulfill its desires. The great power of sin is that it blinds us so that we do not recognize its true character. Remember what God thinks about sin: His holiness burns against it; He sacrificed His Son to conquer sin and to deliver us from it.

Nothing except constant fellowship with God can teach you as His child to hate sin as God hates it. Nothing but the close fellowship of the living Christ can make it possible for you to understand what sin is and to detest it. Without this deeper understanding of sin, we cannot truly appropriate the victory that Christ made possible for us.

Living a Prayerful Life

ALONE WITH GOD

HUMANKIND WAS CREATED for fellowship with God. God made us in His own image and likeness that we might be capable of understanding and enjoying God, entering into His will and delighting in His glory. Because God is everywhere present, we could have lived in unbroken fellowship with Him. But sin robbed us of this fellowship. And nothing short of it can satisfy us or the heart of God. It was this fellowship that Christ came to restore; to bring back to God His lost creatures.

"But when you pray, go into your room, close the door and pray to your Father, who is unseen. Then your Father, who sees what is done in secret, will reward you."
MATTHEW 6:6

This communion with God is meant to be ours every day, no matter our state of mind or the circumstances that surround us. But its enjoyment depends upon the reality of our fellowship in the quiet place. The power to maintain close fellowship with God all day will depend entirely upon the intensity with which we seek to secure it in the hour of secret prayer. The one essential in the morning watch is *fellowship with God*. Of course, there is the danger of substituting prayer and Bible study for fellowship with God. True fellowship is giving your love, your heart, and your life to Him and receiving from Him His love, life, and Holy Spirit. Your needs may so distract you that the light of His countenance and the joy of His love cannot enfold you. Your Bible study may so pique your interest and so awaken pleasant feelings that the Word of God may become a substitute for God himself. If this happens, we will go out into the day's work without the power of an abiding fellowship because in our morning devotions the blessing was not secured.

What a difference it would make if everything in our prayer life were subject to the one goal: *I want to walk through the day with God*. What strength would be imparted by the awareness that God has taken charge and He is with us: We are going to do His will all day in His strength.

The Believer's Daily Renewal

OBEDIENCE

"My food," said Jesus, "is to do the will of him who sent me and to finish his work."

JOHN 4:34

JESUS HAD HIDDEN manna that He received from the Father, and that was the secret of His power. No one could have discovered what it was; but when He tells us, it appears so simple that many are puzzled over it. His food was to do the will of God.

Food meets a felt need. Jesus' hunger was for one thing: to please God. Without that He could not rest; in that one thing He had all He needed. And when He found the will of God, He did it, and thereby fed His soul with its appropriate food and was satisfied.

Food involves appropriation, like the exercise of fellowship. The weak soul who truly surrenders himself to do the will of God becomes wonderfully strengthened by it. Obedience to God, instead of exhausting the energies, renews them. The doing of God's will was Jesus' food.

Food brings both quickening and joy. Eating is not only necessary for strength but is also enjoyable. To observe a feast in the Spirit is itself equivalent to food. Obedience to the will of God was Jesus' highest joy.

Jesus has become my food, and He dwells in me as the power of my life. Now I know the means by which this life must be fed and strengthened within me. The doing of God's will is my food. The doing of God's will was for Jesus the bread of heaven; and since I have now received Jesus as my heavenly Bread, He teaches me to eat what He ate; He teaches me to do the will of God. And so the feast of the Supper is prolonged in the continued life of obedience to the will of God.

The Lord's Table

A MODEL OF INTERCESSION

IN TRUE, UNSELFISH prayer there is little thought of personal need or happiness. If we would be delivered from the sin of limiting prayer, we must enlarge our hearts for the work of intercession.

To pray constantly only for ourselves is a mark of failure in prayer. It is in intercession for others that our faith and love and perseverance will be stirred up and that the power of the Spirit will be found to equip us for bringing salvation to people. How can we become more faithful and successful in prayer? See in the parable of the friend at midnight how the Master teaches us that intercession for the needy is the highest exercise of believing and prevailing prayer. Here are the elements of true intercession:

Urgent need. If we are to learn to pray as we should, we must open our eyes and heart to the needs around us.

Willing love. It is the very nature of love to give up and forget itself for the sake of others.

The sense of powerlessness. "I have nothing to set before him."

Faith in prayer. What the man himself doesn't have, another can supply. To get from God, and then to give to others what we ourselves receive from day to day, is the secret of successful work. Intercession is the blessed link between our powerlessness and God's omnipotence.

Then he said to them, "Suppose one of you has a friend, and he goes to him at midnight and says, 'Friend, lend me three loaves of bread, because a friend of mine on a journey has come to me, and I have nothing to set before him.'

Then the one inside answers, 'Don't bother me. The door is already locked, . . . I can't get up and give you anything.' I tell you, though he will not get up and give him the bread because he is his friend, yet because of the man's persistence he will get up and give him as much as he needs."

LUKE 11:5–8

The Ministry of Intercessory Prayer

God's Provision for Holiness

To those sanctified in
Christ Jesus and called
to be holy.
1 CORINTHIANS 1:2

HOLY AND IN CHRIST are perhaps the most wonderful words in all the Bible.

Holy is a word of unfathomable meaning. Even seraphs utter it with veiled faces. *Holy* is the word in which all God's perfections center and of which His glory is but the pouring forth. *Holy* is the word that reveals the purpose with which God from eternity thought of humankind and foretells our highest glory in the coming eternity—to be partakers of God's holiness!

In Christ—here all the wisdom and love of God are unveiled: the Father giving His Son to be one with us; the Son dying on the cross to make us one with Him; the Holy Spirit of the Father dwelling in us to establish and maintain that union! *In Christ* is a summary of what redemption has done and of the inconceivably blessed life in which the child of God is permitted to dwell. *In Christ* is the one lesson we have to study on earth, God's one answer to all our needs and prayers and the guarantee and foretaste of eternal glory.

What wealth of meaning and blessing when the words are combined: *holy in Christ*. Here is God's provision for our holiness, God's response to our question "How can we be holy?" When we hear the call "Be holy, even as I am holy," it seems as if there is, and ever must be, a great gulf between the holiness of God and that of humankind. But *in Christ* is the bridge that spans the gulf—or better, His fullness has filled it up.

The Spirit of God's holiness is given from the throne and represents, reveals, and communicates the unseen Christ. In this gift the holy life of Christ descends and takes possession of His people, and they become one with Him. Abiding and growing up in Him, I can be holy in all manner of living, just as God is holy.

The Path to Holiness

THE PROMISE OF THE COVENANT

"IT IS NOT the natural children who are God's children, but it is the children of the promise who are regarded as Abraham's offspring" (Romans 9:8).

Here we have the first full revelation of the terms of God's covenant, of God's dealing in grace with Abraham, the father of all who believe. Here is the foundation promise for what God calls "an everlasting covenant." God had revealed himself to Abraham as his God and as the God who would give him a child. The thing that is new and remarkable here is the assurance that the covenant to be established was to be with his seed as much as with himself.

"I will establish my covenant as an everlasting covenant between me and you and your descendants after you for the generations to come, to be your God and the God of your descendants after you."
GENESIS 17:7

The matter of the promise is the same in each case: "I will establish my covenant . . . to be your God and the God of your descendants after you." It is God's purpose to stand in the same relationship to the child as the father stands; the believing parent and the innocent child are to have the same place before Him. God longs to take possession of children before sin gains a mastery; from birth—yes, even from before birth—He would secure them as His own and have the parents' heart and the parents' love sanctified, guided, and strengthened by the thought that the child is His: "your God and the God of your descendants."

The condition of the promise is the same in each case. In its twofold blessing it is offered to the faith of the parent and must be accepted by faith alone. If the promise "I will be your God" is not received, unbelief renders the promise of no effect. God is true, His promise faithful, and His offer of mercy real. But if there is unbelief, the blessing is lost.

Let us believe God for the protection and salvation of our children.

Raising Your Child to Love God

WORSHIP IN THE SPIRIT

"But the hour is coming, and now is, when the true worshipers will worship the Father in spirit and truth; for the Father is seeking such to worship Him. God is Spirit, and those who worship Him must worship in spirit and truth."
JOHN 4:23–24 (NKJV)

TO WORSHIP IS OUR highest privilege. We were created for fellowship with God: of that fellowship, worship is the most sublime expression. All the disciplines of the Christian life—meditation and prayer, love and faith, surrender and obedience—culminate in worship. Recognizing what God is in His holiness, His glory, and His love; realizing what I am as a sinful creature and as the Father's redeemed child, in worship I gather up my whole being and present myself to my God. I offer Him the adoration and the glory that is due Him. The truest, fullest, and nearest approach to God is worship.

When God created man a living soul, that soul, as the seat of his personality and consciousness, was linked on the one side, through the body, with the outer visible world, and on the other side, through the spirit, with the unseen and the divine. The soul had to decide whether it would yield itself to the spirit and by it be linked with God and His will, or to the body and the solicitations of the visible. In the Fall, the soul refused the rule of the spirit and became the slave of the body with its appetites. Man became flesh, and the spirit lost its rule and became little more than a dormant power. It was no longer a ruling principle but a struggling captive. The spirit now stands in opposition to the flesh (the word for the life of the soul and the body together) in its subjection to sin.

True worshipers worship the Father in spirit and in truth. In order to be a true worshiper, there must be accordance, harmony, and unity between God, who is Spirit, and our own spirit.

The Spirit of Christ

THE ONLY TEACHER

THE DISCIPLES had been with Christ and had seen Him pray. They had learned to understand something of the connection between His public life and His private life of prayer. They had learned to believe in Him as a Master in

One day Jesus was praying in a certain place. When he finished, one of his disciples said to him, "Lord, teach us to pray."
LUKE 11:1

the art of prayer—none could pray like Him. So they came to Him with the request "Lord, teach us to pray." In hindsight they surely would have told us that few things surpassed what He taught them about prayer.

As we see Him pray, and we remember that no one can pray or teach like Him, we agree with the disciples and say, "Lord, teach *us* to pray." As we think about the fact that He is our very life, we feel assured that we have but to ask and He will be delighted to take us into closer fellowship with himself and to teach us to pray as He prays.

Prayer is what we need to be taught. And though in its beginnings prayer is so simple that even a small child can pray, it is at the same time the highest and holiest work to which anyone can rise. It is fellowship with the unseen and most holy One. The powers of the eternal world have been placed at its disposal. It is the channel of all blessings and the secret of power and life. Through prayer, God has given to everyone the right to take hold of Him and His strength. It is on prayer that promises wait for their fulfillment, the kingdom for its coming, and the glory of God for its full revelation.

Even when we know what to ask, how much is still needed to make our prayer acceptable? It must be to the glory of God, in full surrender to His will, in full assurance of faith, in the name of Jesus, and with a perseverance that refuses to be denied. All this must be learned. And it can only be learned in the school of much prayer, for it is practice that makes perfect.

Teach Me to Pray

BE STRONG AND OF GOOD COURAGE

Wait on the LORD; be of good courage, and He shall strengthen your heart; wait, I say, on the LORD!
PSALM 27:14 (NKJV)

THE PSALMIST SAID in the previous verse, "I would have lost heart, unless I had believed that I would see the goodness of the LORD in the land of the living." If it had not been for his faith in God, his heart would have given up. But in the confident assurance in God that faith gives, he urges himself and us to remember one thing above all—to wait on God. The deliverance we often wait for is from our enemies, in whose presence we are powerless. The blessings we plead for are spiritual and unseen, things impossible with men. Our heart may well faint and fail. Our souls are unaccustomed to holding intimate fellowship with God. The God we wait on often appears to hide.

We are in such a habit of evaluating God and His work in us by what we *feel* that it is very likely that on some occasions we will be discouraged because we do not feel any special blessing. Above everything, when you wait on God, do so in the spirit of hope. It is God in His glory, His power, and His love who is longing to bless you.

The blessedness of waiting on God has its root in the fact that He is such a blessed being, full of goodness and power and life and joy. God is love! That is the one and only all-sufficient reason for your expectation. Love seeks out its own: God's delight is to impart himself to His children. Come. However weak you *feel*, wait in His presence. Just as a weak and sickly invalid is brought out into the sunshine to allow its healing warmth to go through his body, come with all that is dark and cold in you into the sunshine of God's holy, omnipotent love, and sit and wait there. As the sun does its work in the weak who seek its rays, God will do His work in you. Trust Him!

Waiting on God

ALL YOU WHO HAVE COME TO HIM

NO DOUBT YOU HAVE never regretted responding to His call and com-

"Come to me."
MATTHEW 11:28

ing to Him. You experienced that His word was truth; all His promises He fulfilled; He made you a partaker of the blessings and the joy of His love. His welcome was heartfelt, His pardon full and free, His love most sweet and precious, was it not? You more than once, at your first coming to Him, had reason to say, "The half was not told me."

And yet you have had some disappointment. As time went on, your expectations were not always realized. The blessings you once enjoyed were lost; the love and joy of your first meeting with your Savior, instead of deepening, have become faint and weak. And you have often wondered why, with such a mighty and loving Savior, your experience of salvation was not a fuller one.

The answer is very simple. You wandered from Him. The blessings He bestows are all connected with His "Come to me," and are only to be enjoyed in close fellowship with Him. You either did not fully understand, or did not rightly remember, that the call meant "Come to me and remain with me." This was His object and purpose when He first called you to himself. It was not to refresh you for a few short hours after your conversion with the joy of His love and deliverance, and then to send you forth to wander in sadness and sin.

No, indeed, He has prepared for you an abiding dwelling with himself, where your whole life and every moment of it might be spent and where the work of your daily life might be done as you enjoy unbroken communion with Him. Who would be content, after seeking the King's palace, to stand in the door, when he is invited in to dwell in the King's presence and share with Him in all the glory of His royal life? Let us enter in and abide and enjoy fully all the rich supply His wondrous love has prepared for us!

Abiding in Christ

THE JOY OF BEING FILLED WITH THE SPIRIT

When the day of Pentecost came, they were all together in one place. . . . All of them were filled with the Holy Spirit.
ACTS 2:1, 4

THE CLEAREST illustration of the joy of being filled with the Spirit is seen in the wonderful change that Pentecost brought to the lives of the disciples. It is one of the most wonderful object lessons in all of Scripture—the Twelve, under Christ's training for three years, and yet remaining, apparently, at some distance from the life they were meant to live; and then all at once, by the blessed incoming of the Holy Spirit, being made just what God wanted them to be.

Isn't that what your heart longs for? I have thought and thought of Jesus in Bethlehem, of Jesus on Calvary, of Jesus upon the throne, and I have worshiped and rejoiced exceedingly in Him; but all the time I wanted something better, something nearer. The answer is to have the living Jesus within. That is what the Holy Spirit will give you, and that is why we plead with you: Will you not yield yourself to receive this blessing—to be filled with the Spirit—that the blessed Jesus may be able to take possession of you? Jesus *within*—the very Jesus who is the Almighty One, who died on the cross and sits upon the throne, condescending to be your life.

I would like to convince every believer that Jesus loves you; He does not wish to be separated from you for a moment. He cannot bear it. No mother has delighted more in the baby in her arms than does Christ delight in you. He wants both intimate and unceasing fellowship with you. Receive it, dear believer, and say, "If it is possible, God helping me, I must have this filling of the Holy Spirit so that I may know and sense the presence of Jesus always dwelling in my heart."

Absolute Surrender

THE ENTRANCE INTO A LIFE OF FULL OBEDIENCE

YOU MIGHT THINK citing a text in which obedience is seen at its highest state of perfection is a mistake for our consideration of entrance onto this course. But it is no mistake. The secret of success in a race is to have the goal clearly defined and to have it as our aim from the outset.

He humbled Himself and became obedient to the point of death, even the death of the cross. Therefore God also has highly exalted Him.
PHILIPPIANS 2:8–9 (NKJV)

From the very outset of the Christian life, let us avoid the fatal mistake of calling Christ "Master" but not doing what He says. Let all who are to any degree convicted of the sin of disobedience come and listen. God's Word will show the way to escape from such a life and gain access to the life Christ alone can give—a life of full obedience.

To be as merciful as the Father in heaven, to forgive just as He does, to love our enemies and do good to them that hate us, and live lives of self-sacrifice and benevolence—this was the walk Jesus taught while on earth. If you would hope to lead different lives, to possess a Christlike obedience unto death, begin by seeking God for the Holy Spirit of conviction to show you your disobedience and to lead you in humble confession to the cleansing God has provided.

Our Lord called us to deny ourself and to take up our cross, to forsake all, to hate and lose our own life, to humble ourself and become a servant of all.

God sent Christ into the world to restore obedience to its rightful place in our hearts and lives. Christ came, becoming obedient unto death, showing what true obedience is like. Obedience unto death is the essence of the life He imparts. Shall we not accept it and trust Him to perfect it in us?

A Life of Obedience

Cleansing Through the Blood

But if we walk in the light, as he is in the light, we have fellowship with one another, and the blood of Jesus, his Son, purifies us from all sin.
1 John 1:7

THE WORD *purifies* here does not refer to the grace of pardon received at conversion, but to the effect of grace *in* God's children who walk in the light. Cleansing is something that comes after pardon and is the result of it.

This takes place, according to the Word, first in the purifying of the conscience: "How much more, then, will the blood of Christ, who through the eternal Spirit offered himself unblemished to God, cleanse our consciences from acts that lead to death, so that we may serve the living God!" (Hebrews 9:14).

"The blood of Jesus . . . purifies us from all sin"—from original sin (Adam's) as well as from actual sin. The blood exercises its spiritual, heavenly power in the soul. The believer in whose life the blood is efficacious experiences the old nature as hindered from manifesting its power. Through the blood, its lusts and desires are subdued and slain, and everything is so cleansed that the Spirit can bring forth His glorious fruit. Even unconscious sins are rendered powerless through its efficacy.

Many seem to think that the blood is there so that if we sin we can turn to it again to be cleansed. But this is not exactly true. Just as a fountain continues to flow and always purifies what is placed in it or under its stream, so it is with this fountain. It is open for sin and uncleanness at all times, and we can remain under its cleansing flow (Zechariah 13:1). The eternal power of the life of the Spirit works through the blood. Through Him the heart can abide always under the flow and cleansing of the blood. Count on the cleansing from sin by His blood as a blessing you can be confident of and enjoy every day.

The Blood of Christ

THE CURE FOR UNBELIEF

WHEN THE DISCIPLES saw Jesus cast the evil spirit out of the epileptic boy, they asked the Master for the cause of their failure. He had given them power and authority over all demons and diseases. They had often exercised that power and joyfully told how the demons were subject to them. Yet this time they had utterly failed.

There had been nothing in the will of God or in the nature of the case to render deliverance impossible—at Christ's bidding the evil spirit had gone out. From their question "Why couldn't we drive it out?" it is evident that they had tried to do so. Their efforts had been in vain, however, and in front of the multitude, they had been put to shame.

Then the disciples came to Jesus in private and asked, "Why couldn't we drive it out?" He replied, "Because you have so little faith. I tell you the truth, if you have faith as small as a mustard seed, you can say to this mountain, 'Move from here to there' and it will move. Nothing will be impossible for you."
MATTHEW 17:19–20

Christ's answer was direct and plain: "Because you have so little faith." Their failure was not due to some special power that was unavailable to them. He had often taught them that there is one power—that of faith—to which everything in the kingdom of darkness and in the kingdom of God must bow; in the spiritual world, failure has but one cause: lack of faith.

The power the disciples received to cast out demons was not a power they held in themselves as a permanent gift or possession; rather, it was the power of Christ to be received and used by faith alone. Had they been full of faith in Him as Lord and Conqueror of the spirit world, full of faith in Him as having given them authority to cast out demons in His name, they would have had the victory.

Believing Prayer

Commitment—The New Testament Standard

However, for this reason I obtained mercy, that in me first Jesus Christ might show all longsuffering, as a pattern to those who are going to believe on Him for everlasting life.

1 Timothy 1:16 (NKJV)

IN ANY JUDGMENT we pronounce, everything will depend upon the standard we use. Those who are content with a level of ordinary Christianity, though they may admit that their own commitment is lacking, will not be deeply convicted of its sinfulness or of the need or the possibility of any higher attainment. But when we begin to see what the New Testament standard is, and its universal obligation, we see how far we fall short of it. We then become convicted of the sin of unbelief in the power of Jesus to keep us from sin and to enable us to live a life that is pleasing to God. We find in God's Word that no matter how impossible humanity's standard is, it is not impossible to God, who works in us to will and to do through the power of His Holy Spirit.

Discovering the New Testament standard of commitment is not an easy matter. Our preconceived opinions blind us; our surroundings will exercise a powerful influence. Unless there is a sincere desire to truly know the entire will of God, and a prayerful dependence on the Holy Spirit's teaching, we will search in vain. Let everyone who is willing to live entirely for God, and desires in everything to please Him, be encouraged: God wants us to know His will and promises to reveal it to us by His Spirit.

Many look upon Christ's sinless perfection as so utterly beyond what we can attain that His example loses its power. In Paul, the chief of sinners, we see a man of like passions and desires. In him, Christ proved for all time what He could do to save and keep a sinner from sin.

The Believer's Call to Commitment

ANOINTING WITH OIL IN THE NAME OF THE LORD

IT WAS THE CUSTOM of the people in the East to anoint themselves with oil when they came out of the bath, a most refreshing practice in a hot climate. We see also that all those who were called to the special service of God were to be anointed with oil as a token of their con-

Is any one of you sick? He should call the elders of the church to pray over him and anoint him with oil in the name of the Lord.
JAMES 5:14

secration to God and of the grace they should receive from Him to fulfill their vocation. The oil that was used to anoint the priests and the tabernacle was looked upon as "most holy" (Exodus 30:22–32), and wherever the Bible speaks of anointing with oil, it is a symbol of holiness and consecration. Nowhere in the Bible do we find any proof that oil was used as a remedy.

In the Old Testament, oil was the symbol of the gift of the Holy Spirit: "The Spirit of the Lord GOD is upon Me, because the LORD has anointed me" (Isaiah 61:1 NKJV). It is said of the Lord Jesus in the New Testament, "God anointed Jesus of Nazareth with the Holy Spirit and power, and . . . he went around doing good and healing all who were under the power of the devil, because God was with him" (Acts 10:38). Sometimes man feels the need of a visible sign, appealing to his senses, which may help to sustain his faith and enable him to grasp the spiritual meaning. The anointing, therefore, should symbolize to the sick the action of the Holy Spirit, who gives the healing.

We should regard it not as a remedy but as a pledge of the mighty virtue of the Holy Spirit, as a means of strengthening faith, a point of contact and of communion between the sick and the members of the church who are called to anoint him with oil.

Divine Healing

GOD ASSURES US OF ITS COMING

"If you then, though you are evil, know how to give good gifts to your children, how much more will your Father in heaven give the Holy Spirit to those who ask him!"
LUKE 11:13

THIS DIVINE ASSURANCE was clearly stated by Jesus' word that much more readily than an earthly father who gives his children bread will God give the Holy Spirit to those who ask. We would call it child abuse if a father refused to feed his children; how much more, then, shall not God give the promised fullness of the Spirit to those who ask Him. Among all the aspects of our spiritual life, the fundamental element should be the firm confidence that the Father will give His child His full heritage. God is a spirit. He desires full possession of us, but He can only accomplish this by giving us His Spirit. As surely as He is God, He will fill you with His Holy Spirit. Without faith you will never receive the blessing. That faith will give you the victory over every difficulty.

God takes upon himself the responsibility of your being full of the Spirit, not as a treasure that *you* must carry and keep, but as a power that carries and keeps you.

In His promise of the blessing and the power of the Spirit, the Lord Jesus always pointed to God the Father. He called it "what my Father has promised" (Luke 24:49). He directed us to the love of God: It is as a Father that God is to give this gift to His children. Let every thought of this blessing and every desire for it only lead us to God. Let us in quiet worship set our hearts on God. Let us joyfully trust in Him: He is able to do more than we could ever ask or think. His love will bestow upon us a full blessing. Humbly pray as Mary did, "May it be to me as you have said" (Luke 1:38).

"The one who calls you is faithful and he will do it" (1 Thessalonians 5:24).

The Fullness of the Spirit

THE CARNAL LIFE AND THE SPIRITUAL LIFE

PAUL FELT THAT ALL his preaching would be useless if he talked about spiritual things to men who were unspiritual. They were believers, true Christians, but there was one deadly fault— they were *carnal*. They were very clever and full of knowledge, but when it came to spiritual teaching they could not always grasp it.

What does it mean to be carnal? There are four characteristics of the carnal state. First, it is a state of protracted infancy. Babyhood is a beautiful thing, but not when its characteristics continue beyond babyhood. A six-month-old child is only expected to do certain things, but if that same child has not progressed six months later, something is wrong. The second characteristic of a carnal state is when sin and failure are the masters. Sin has the upper hand in your life. The flesh is selfish and proud; every sin against love is only proof that the person is carnal.

A third identifying trait of carnality is that although a person may exercise spiritual gifts, he will not readily exemplify the spiritual graces. There is a great difference between spiritual gifts and spiritual graces, and that is what many people do not understand. Fourth, the carnal state renders it impossible for a man to receive spiritual truth in a way that he can truly benefit from it. This is characterized by believers who hunger for the Word, listen to it, and even study it, and yet they receive no help from it; or they are helped for two or three weeks and the blessing passes away. The carnal state hinders the reception of spiritual truth.

For when we were controlled by the sinful nature, the sinful passions aroused by the law were at work in our bodies, so that we bore fruit for death. But now, by dying to what once bound us, we have been released from the law so that we serve in the new way of the Spirit, and not in the old way of the written code.
ROMANS 7:5–6

Absolute Surrender

ARE WE CARNAL OR SPIRITUAL?

*Those who belong to
Christ Jesus have crucified
the sinful nature with its
passions and desires.*
GALATIANS 5:24

THERE IS A GREAT difference between being carnal (living after the flesh) and being spiritual. This fact is little understood or pondered. The Christian who walks in the Spirit, and has crucified the flesh, is spiritual (Galatians 5:24). The Christian who walks after the flesh, and wishes to please the flesh, is carnal (Romans 13:14). The Galatians, who had begun in the Spirit, reverted to a life in the flesh. Yet there were among them some spiritual members, who were able to restore the wandering with true meekness.

With the carnal Christian, there may be the appearance of virtue and zeal for God and His service, but it is for the most part a manifestation of human power. With the spiritual Christian, on the other hand, there is a complete submission to the leading of the Spirit, a sense of personal weakness and total dependence on the work of Christ—it is a life of abiding fellowship with Christ brought into being by the Spirit.

A minister may be very faithful in his teaching of doctrine and be enthusiastic in his service, and yet be so, for the most part, in the power of human wisdom and zeal. One of the signs of this is little pleasure or perseverance in fellowship with Christ through prayer. A love of prayer is one of the marks of the Spirit.

A tremendous change is in store for the carnal Christian who would become truly spiritual. At first he cannot understand what needs to change or how it will take place. But the more the truth dawns upon him, the more he is convinced that it is impossible unless God does the work. Yet to believe that God will do it requires diligent prayer. Meditation and a quiet, solitary place are indispensable, along with the end of all confidence in self. But along this road there comes the faith that God is willing, and He will do it.

Living a Prayerful Life

OBEDIENCE TO THE LAST COMMAND OF JESUS

"Go therefore and make disciples of all the nations, baptizing them in the name of the Father and of the Son and of the Holy Spirit."

MATTHEW 28:19 (NKJV)

THESE WORDS BREATHE nothing less than the spirit of world conquest. In other passages Jesus spoke of "all the world, every creature, and the uttermost parts of the earth." Each expression indicates that the heart of Christ was set on claiming His rightful dominion over the world He had redeemed and won for himself. And He counts on His disciples to undertake and carry out the work. He himself will carry on the war. He seeks to inspire them with His own assurance of victory, with His own purpose of making this the only thing worth living or dying for—the winning back of all the world to God.

Christ does not teach or argue, ask or plead; He simply commands. He has trained His disciples in obedience. He has linked them to himself in a love that is able to obey. He can count on them. Within a generation, simple men, whose names we do not even know, had preached the Gospel in Antioch and Rome and the regions beyond. The command was passed on and absorbed into the heart and life, as meant for all ages and for every disciple.

The command is for each one of us, too. We are His body. We now occupy His place on earth. His will and love carry out through us the work He began, and now in His stead we live to seek the Father's glory in winning a lost world back to Him.

Have you ever wondered how the disciples accepted the great command so easily and so heartily? They came fresh from Calvary. To them Jesus was Savior, Master, Friend, and Lord. His Word had divine power; they could only obey. Let us unhesitatingly and with our whole heart accept the command and our life's sole purpose: the Gospel to every creature!

A Life of Obedience

SANCTIFICATION

"Stop sinning or something worse may happen to you. . . . Go now and leave your life of sin."
JOHN 5:14; 8:11

JESUS SPOKE TO the sick man whom He had healed at the pool of Bethesda. He spoke also to the woman whom He liberated from the hand of her persecutors. He speaks to every soul to which He has shown mercy, whose sickness He has healed, and whose life He has redeemed from destruction. He speaks to everyone who goes forth from the blessed feast of the Supper: "Go now and leave your life of sin."

It was in order to save us from sin that God sent His Son, Jesus gave His lifeblood, and the Spirit came down from heaven. The Redeemer cannot allow a ransomed soul to go from the table of the covenant without hearing this glorious word: "Go now and leave your life of sin." In the presence of the cross and what your sin cost Him, in view of His love and all the blessings He has bestowed upon you, this word comes with divine power.

We may ask, "But, Lord, must I never sin? In me dwells no good thing. I thought the Christian must continue to sin to the end."

He will answer, "Have I not redeemed you from the power of sin? Does not my Spirit dwell in you? Am I not your sanctification?"

Again, "But, Lord, can anyone in this life be holy?"

"You will continue to have the sinful nature, but its workings can be overcome. You may become more holy every day. I am prepared to do for you above all that you dare ask or think."

Of course we long to be holy. Sin grieves us. We only long to be taught how we can be holy. Jesus would say to us that He is our sanctification. We must abide in Him. We must entrust ourselves to Him. He will keep us. He will do in us what we cannot do.

The Lord's Table

BECAUSE OF HIS BOLDNESS

IT IS NOT BECAUSE GOD has to be made willing or available to bless that urgent prayer is necessary. The difficulty is not in God's love or power but in us and in our own incapacity to receive the blessing. But because there is this difficulty with us, this lack of spiritual preparedness, there is also a difficulty with God. His wisdom, His righteousness, even His love, dare not give us what would do us harm if we received it too soon or too easily.

In the very difficulty and delay that calls for persevering prayer, the true blessedness of the spiritual life is found. There we learn how little we delight in fellowship with God and how small our faith is in Him. We discover how earthly and unspiritual our heart is, and how we need God's Holy Spirit. There we are brought to know our own weakness and unworthiness and to yield to God's Spirit to pray through us. There we take our place in Christ Jesus and abide in Him as our only advocate with the Father. There our own will and way are crucified. And there we rise in Christ to newness of life, because now our whole will is dependent upon God and fixed upon His glory. Let us begin to praise God for the need and the difficulty of persistent prayer as one of His choicest means of grace.

Let us acknowledge how vain our work for God has been due to our lack of prayer. Let us change our methods and make continuing, persistent prayer the proof that we look to God for all things and that we believe that He hears us and answers us.

Then Jesus told his disciples a parable to show them that they should always pray and not give up. . . . "Listen to what the unjust judge says. And will not God bring about justice for his chosen ones, who cry out to him day and night? Will he keep putting them off? I tell you, he will see that they get justice, and quickly."
LUKE 18:1, 6–8

The Ministry of Intercessory Prayer

GOD'S CALL TO HOLINESS

But just as he who called you is holy, so be holy in all you do; for it is written: "Be holy, because I am holy."
1 PETER 1:15–16

IN GOD'S CALL to holiness He reveals to us what His thoughts and His will are concerning us and what the life is to which He invites us. He makes clear to us what the hope of our calling is, and as we spiritually apprehend and enter into this, our life on earth will be the reflection of His purpose for us in eternity.

Our calling, before and above everything else, is to holiness. The quality is not something we do or attain by our own power: it is the communication of the divine life, the inbreathing of the divine nature, the power of the divine presence resting on us. Our power to become holy is to be found in the call of God. He not only says, "I am holy," but "I am the LORD, who makes you holy" (Leviticus 22:32).

Because the call comes from the God of infinite power and love, we may have confidence that we can be holy. Child of God, have you ever heard this call from God? Shouldn't we confess that happiness has been to us more than holiness, and salvation more than sanctification? But it is not too late to redeem the error.

Listen to the voice that calls, draw close, and find out what holiness is, or better, find out and know Him who is the Holy One. If the first approach to Him fills us with shame and confusion, makes us fear and hold back, let us still listen to the voice that tells us to be holy, as He is holy. "The one who calls you is faithful and he will do it" (1 Thessalonians 5:24). All our fears and questions will be met by this One who has revealed His holiness with one purpose in view: that we might share it with Him.

The Path to Holiness

PROTECTING THE FAITH

IT WAS BY FAITH Moses' parents saw that he was no ordinary child. The natural love of a parent's heart sees the child as beautiful, but faith sees even more. God opened their eyes, and there was the consciousness of something special in Moses. Perhaps it was a spiritual beauty that made their baby doubly pre-

By faith Moses' parents hid him for three months after he was born, because they saw he was no ordinary child, and they were not afraid of the king's edict.
HEBREWS 11:23

cious. And so the eye of faith sees in each little one the image of God.

Here is a picture of our great redemption. We are loved and destined to be partakers of the precious blood and Holy Spirit of Jesus, to be the object of the joy of angels and God's everlasting pleasure. As His child our worth exceeds that of the whole world. Even in this life, we can be a brother of Jesus, a servant of God, a blessing to the spirits of our fellowmen. Faith calls the newborn unspeakably fair, seeing him as a jewel in the crown of the Lamb—His joy and His glory. We have indeed a surer hope than ever Moses' parents had, and a brighter light in which the heavenly beauty of our offspring is reflected.

It is faith that sees but fears not the danger. Pharaoh commanded that all the children of God's people should be destroyed. He knew that if the children were cut off, the people would soon die out. The prince of this world still pursues the same agenda. When parents take a decided stand for God, the world may despise or hate them, but it soon learns that it is of little use to attempt to conquer them. Instead, the spirit of the world claims possession of the children; if these are won, all are won. Too often children grow up in comparative ignorance about the blessed Savior and are entrusted to the care of worldly teachers. Then they are allowed to associate with those whose spirit and influence is altogether opposed to the ways of God. A wise parent will take heed to these words.

Raising Your Child to Love God

The Spirit and the Word

> *"It is the Spirit who gives life; the flesh profits nothing. The words that I speak to you are spirit, and they are life." . . . "Lord, to whom shall we go? You have the words of eternal life."*
> John 6:63, 68 (NKJV)

OUR LORD HAS BEEN speaking of himself as the bread of life, and of His flesh and blood as the meat and drink of eternal life. To many of His disciples it was a hard saying, which they could not understand. Jesus tells them that when the Holy Spirit comes, and they have Him, that His words will become clear to them.

"It is the Spirit who gives life." Here we have the closest definition of the Spirit. The Spirit always acts, whether in nature or in grace, as a life-giving principle. The flesh profits nothing.

The Holy Spirit has for all ages embodied the thoughts of God in the written Word, and lives now for this very purpose in our hearts—to reveal the power and the meaning of the Word. If you would be full of the Spirit, be full of the Word. If you would have the divine life of the Spirit in you grow strong and exercise power in every part of your nature, let the Word of Christ dwell in you richly. As the Word abides in you, the Spirit will reveal to you the will of God in every circumstance of your life. Let the written Word be transcribed on your heart.

The Word is like a seed. In every natural seed there is a fleshy part in which the life is hidden. We can have the most perfect seed to all outward appearances, but unless that seed has the influence of the sun and good soil and moisture, its life will never develop and grow. We may hold the words and the doctrines of Scripture in the intelligent sense, and yet know little of their life and power. Just as the Scriptures were spoken and written down as men were moved by the Spirit of God, it is only by the Spirit of God that they can be fully understood.

The Spirit of Christ

THE TRUE WORSHIPERS

JESUS' WORDS TO the woman of Samaria make up His first recorded teaching on prayer. The Father *seeks* worshipers. Our worship satisfies His loving heart and is a joy to Him. He seeks *true worshipers* but does not find many.

> *"Yet a time is coming and has now come when the true worshipers will worship the Father in spirit and truth, for they are the kind of worshipers the Father seeks. God is spirit, and his worshipers must worship in spirit and in truth."*
> JOHN 4:23–24

Our Lord spoke of a threefold worship to the woman of Samaria. There is the unlearned worship of the Samaritans: "You Samaritans worship what you do not know" (John 4:22a); the intelligent worship of the Jew, having the true knowledge of God: "We worship what we do know, for salvation is from the Jews" (John 4:22b); and the new spiritual worship that He himself came to introduce: "Yet a time is coming and has now come when the true worshipers will worship the Father in spirit and truth" (John 4:23). From the connection, it is evident that the words *in spirit and truth* do not mean "from the heart, in sincerity." The Samaritans had the five books of Moses and some knowledge of God; there was doubtless more than one among them who sincerely sought God in prayer. The Jews had the full revelation of God in His Word as had been given up to that time; there were among them godly men who called upon God with their whole heart. But worshiping "in spirit and truth" was not yet fully realized.

Among Christians there are still three classes of worshipers: some, in their ignorance, hardly know what they are asking. They pray earnestly but receive little. Others, with more knowledge, try to pray with all their mind and heart, but do not attain the full blessing. We must ask our Lord Jesus to take us into the third class: We must be taught of Him how to worship in spirit and truth.

Teach Me to Pray

HIS LIGHT IN THE HEART

I wait for the LORD, my soul waits, and in His word I do hope. My soul waits for the Lord more than those who watch for the morning— yes, more than those who watch for the morning.
PSALM 130:5–6 (NKJV)

THERE ARE TIMES and situations in which dawn is awaited with intense longing: sailors in a shipwrecked vessel, a nighttime traveler in a dangerous country, an army that finds itself surrounded by an enemy, are just a few examples. The morning light reveals what hope of escape there may be. In the same way, the saints of God living in the darkness of this world have longed for the light of His countenance—more than those who wait for the dawn. Can we say that we wait for God with this kind of fervency and expectancy? Our waiting on God can have no higher goal than to have His light shine on us and in us and through us all day.

God is light. Paul says, "For it is the God who commanded light to shine out of darkness, who has shone in our hearts to give the light of the knowledge of the glory of God in the face of Jesus Christ" (2 Corinthians 4:6 NKJV). Just as the sun shines its life-giving light on our Earth, so God shines in our hearts the light of His glory and His love. Our hearts are meant to have this light filling them every day.

Simple faith in God's Word and His love opens the eyes and the heart to receive and enjoy the indescribable glory of His grace.

Simply bow, even now, in stillness before God and wait on Him to shine in you. Say in humble faith, God is light, infinitely brighter and more beautiful than the light of the sun. The light will shine in me and make me full of light. And I shall learn to walk in the light and the joy of God.

Waiting on God

AS THE BRANCH
IN THE VINE

IT WAS IN CONNECTION with the parable of the vine that our Lord first used the expression "Abide in Me." That

"I am the vine; you are the branches."
JOHN 15:5 (NKJV)

parable, so simple and yet so rich in its teaching, gives us the best and most complete illustration of the meaning of our Lord's command and the union to which He invites us.

The parable teaches us *the nature* of that union. The connection between the vine and the branch is a living one. No external, temporary union is described here, and no work of man can make it happen. The branch, whether an original or an engrafted one, is the Creator's own work; the life, the sap, the fatness, and the fruitfulness of the branch are only possible because of its attachment to the vine. And so it is with the believer, too. His union with his Lord is no work of human wisdom or human will, but an act of God by which the closest and most complete life-union possible is forged between the Son of God and the sinner. "God has sent forth the Spirit of His Son into your hearts" (Galatians 4:6 NKJV). The same Spirit that dwelt and still dwells in the Son becomes the life of the believer; in the unity of that one Spirit, and the fellowship of the same life that is in Christ, he is one with Him. As between the vine and branch, it is a life-union that makes them one.

It will be as if He says, "Think, believer, how completely I belong to you. I have joined myself inseparably to you; all the fullness and fatness of the Vine are yours. It is My desire and My honor to make you a fruitful branch; only *Abide in Me*. You are weak, but I am strong; you are poor, but I am rich. Only abide in Me; yield yourself wholly to My teaching and rule; simply trust My love, My grace, and My promises. Only believe; I am wholly yours; I am the Vine, you are the branch. Abide in Me."

Abiding in Christ

THE GLORIFIED ONE

Your life is hidden with Christ in God. When Christ who is our life appears, then you also will appear with Him in glory.
COLOSSIANS 3:3–4 (NKJV)

THE ONE WHO ABIDES in Christ, the Crucified One, learns what it is to be crucified with Him and in Him to be dead to sin. The one who abides in Christ, the Risen and Glorified One, becomes a partaker of His resurrection life and the glory He is now crowned with in heaven. Unspeakable are the blessings that flow out of our union with Jesus in His glorified life.

This life is a life of *perfect victory and rest.* Before His death, the Son of God had to suffer and struggle, could be tempted and troubled by sin and its assaults. But as the Risen One, He has triumphed over sin; and, as the Glorified One, His humanity has participated in the glory of Deity. The believer who abides in Him as such is led to see how the power of sin and the flesh are indeed destroyed; the consciousness of complete and everlasting deliverance becomes increasingly clear, and blessed rest and peace—the fruit of such a conviction that victory and deliverance are an accomplished fact—take possession of the life.

It is a life of *wondrous expectation and hope.* Christ sits at the right hand of God, *waiting in expectation* till all His enemies are made His footstool (Hebrews 10:13), looking forward to the time when He will receive His full reward, when His glory will be known to all, and His beloved people will be with Him forever in that glory.

May our daily lives be the bright and blessed proof that a hidden power dwells within, preparing us for the glory to be revealed. May our abiding in Christ the Glorified One be our strength to live to the glory of the Father, our enabling to share in the glory of the Son.

Abiding in Christ

HUMILITY AND EXALTATION

TAKE EVERY OPPORTUNITY to humble yourself before God and man. Accept with gratitude everything that God allows from within or without, from friend or enemy, in nature or in grace, to remind you of your need for humbling and to help you in it. Reckon humility to be the mother-virtue, your very first duty before God, the one perpetual safeguard of the soul, and set your heart upon it as the source of all blessing. The promise is divine and sure: He that humbles himself shall be exalted.

Humble yourselves, therefore, under God's mighty hand, that he may lift you up in due time.
1 PETER 5:6

All God's dealings with us are characterized by two stages. First, is a time of preparation, when command and promise, with the mingled experience of effort and failure, and a holy expectancy of something better, awakens, trains, and disciplines us for a higher stage. The second stage is fulfillment, when faith inherits the promise and enjoys what it had so often struggled for in vain.

To every Christian the command comes from the throne of God himself: humble yourself. The earnest attempt to listen and obey will be rewarded with the painful discovery of two things: the depth of our pride, and the powerlessness of all our efforts to destroy it. Blessed is the man who has learned to put his hope in God.

Water always fills first the lowest places. The lower, the emptier a man lies before God, the speedier and the fuller will be the inflow of the divine glory. The exaltation God promises is not, cannot be, any external thing apart from himself: All that He has to give or can give is only more of himself, in order that He might take the more complete possession. The presence and the power of the glorified Christ will come to them that are of a humble spirit.

Humility

THE OPEN REWARD

When they saw the courage of Peter and John and realized that they were unschooled, ordinary men, they were astonished and they took note that these men had been with Jesus.
ACTS 4:13

THE TRANSITION FROM fellowship with God in the morning hour to interaction with others is sometimes difficult. If we have met God, we long to maintain the sense of His presence and our surrender to Him. We go to the breakfast table, where perhaps the atmosphere is suddenly changed, and when the presence of others and the mundane asserts itself, we begin to lose what we had so recently found. Many a young Christian has been perplexed with the question of how to keep his heart filled with what he does not feel at liberty to discuss or does not have the opportunity to share.

The blessing of communion with God may easily be lost by entering into meaningless conversation with people. The spirit of prayer must be sustained by watchfulness throughout the day; we do not know at what hour the enemy may come. This continuance of the morning watch may be maintained by a quiet self-restraint, not giving in to the pull of the flesh.

In the circle of a Christian home, it is a wonderful thing if each member repeats a text at the breakfast table on some particular subject, allowing occasion for spiritual conversation. Once the abiding sense of God's presence and communion with Him has become the goal of the morning hour as well as deep humility and loving relationship with those around us, grace will be found to proceed into the day's duties with unbroken fellowship. It is a great privilege to enter the inner chamber, to shut the door, and to meet the Father in secret. It is a further privilege to open the door and continue to enjoy that presence that nothing can disturb.

The Believer's Daily Renewal

DWELLING IN THE HOLY PLACE THROUGH THE BLOOD

THROUGH SIN MAN WAS driven out of paradise and away from the presence and fellowship of God. God in His mercy sought from the beginning to restore this broken fellowship. To this end He gave to Israel, through the shadow types of the tabernacle, the expectation of a time to come, when the wall of partition would be removed so that His people might dwell in His presence.

Therefore, brothers, since we have confidence to enter the Most Holy Place by the blood of Jesus, by a new and living way opened for us . . . and since we have a great priest over the house of God, let us draw near to God with a sincere heart in full assurance of faith.
HEBREWS 10:19–22

What is this Holy Place? It is the place where God dwells, the dwelling place of the Most High. This does not refer only to heaven, but to the *spiritual* Holy Place of God's presence.

What a glorious privilege it is to enter into the Holy Place and dwell there, to walk all day in the presence of God. What a rich blessing is poured out there. In the Holy Place, the favor and fellowship of God are enjoyed; the life and blessing of God are experienced; the power and joy of God are found. It is a holy life of prayer and blessedness.

Admission to the Holy Place, like the place itself, belongs to God. God himself thought of it and prepared it; we have the liberty, the freedom, and the right to enter by the blood of Jesus.

Believer in Jesus Christ, do you have liberty to enter into and abide in the Holy Place as one who has been redeemed? It is fitting for you to make your home there, for Christ cannot reveal the full power of His redemption anywhere else. There He can bless you richly. May it be the one desire of our hearts to enter into the Holy Place and to abide there.

The Blood of Christ

THE RELATIONSHIP OF PRAYER AND LOVE

"And when you stand praying, if you hold anything against anyone, forgive him, so that your Father in heaven may forgive you your sins."
MARK 11:25

THESE WORDS IMMEDIATELY follow the great prayer promise "Whatever you ask for in prayer, believe that you have received it, and it will be yours." We have already seen how the words that preceded our promise "Have faith in God" show that in prayer everything depends upon our relationship to God being clear. The words that follow it remind us that our relationship with others must also be unhindered. Love for God and love for our neighbor are inseparable; prayer from a heart that is not right with God or that cannot get along with others can have no real effect. Faith and love are interdependent.

Every prayer depends upon our faith in God's pardoning grace. If God dealt with us according to our sins, not one prayer would be heard. Pardon opens the door to all of God's love and blessing; because God has pardoned our sins, our prayers can prevail. The ground for answered prayer is God's forgiving love. When God's love and forgiveness have taken possession of our hearts, we will pray in faith and we will live in love. God's forgiving disposition, revealed in His love to us, will become our disposition as the power of His forgiving love is shed abroad in our hearts.

If an injury or injustice is done to us, we must seek first of all to maintain a godlike disposition—to be kept from a desire to maintain our rights or to punish the offender. In the annoyances of daily life, we must be careful not to excuse a hasty temper, sharp words, or rash judgment by saying that we meant no harm, that we did not hold the anger long, or that it is too much to ask of our human nature not to behave in such a manner. Instead, we must seek to forgive as God in Christ has forgiven us, diffusing anger and judgment.

Believing Prayer

COMMITMENT—THE GREAT NEED OF THE CHURCH

WHEN GOD REVEALED His love in the gift of His Son, His great work was completed. When Christ died on the cross, was raised again, and seated on the throne of God, His work was completed. Then began the dispensation of the

Because you are sons, God has sent forth the Spirit of His Son into your hearts, crying out, "Abba, Father!"
GALATIANS 4:6 (NKJV)

Spirit, whose office it was to reveal and impart all that the work of God through Christ had prepared. This work of the Holy Spirit has not yet been totally accomplished; it is for this that Christ sits upon the throne until all His enemies are made His footstool.

There is a great difference between the work of the Father, the Son, and the Holy Spirit. The Father and the Son accomplished their work for and on behalf of humankind: salvation that prepared them for their acceptance. The Holy Spirit's work is to impart to us the grace that enables us to accept and live out what the Father and the Son have provided. The distinguishing mark of the operation of the Spirit is that His work and our work are inextricably linked together. When Paul spoke of God in Christ reconciling the world to himself, he added, "and has committed to us the word of reconciliation" (2 Corinthians 5:19 NKJV). Making the reconciliation known was entrusted to the church.

Thank God for the assurance that the Holy Spirit has been given, that He is ready and able to indwell His church. Let us readily confess to the true condition of the church and our responsibility in it. Let all who believe in God, in His love and His almighty power, bear testimony to the one thing needful: God is longing to enter by the power of the Spirit into possession of His redeemed people. May our one desire be that of being filled with His power, yielded completely to be made suitable for the dwelling, the worship, and service of the living God.

The Believer's Call to Commitment

Because of Your Unbelief

Then the disciples came to Jesus in private and asked, "Why couldn't we drive it out?" He replied, "Because you have so little faith."
Matthew 17:19–20

WHEN THE LORD JESUS sent His disciples into different parts of Palestine, He endued them with authority to drive out evil spirits and to heal every disease and sickness (Matthew 10:1). On the day of the Transfiguration, while the Lord was still on the mountain, a father brought his son who was possessed with a demon to His disciples, begging them to cast out the evil spirit, but they could not. After Jesus had delivered the child, the disciples asked Him why they had been unable to do it. He answered them, "Because you have so little fiath."

Today divine healing is scarcely believed in. One may ask the reason, and here are two answers that have been given: The greater number think that miracles, the gift of healing included, were limited to the time of the primitive church, that their object was to establish the first foundation of Christianity. Other believers say that if the church has lost these gifts it is her fault. It is because she has become worldly that the Spirit does not act on her behalf, and because she has not remained in direct relationship with the power of the unseen world.

What do the Scriptures say? The Bible does not authorize us, either by the words of the Lord or His apostles, to believe that the gifts of healing were granted only to the early church; on the contrary, the promise that Jesus made to the apostles when He gave them instructions concerning their mission, shortly before His ascension, appear to us applicable to all times (Mark 16:15–18). Paul places the gift of healing among the operations of the Holy Spirit. James gives a precise command on this matter without any restriction of time. The entire Scriptures declare that these graces will be granted according to the measure of the Spirit and of faith.

Divine Healing

How Glorious the Experience!

All of them were filled with the Holy Spirit and began to speak in other tongues as the Spirit enabled them.
ACTS 2:4

DURING THE LORD'S training of His disciples, He spared no pains in teaching and exhorting them with the goal to renew and sanctify them. In most respects, however, they remained just what they were. The reason they did not change was that up to this point He was to them only the "external" Christ, one who stood outside of them and sought to work in them through His Word and His personal influence. With the advent of Pentecost, this relationship was entirely changed. Through the Holy Spirit He came as the indwelling Christ to become in the innermost recesses of their being the life of their life.

Jesus Christ, the crucified, glorified Lord from heaven, came in power by the Spirit to impart to them the ever-abiding presence of their Lord that had been promised to them, and in a way that was intimate, all-powerful, and wholly divine. Instead of the Jesus they knew in the flesh, He became Jesus within them.

This, in truth, is still the only way to real sanctification, to a life that actually overcomes sin. Many believers keep their minds occupied only with the external Christ on the cross or in heaven, and wait for the blessing of His teaching and His working without understanding that the blessing of Pentecost brings Him *into us,* to work His life *in us.*

If you would taste the joy, if you would know by personal experience the blessedness of having Jesus in your heart, of having within you His Spirit of holiness and humility, love and self-sacrifice, courage and power, as naturally and continuously as your own spirit—then separate yourselves from everything that is of this world and cast it from your heart; fix your desire on this one thing: to be filled with the Spirit of God.

The Fullness of the Spirit

HUMILITY AND FAITH

"How can you believe if you accept praise from one another, yet make no effort to obtain the praise that comes from the only God?"
JOHN 5:44

THE PROMISES MADE to faith are free and sure; the invitation and encouragement strong; the mighty power of God close at hand and free. All that hinders the blessing being ours is pride or a lack of faith. In our text, Jesus reveals to us that it is indeed pride that makes faith impossible: "How can you believe if you accept praise from one another?" As we see how in their very nature pride and faith are irreconcilably at odds, we learn that faith and humility are at their root one, and that we can never have more of true faith than we have of true humility. It is possible to have strong intellectual convictions and assurance of the truth while pride is still in the heart, but it makes living faith, which has power with God, impossible.

Humility is simply the disposition that prepares the soul for living in trust. Even the most secret breath of pride, in self-seeking, self-will, self-confidence, or self-exaltation, is only the strengthening of that self that cannot enter the kingdom or possess the things of the kingdom because it refuses to allow God to be who He is.

"How can you believe if you accept praise from one another?" Nothing can cure you of the desire to receive glory from men or of the sensitiveness and pain and anger that come when it is not given, but seeking alone the glory that comes from God. Let the glory of the all-glorious God be everything to you. You will be freed from the glory of men and of self and be content and glad to be nothing. Out of this nothingness you will grow strong in faith, giving glory to God, and you will find that the deeper you sink in humility before Him, the nearer He is to fulfill every desire of your faith.

Humility

CHRIST, OUR EXAMPLE

OUR HEAD, CHRIST, took the lowest place on the cross, and so He has marked out for us, His members, the lowest place. The radiance of God's glory (Hebrews 1:3) became the afflicted One of men (Isaiah 53:4). Since that time the only right we have is to be the last and the lowest. When we claim anything more, we have not yet fully understood the cross.

We seek for a higher life, and we will find it if we go deeper into the fellowship of the Cross with our Lord. We long for full victory. And we find it as we more fully enter into the fellowship of His Cross. The Lamb obtained His greatest victory with His hands and feet nailed to a cross. We abide in the shadow of the Almighty only so long as we abide under the shadow of that cross. The Cross must be our home. There alone are we sheltered and protected. We first understand our own cross when we have understood His. May we desire to get so close to it that we not only see it but we also embrace it, take it up, and make it our own. Then the Cross asserts itself in us, and we experience His power—to the point that we do not faint under it but carry it with joy.

What would Jesus be without His cross? His pierced feet have bruised the head of the Enemy, and His pierced hands have spoiled the devil's tactics completely. What are we without the cross of Christ? Do not let it go, but hold it securely. Do we think we can go by any other road than that which the Master trod?

The grace of God that brings salvation has appeared to all men. It teaches us to say "No" to ungodliness and worldly passions . . . while we wait for the . . . glorious appearing of our great God and Savior, Jesus Christ, who gave himself for us to redeem us from all wickedness and to purify for himself a people that are his very own, eager to do what is good.
TITUS 2:11–14

Living a Prayerful Life

THE IMPORTANCE OF THE MORNING WATCH

For if the firstfruit is holy, the lump is also holy; and if the root is holy, so are the branches.
ROMANS 11:16 (NKJV)

THERE IS GRACIOUS provision suggested by many types and examples of the Old Testament by which an hour set aside at the beginning of each day enables us to assimilate a blessing for our work and gives us the assurance of victory over temptation. What cause for praise and joy that the morning watch can so renew and strengthen our surrender to Jesus and our faith in Him that the life of obedience can not only be maintained but also go from strength to strength.

Only one thing will suffice to keep us faithful in communing with God—*a sincere desire for fellowship with Him*. It is in the place of quiet where we are alone with God that our spiritual life is both tested and strengthened. There is the battlefield where it is decided every day whether God will have all of us and whether our life will be one of absolute obedience. If we truly conquer there, committing ourselves into the hands of our Lord and finding a refuge in Him, the victory during the day is certain.

The superficiality of our Christian service comes from having so little real contact with God. If it is true that God alone is the source of love, goodness, and happiness, and that to have as much as possible of His presence, His fellowship, and His blessing is our highest joy, then surely to meet Him alone in the morning ought to be our aim. To have had God appear to them and speak to them was the secret of the strength of the Old Testament saints.

God has called us to live a life in the supernatural. Allow your devotional time each day to be as the open gate of heaven through which light and power stream into your waiting heart and from which you go out to walk with God all day.

A Life of Obedience

THE POWER OF FOOD

LIFE MUST BE FED with life. In a seed the life of nature is hidden, and we enjoy the power of that life in bread. As with the body so it is with the spirit. The body is fed by the visible, the changeable life; the spirit must be fed with the invisible, unchangeable life of heaven.

"For my flesh is real food and my blood is real drink. Whoever eats my flesh and drinks my blood remains in me, and I in him."
JOHN 6:55–56

It was to bring to us this heavenly life that the Son of God descended to earth. It was to make this life accessible to us that He died like the seed in the earth, that His body was broken like the grain of wheat. It is to communicate this life to us and to make it our own that He gives himself to us in the Lord's Supper.

By His death Jesus took away the cause of our everlasting hunger and sorrow; namely, sin. The spirit of man, his part that does not die, can live only by God, who only has immortality. Sin separated man from God, and an eternal hunger and an eternal thirst of death are now his portion. He lost God, and nothing in the world can satisfy his infinite cravings. But Jesus comes and takes sin away and brings it to nothing in His body and gives us that body to eat and to do away with sin in us. Since in Him dwells the fullness of the Godhead bodily, when I receive and enjoy Him, not only do I have the forgiveness of sins but I have the life of God.

Wonderful grace! May we come to understand it. The one who benefits from the Lord's Supper is the one who is distinguished from others by the fact that he or she has partaken of the Bread of Life.

Glorious food! Heavenly bread! It imparts heavenly life to us. Love to God, blessed rest, true holiness, inward power, all that characterizes the life that is enjoyed in heaven. Let us be encouraged. We can do all things through Christ, who strengthens us. He dwells in us. He is our food.

The Lord's Table

GOD SEEKS INTERCESSORS

"You did not choose me, but I chose you . . . to go and bear fruit—fruit that will last. Then the Father will give you whatever you ask in my name."
JOHN 15:16

THERE IS A WORLD out there with millions who are perishing without Christ. The work of intercession is its only hope. Much of our expressions of love and work in ministry are comparatively vain because there is so little real intercession connected with it. Millions live as though there never were such a one as the Son of God who died for them. Millions pass into outer darkness without hope year after year. Of the millions who bear the name of Christ the great majority live in utter ignorance or indifference.

Every soul is worth more than the world and nothing less than the price paid for it by Christ's blood. Each is within reach of the power that can be tapped through intercession. We have no concept of the magnitude of the work to be done by God's intercessors or we would cry out to God for an outpouring of the Spirit of intercession.

When God called His people out of Egypt, He separated the priestly tribe to draw near to Him, stand before Him, and bless the people in His name. From time to time He sought, found, and especially honored intercessors, for whose sake He spared or blessed His people.

We may praise God that in our day, too, there is an ever-increasing number who are beginning to see and prove that in the church and in missions, in large organizations as well as small groups and individual efforts, intercession is being acknowledged as the primary power by which God moves and opens heaven.

Because there is lack of intercession there is lack of blessing. Oh, that we would turn our eyes and heart from everything else and fix them upon the God who hears our prayers until the magnificence of His promises and His power and His purpose of love overwhelms us!

The Ministry of Intercessory Prayer

HOLINESS AND CHASTISEMENT

WHAT CHRIST WAS and won was all for us. And it is the power of the new life that comes from Him to us. In the light of His example, we can prove that suffering is to God's child the token of the Father's love and the channel of His richest blessing. To such faith the apparent mystery of suffering is seen to be nothing but a divine need—the light affliction that works out the exceeding weight of glory.

> *But God disciplines us for our good, that we may share in his holiness. . . . Without holiness no one will see the Lord.*
> HEBREWS 12:10, 14

"God disciplines us for our good, that we may share in his holiness." Of all the precious words Holy Scripture has for the sorrowful, there is hardly one equal to this in leading us more directly and more deeply into the fullness of blessing that suffering is meant to bring. It is His holiness, God's own holiness, of which we are to partake.

Sometimes it is difficult to see the blessing in affliction, even to God's children. Affliction by nature stirs up opposition to God's will because a loss of peace and happiness has been suffered. But in spite of an initial negative response, the affliction is working out God's purposes: "To humble [us] and to test [us] in order to know what was in [our] heart" (Deuteronomy 8:2) is still His object in leading us into the wilderness. To a great extent we are not aware that the practice of our Christianity is often selfish and superficial. When we accept the teaching of chastisement in unmasking the self-will and love of the world that still prevails, we have learned one of its first and most necessary lessons.

Chastisement leads to the fellowship of God's Son. Only in Christ do we have the power to love and rejoice in the will of God. In Him we have the power. In suffering He draws near; He makes our suffering the fellowship of His suffering, and in it makes himself—who was perfected through suffering—our sanctification.

The Path to Holiness

A CONSECRATED HOME

*"But if serving the LORD
seems undesirable to you,
then choose for yourselves
this day whom you will
serve, whether the gods
your forefathers served
beyond the River, or the
gods of the Amorites, in
whose land you are living.
But as for me and my
household, we will
serve the LORD."*
JOSHUA 24:15

IN GOD'S DEALINGS with Noah and Abraham, and with Israel in the Passover and at Mount Sinai, we see repeatedly the mention of father and children as these relate to His commands and promises. Such is always the language of the covenant God. In the words of Joshua we have the response from earth, "As for me and my household. . . ." The parent boldly vouches for his family as well as for himself; the covenant engagement of the Father in heaven is met by the covenant obligation of the father on earth.

Here Joshua is to us the model of a godly parent, and in him we can see what parental guidance in the faith ought to be.

Let it be a *personal* faith. "But as *for me* and my household"—he began with himself. For a godly education the first and the most essential prerequisite is personal consecration. It is good to reflect on our responsibility, to examine our duties and the best way of fulfilling them, to speak with our children and to pray continually for them—but all these may be called accessories. The first and most important action on the part of the parent is to maintain a life devoted to God and His service. It is this commitment that creates the spiritual atmosphere for the children.

There must be no hesitation or halfheartedness in the confession of our devotion to God's service. In the home and out of it, it must be a settled thing in the heart of a parent: "But as for me . . . [I] will serve the Lord."

Raising Your Child to Love God

THE SPIRIT OF THE GLORIFIED JESUS

OUR LORD SAID that those who come to Him, believing, will not only never thirst again, but will become as living fountains, flowing out to others in new life and blessing.

When Jesus, who had been from eternity with His Father, became flesh, He entered upon a new stage of existence. He was still the only begotten Son of God, and yet not altogether the same. For He was now also, as Son of Man, the first-begotten from the dead, clothed

"He who believes in Me, as the Scripture has said, out of his heart will flow rivers of living water."
But this He spoke concerning the Spirit, whom those believing in Him would receive; for the Holy Spirit was not yet given, because Jesus was not yet glorified.
JOHN 7:38–39 (NKJV)

with that glorified humanity that He had perfected and sanctified for himself. Likewise, the Spirit of God poured out at Pentecost was indeed something new. Through the Old Testament, He was always called the Spirit of God or the Spirit of the Lord. The name "Holy Spirit" was not yet used. It was only in connection with His work in preparing the way for Christ, and a body for Him, that the proper name comes into use (Luke 1:15, 35). When poured out at Pentecost, He came as the Spirit of the glorified Jesus, the Spirit of the incarnate, crucified, and exalted Christ, the bearer and communicator of that life as it had been interwoven into the human nature of the person of Christ. It is in this capacity that He can dwell in us also.

These thoughts open to us further the reason why it is not the Spirit of God (as spoken of in the Old Testament) but the Spirit of Jesus that was sent to dwell in us. Sin had not only disturbed our relationship to God's law, but to God himself; with divine favor lost, we lost divine life. Christ came not only to deliver us from the law and its curse, but to bring human nature back into fellowship with divine life.

The Spirit of Christ

THE SECRET PLACE
OF PRAYER

*"Ane when you pray, do
not be like the hypocrites,
for they love to pray
standing in the synagogues
and on the street corners
to be seen of men."*
MATTHEW 6:5

JESUS GAVE HIS FIRST disciples
their first public teaching in the Sermon
on the Mount. He expounded to them
the kingdom of God, its laws and its life.
In that kingdom God is not only King
but Father. He not only gives all but is
all. The knowledge and fellowship of
Him alone is its own reward. So the revelation of prayer and the prayer
life was a part of His teaching concerning the new kingdom He came to
set up. Moses gave neither command nor regulation with regard to
prayer. Even the prophets say very little in direct reference to the practice of prayer. *It is Christ who teaches us to pray.*

The first thing the Lord teaches His disciples is that they must have a
secret place for prayer. Jesus is our teacher in the school of prayer. He
taught us at Samaria that worship is no longer confined to times and
places, but that true spiritual worship is something of the spirit and of
life. But He still sees it as important that each one choose a location where
he can daily meet with Him. That inner room, that solitary place, is Jesus'
schoolroom. That spot could be anywhere. It may even change from day
to day if we have to move for the sake of family or schedules, but there
must be a secret place and a quiet time in which the student places himself in the Master's presence to be prepared by Him to worship the Father.
Jesus comes to us in that place and teaches us to pray.

God hides himself from the carnal eye. If in worship we are primarily
occupied with our own thoughts and exercises, we will not meet Him
who is spirit. But to the one who withdraws himself from all that is of
the world and the flesh and prepares to wait upon God alone, the Father
will reveal himself.

Teach Me to Pray

KEEPING ALL HIS WAYS

IF WE WANT TO FIND someone, we ask where he lives and how to get there. When we wait on God, we must be sure we are in His way; outside of it we cannot expect to find Him. "You meet

Wait on the LORD, and keep His way, and He shall exalt you to inherit the land.
PSALM 37:34 (NKJV)

him who rejoices and does righteousness, who remembers You in Your ways" (Isaiah 64:5 NKJV).

The connection is very close between the two parts of the command in our text: "Wait on the Lord"—having to do with worship and attitude—"and keep His way"—dealing with our walk and work. The outer life must be in harmony with the inner life; the inner is the inspiration and the strength for the outer. God has made known in His Word His way for our conduct and invites our confidence that His grace and help will come when we need it. If we do not keep His way, our waiting on Him will be futile. Surrender in full obedience to all His will is the secret of access to the blessings of His fellowship.

Do not harbor the fear that you cannot keep His way. None of us has the strength in ourselves, but if we surrender to God and trust Him, the strength will come. He will prove himself to you and work in you that which is pleasing in His sight through Jesus Christ. It is important to be *willing* to walk in His ways. Do not think about waiting on God while in your heart you are not willing to be obedient. However weak you feel, only be willing, and He who has worked to *will*, will work to *do* by His power.

Come and learn that He is the God who is good and who alone can work any good thing. Be content to receive from God each moment of the day His grace to wait, to believe, and to see Him work all that is good in your life.

Waiting on God

AT THIS MOMENT

Behold, now is the accepted time; behold, now is the day of salvation.

2 CORINTHIANS 6:2 (NKJV)

IT HAS BEEN WELL SAID that in that little word *now* lies one of the deepest secrets of the life of faith. At the close of a conference on the spiritual life a minister of experience rose and spoke. He said he did not know if he had learned any truth he did not know before, but he had learned how to use correctly what he already knew. He had learned that it was his privilege at each moment, whatever his surrounding circumstances might be, to say, "Jesus saves me *now*." This is the secret of rest and victory.

Whatever the present moment may hold, however unprepared the message finds you, however sad the divided and hopeless state of your life may be, do come and surrender—this very moment. I know that it will take time for the Lord to assert His power and arrange all within you according to His will, time to conquer your enemies and train all your powers for His service. This is not the work of a moment. But there are things that *are* the work of a moment—of this moment. One is your surrender of all to Jesus, your surrender of yourself entirely to live only in Him. As time goes on, and exercise has made faith stronger and brighter, that surrender may become clearer and more intelligent. But for this you cannot wait. The only way to attain it is to begin at once.

Let any Christian begin, then, and he will quickly experience how the blessing of the present moment is passed on to the next. It is the unchanging Jesus to whom he links himself; it is the power of a divine life, in its unbroken continuity, that takes possession of him. The *do it now* of the present moment—although it seems such a little thing—is nothing less than the beginning of the ever-present now, which is the mystery and the glory of eternity.

Abiding in Christ

THAT GOD MAY BE
ALL IN ALL

WHAT MYSTERY THERE is in this section of Scripture! We speak of the two great acts of humility on the part of the Lord Jesus: His descending from the throne in heaven and becoming a man upon earth, a servant among men, and His descent through the cross, into the grave, and the depth of humiliation under the curse of sin. But another mystery is spoken of here: The time is coming when the Son of Man will be subjected to the Father and will give the kingdom into the Father's hands that "God may be all in all"! It is hard to grasp this; it passes our human understanding.

Then the end will come, when he hands over the kingdom to God the Father after he has destroyed all dominion, authority and power. . . . When he has done this, then the Son himself will be made subject to him who put everything under him, so that God may be all in all.
1 CORINTHIANS 15:24, 28

Here we learn a precious lesson: *The whole aim of Christ's coming, the whole aim of redemption, the whole aim of Christ's work in our hearts is summed up in the one goal: "That God may be all in all."* Let us take this as our life motto. If we fail to see that this is Christ's object, we will never understand what He desires to work in us. But if we realize that everything must be subordinated to God the Father, then we will have the same principle ruling our life that ruled the life of Christ. Let us meditate upon it with the earnest prayer: *Father, we hope to be present on that wondrous day when Christ will give up the kingdom, and when you will be all in all. We hope to be there to see it, to experience it, and to rejoice in it throughout all eternity. Help us to know something of it now, Lord. Take your place and reveal your glory that our hearts may bow before you, having but one song and one hope:* that God may be all in all. *Amen.*

Absolute Surrender

PRAYER AND THE WORD OF GOD

When Moses entered the Tent of Meeting to speak with the LORD, he heard the voice speaking to him from between the two cherubim above the atonement cover on the ark of the Testimony. And he spoke with him.
NUMBERS 7:89

WITH REGARD TO the connection between prayer and the Word in our private devotions, the expression of a new convert has often been quoted: "When I pray, I speak to God; when I read the Bible, God speaks to me." When Moses prayed for himself or his people and waited for instructions, he found God waiting for him. What a lesson for our morning watch! A prayerful spirit is the spirit God will speak to. A prayerful spirit will be a listening spirit waiting to hear what God will say.

As we enter the place of secret prayer, let us be as eager to hear Him speak as we are to say what is on our heart. The highest blessing of prayer will come as we cease to pray and let God speak.

Prayer and the Word are inseparably linked; power in the use of either depends upon the presence of the other. The Word gives you a subject for prayer. It shows you the path of prayer, telling you how God would have you come. It gives you the power for prayer—courage in the assurance that you will be heard. And it brings you the answer to prayer as it teaches what God will do for you. On the other hand, prayer prepares your heart to receive the Word from God himself, to receive spiritual understanding from the Spirit, and to build faith that participates in its mighty working.

In prayer and His Word, God must be everything. Make God the aim of your heart, the one object of your desire. Prayer and His Word will result in blessed fellowship with God, the interchange of thought, love, and life—dwelling in God and God in you.

The Believer's Daily Renewal

JESUS CHRIST IS NOT only Priest to purchase and King to secure, but also Prophet to reveal to us the salvation that God has prepared for those who love Him. Just as at creation the light was first called into existence, that in it all God's other works might have their life and beauty, so in our text wisdom is men-

Of Him [God] you are in Christ Jesus, who became for us wisdom from God—and righteousness and sanctification and redemption.
1 CORINTHIANS 1:30
(NKJV)

tioned first as the treasury in which are found the three precious gifts that follow. The life is the light of man (John 1:4); in revealing this to us, and enabling us to see the glory of God in His own face, Christ makes us partakers of eternal life. It was by the Tree of Knowledge that sin came; it is through the knowledge that Christ gives that salvation comes. He is made by God wisdom for us. *In Him* are hidden all the treasures of wisdom and knowledge (Colossians 2:3).

It is this connection between what Christ has been made for us and how we have it only as we are in Him that we need to understand better. The blessings prepared for us in Christ cannot be obtained as special gifts in answer to prayer *apart from abiding in Him*. The answer to each prayer must come in a closer union and deeper abiding in Him; in Him—the unspeakable gift—all other gifts are treasured up, including the gifts of wisdom and knowledge.

Let us be content to possess Christ, to dwell in Him, to make Him our life. Only in a deeper searching into Him will we find the knowledge we desire. Just as much as you need to know and are capable of understanding will be communicated, *if you only trust Him*. Never think of the riches of wisdom and knowledge hidden in Jesus as treasures without a key or of your way as a path without a light. Jesus, your wisdom, is guiding you in the right way, even when you do not see it.

Abiding in Christ

A MAN OF PRAYER

MOSES IS THE FIRST man appointed to be a teacher and leader of others. After his first call in Egypt, Moses prayed. He asked God what he saw in him and why He would choose him and then what he was to say when people asked him who God was. He argued with God about all his weaknesses and begged Him to be relieved of his mission. When the people reproached him because their workload was increased, he told God about it and expressed to Him all his fears. This was a time of training for Moses. Out of his trouble was born his power in prayer, when time after time Pharaoh asked him to entreat the Lord for him, and deliverance came at Moses' request.

At the Red Sea, Moses cried to God with the people and the answer came. In the wilderness, when the people thirsted and when Amalek attacked them, it was prayer that brought deliverance.

At Sinai, when Israel made the golden calf, it was prayer that averted the threatened destruction. It was renewed prayer that gained them restoration. It was more prayer that secured God's presence to go with them, and once again it was prayer that brought the revelation of God's glory. And when that had been given, it was fresh prayer that received the renewal of the covenant.

Moses was devoted to God, zealous, even jealous for God, for His honor and will. He was devoted to his people, ready to sacrifice himself if it meant they could be saved. He was conscious of a divine calling to act as mediator, to be the channel of communication and of blessing between God in heaven and men on earth.

The Believer's Daily Renewal

THE TRUE PLACE OF
THE CREATURE

THIS PSALM, in praise of the Creator, has been speaking of the birds and the beasts of the forest; of the young lions, and of man going forth to his work; of the great sea, in which there are innumerable creeping organisms, both small and large. And it sums up the whole relationship of all creation to its Creator and

*These all wait for You,
that You may give them
their food in due season.
What You give them they
gather in; You open
Your hand, they are
filled with good.*
PSALM 104:27–28 (NKJV)

its continuous and universal dependence on Him in the one phrase: "These all wait for You"! Just as much as it was God's work to create, it is His work to maintain. The whole creation is ruled by the one unalterable law of *waiting on God*!

The phrase is the simple expression of the very reason for which the creature was brought into existence, the very foundation of its makeup. The one purpose for which God gave life to creatures was that in them He might prove and show forth His wisdom, power, and goodness, in His being each moment their life and happiness, and in pouring out to them, according to their capacity, the riches of His goodness and power. And just as this is the place and nature of God to be the constant supplier of everything the creature needs, so the place and nature of the creature is nothing but this: to wait on God and receive from Him what He alone can give.

If our eyes are once opened to this precious truth, all nature will become a preacher, reminding us of the relationship that was begun in creation and is continued in grace. We may rest assured that the One who made us for himself that He might give himself to us and dwell in us will *never* disappoint us. In waiting on Him we will find rest and joy and strength and the supply of every need.

Waiting on God

FAITH IN THE BLOOD

God presented him as a sacrifice of atonement, through faith in his blood.
ROMANS 3:25

FAITH IN THE BLOOD of Christ is the one thing that makes the doctrines of the holiness and grace of God, of the divine and human nature of Christ, and of our deliverance from sin and union with God, understandable. In the history of the kingdom of God covering the period from the first to the second paradise (the first being the Garden of Eden), as well as in the experience of each believer, it becomes manifest that we have in the blood of Christ the supreme revelation of the wisdom, power, and love of God.

Faith is the ear that hears and receives the Word of God. It listens attentively to understand what God says. Faith is the eye that seeks to place before itself as an object of vital importance what would otherwise remain only a thought. Faith sees the invisible; it observes the things that are not seen; it is the evidence of things hoped for. So it seeks to behold, through the Spirit, the blood being brought into heaven and sprinkled upon the throne and upon the soul with powerful results.

Faith is not only an ear and an eye to ascertain but it is also a hand and mouth to receive. What it hears from the Word, and in the spirit beholds, it appropriates for itself. Faith accepts as certainty that what the Word of God says the power of God is prepared to make real.

A Christian writer has testified that the insight into what the blood can do in its ever-cleansing power was the beginning of a new experience in her spiritual life. Some time later she wrote, "I see more and more clearly that it is only by the abiding indwelling of the Holy Spirit that this hidden power of the blood can be revealed and experienced" (P. R. Havergal). May our lives also be under the teaching of the Holy Spirit that He may constantly keep us in the heavenly blessedness and joy that the blood has procured for us.

The Blood of Christ

THE PRAYERS OF MANY

UNITED PRAYER is a great privilege, and its power waits to be experienced. If the believing couple knew they were joined together in the name of Jesus to experience His presence and power in united prayer; if friends believed how effective two or three praying in concert could be; if in every prayer meeting faith in His presence and expectation of an answer were foremost; if in every church

On him we have set our hope that he will continue to deliver us, as you help us by your prayers. Then many will give thanks on our behalf for the gracious favor granted us in answer to the prayers of many.
1 CORINTHIANS 1:10–11

united prayer was regarded as one of the chief purposes for which Christians come together—the highest exercise of their power as a church; if in the church universal the coming of the kingdom, and the King himself, first in the mighty outpouring of His Holy Spirit, and then in His own glorious person, were matters of ceaseless pleading with God, who could predict what blessing might come through those who agree to prove God's promises?

The apostle Paul is a great example of faith in the power of united prayer. To the Romans he wrote and urged: "Join me in my struggle by praying to God for me" (15:30). As a result, he expected to be delivered from his enemies and to prosper in his work. Their prayer was to have a significant share in his deliverance. Of the Ephesians, he requested, "Pray in the Spirit on all occasions with all kinds of prayers and requests . . . always keep on praying for all the saints. Pray . . . that whenever I open my mouth, words may be given me so that I will fearlessly make known the mystery of the gospel" (6:18–19). Power and success in his ministry depended on their prayers.

There will be untold blessing when we meet as one in the name of Jesus and boldly claim the promise that the Father will do what we agree to ask.

Believing Prayer

COMMITMENT AND THE SPIRITUAL LIFE

Blessed be the God and Father of our Lord Jesus Christ, who has blessed us with every spiritual blessing in the heavenly places in Christ.

EPHESIANS 1:3 (NKJV)

THESE OPENING WORDS of the epistle to the Ephesians not only give us a summary of the truth of the gospel, but reveal from the depths of Paul's experience what the true Christian life is.

"Every spiritual blessing" is "in Christ." The expression *in Christ* is the keynote of the epistle, occurring more than twenty times. The words of the text are the beginning of a sentence running nonstop from verses 3 to 14, in which we find "chose us in him"; "predestined us to adoption as sons"; "accepted in the Beloved"; "redemption through His blood"; "according to the purpose of Him who works all things"; "in Him you also trusted"; "in whom . . . having believed"; and "were sealed with the Holy Spirit" (NKJV). All our blessings are stored up *in Christ*, and we are in Him.

As surely as our blessings are in Christ, so is our life in Him. Abiding in Christ means abiding in the heavenly places with all the spiritual blessings God bestows through Him. Faith in Christ is unceasing dependence on Him, fellowship with Him, and receiving every grace the soul needs from His hand. As absolutely necessary as air is to my physical needs, so is my soul kept alive through fellowship with the Lord Jesus. This is what Scripture means when it says that Christ is our life.

After grace comes the love of God. It is the Father who has blessed us in the Son. Christ is the Father's gift to us; all blessings come through Him. God's purpose was to bring us back to himself as our Creator, in whose fellowship and glory our happiness can alone be found. God could attain His purposes and satisfy the love of His own heart only by bringing us into complete union with Christ, so that in Him we can be as near to God as Christ is. Oh the mystery of the love of God!

The Believer's Call to Commitment

DISCIPLINE AND SANCTIFICATION

"IN A LARGE HOUSE there are articles . . . for noble purposes and . . . ignoble. If a man cleanses himself from the latter, he will be an instrument for noble purposes, made holy, useful to the Master and prepared to do any good work" (2 Timothy 2:20–21).

Endure hardship as discipline; God is treating you as sons. For what son is not disciplined by his father? . . . Our fathers disciplined us for a little while as they thought best; but God disciplines us for our good, that we may share in his holiness.
HEBREWS 12:7, 10

To sanctify anything is to set it apart, to consecrate it to God and to His service. God is forming for himself a holy people, and Jesus sets us free that we may be a part of that people. It is the Lord who breaks the chains by which Satan would hold us in bondage. He would have us free, wholly free to serve Him. He wills to save us, to deliver both the soul and the body, that each of the members of the body may be consecrated to Him and placed unreservedly at His disposal.

A large number of Christians do not yet understand this; they do not know how to take in the fact that the purpose of their deliverance is that they may serve God. They use their life and their members to procure their own satisfaction; consequently, they do not feel at liberty to ask for healing. In these situations, the Lord may allow Satan to inflict sickness upon them, and by it they are bound (Luke 13:11, 16). "God disciplines us for our good, that we may share in his holiness" (Hebrews 12:10).

The discipline that sickness inflicts brings great blessing with it. It is a call to reflect; it leads us to see that God cares about us and seeks to show us what it is that still separates us from God. He urges us to yield to Him, to consecrate our life to Him, and to die to ourself that we may live unto God.

Divine Healing

How It Comes to Full Manifestation

For this reason I kneel before the Father, from whom his whole family in heaven and on earth derives its name. I pray that out of his glorious riches he may strengthen you with power through his Spirit in your inner being, so that Christ may dwell in your hearts through faith. And I pray that you, being rooted and established in love, may have power, together with all the saints, to grasp how wide and long and high and deep is the love of Christ.
Ephesians 3:14–18

I HAVE SAID BEFORE that every blessing God gives is like a seed with the power of an indissoluble life hidden in it. Let no one think that to be filled with the Spirit is a condition of perfection that leaves nothing more to be desired. It was even after the Lord Jesus was filled with the Spirit that He had to be further tested by temptation and so learn obedience.

When the disciples were filled on the Day of Pentecost, power from on high was given them that they might know victory over sin in their own lives. The Spirit must guide us into all truth. But it will be step by step that He leads us into the eternal purposes of God. The fullness of the Spirit is preparation for living and working as a child of God.

The prayer of Paul quoted here is regarded as one of the most glorious representations of what the Christian life should be. He desires that God bring to bear all the wealth of His grace in a fashion consistent with the divine glory of His power, and as the living God to strengthen these believers with might in the inner man.

The gift of the Holy Spirit is God's pledge that He will work everything in us every day of our lives. Our dependence must be entirely on God. He alone can finish the work He has begun in us.

The Fullness of the Spirit

HUMILITY AND HAPPINESS

IT SEEMS THAT PAUL'S thorn in the flesh was sent to humble him so that he might not exalt himself as a result of the great revelations given to him. Paul's first desire was to have the thorn removed, and he asked the Lord three times that it might be taken away. The answer came to him that the trial was a blessing—that through the weakness and humiliation it brought, the grace and strength of the Lord could better be manifested. Paul at once entered upon a new stage in his relationship to the trial: instead of simply enduring it, *he gladly gloried* in it; instead of asking for deliverance, *he took pleasure* in it. He had learned that the place of humiliation is the place of blessing, of power, and of joy.

> *Therefore I will boast all the more gladly about my weaknesses, so that Christ's power may rest on me. That is why, for Christ's sake, I delight in weaknesses. . . . For when I am weak, then I am strong.*
> 2 CORINTHIANS 12:9–10

Many Christians fear and flee and seek deliverance from all that would humble them. At times they may pray for humility, but in their heart of hearts they pray even more to be kept from the things that would bring them to that place.

Paul needed special discipline, and with it special instruction to learn what was more precious than even the unutterable things he had heard from heaven: what it is to glory in weakness and lowliness.

The school in which Jesus taught Paul is our school as well. He watches over us with a jealous, loving care, lest we exalt ourselves. Through trials and failures and troubles, He seeks to bring us to the place where His grace is everything. His strength is made perfect in our weakness; His presence fills and satisfies our emptiness; and becomes the secret of humility. We shall find that the deepest humility is the secret of the truest happiness, of a joy that nothing can destroy.

Humility

Continuing Deliverance
From Prayerlessness

"Do not let your hearts be troubled. Trust in God; trust also in me. . . . I tell you the truth, anyone who has faith in me will do what I have been doing. He will do even greater things than these, because I am going to the Father."
John 14:1, 12

THE LORD WANTED TO teach His disciples that all they had learned from the Old Testament concerning the power and holiness and love of God must now be transferred to Him. They must not believe merely in certain written documents but in Him personally. They must believe that He was in the Father, and the Father in Him, in such a sense that they had one life and one glory. All they knew about God they would find in Christ. He laid great emphasis on this, because it was only through such faith in Him and His divine glory that they could do the works that He did, and even greater works. This faith would lead them to know that just as Christ and the Father are one, so also were they in Christ, and Christ was in them.

It is this intimate, spiritual, personal, uninterrupted relationship to the Lord Jesus that manifests itself powerfully in our lives, and especially in our prayer lives. Do you long to know how you may always experience deliverance from the sin of prayerlessness? Here you have the secret. Believe in the Son of God; give Him time in your quiet place of prayer to reveal himself in His ever-present nearness as the Eternal, Almighty One, the Eternal Love who watches over you.

Take time in your place of prayer to bow down and worship. Wait on Him until He reveals himself, takes possession of you, and goes with you to show you how a person may live and walk in abiding fellowship with Him. Then you will experience something that you possibly have not known before: It has not entered into the heart of man what God can do for those who love Him.

Living a Prayerful Life

UNTIL HE COMES

AT THE SUPPER, Jesus points us not only backward but also forward. From the suffering He points to the glory, out of the depths He calls to the heights. Because the Supper is the remembrance, the communion of Jesus the living Savior, it sets Him before us in all that He was and is and shall be. It is only in the future that we can expect to have the full realization of what was begun at the Lord's Supper. The Supper begins under the Cross with the reconciliation of the world; it is completed before the throne of glory in the new birth of the world.

The true Christian has yet to wait for his inheritance. "Until He comes" is his watchword at every observance of the Lord's Supper. The Lord speaks of drinking the fruit of the vine anew in the kingdom of the Father and of eating and drinking at His table in His kingdom. The Supper is the pledge of the time when they shall cry, "Blessed are they who are called to the marriage supper of the Lamb."

"For whenever you eat this bread and drink this cup, you proclaim the Lord's death until he comes. . . . I tell you, I will not drink of this fruit of the vine from now on until that day when I drink it anew with you in my Father's kingdom. . . . And I confer on you a kingdom, just as my Father conferred one on me, so that you may eat and drink at my table in my kingdom."
1 CORINTHIANS 11:26; MATTHEW 26:29; LUKE 22:29–30

What a prospect! There sin will be forever put away. There the whole church will be eternally united without fault or division. There the whole creation will share in the liberty of the glory of the children of God. Our eyes will see the King in His beauty, and we shall be like Him, for we shall see Him as He is. The Supper here and now is but a prelude, a foretaste of what is to come.

The Lord's Table

IN THE NAME OF CHRIST

"And I will do whatever you ask in my name, so that the Son may bring glory to the Father."
JOHN 14:13

A NAME CALLS TO mind the whole being and nature of a person or thing. When I speak of a lamb or a lion, the name at once suggests the nature peculiar to each. The name of God is meant to express His divine nature and glory. So also the name of Christ means His nature, His person and work, His disposition and Spirit. To ask in the name of Christ is to pray in union with Him.

As Christ's prayer nature lives in us, His prayer power becomes ours as well. The measure of our attainment or experience is not the ground of our confidence; it is the wholeheartedness of our surrender to all that Christ seeks to be in us. If we abide in Him, He says, we can ask whatever we desire.

As we live in Him, we receive the spiritual power to avail ourselves of His name. As the branch wholly surrendered to the life and service of the vine can count upon its sap and strength for its fruit, so the believer who in faith has accepted the fullness of the Spirit to possess his whole life, benefits from the power of Christ's name.

Christ came to earth as a man to reveal what true prayer is. To pray in the name of Christ, we must pray as He prayed. He taught us to pray in union with Him. Let us in love and faith accept Him as our example, our teacher, and our intercessor.

As Christ did, we must make it our primary effort to receive from the Father. No time or trouble will be too great to serve others by prayer and intercession.

Be of good courage as servants of Christ and children of God. Let no weakness or any lack cause you to fear—simply ask in the name of Christ. His name has all the power of Christ himself. His promise still stands: "You may ask me for anything in my name, and I will do it."

The Ministry of Intercessory Prayer

HOLINESS AND CLEANSING

CLEANSING IS THE negative side, washing away defilement; sanctification is the positive union and fellowship with God and the participation of the graces of the divine life and holiness. Of the altar we read that God said to Moses: "Purify the altar by making atonement for it, and anoint it to consecrate it" (Exodus 29:36).

Since we have these promises, dear friends, let us purify ourselves from everything that contaminates body and spirit, perfecting holiness out of reverence for God.
2 CORINTHIANS 7:1

Cleansing, then, prepares the way, and should always lead on to holiness.

Just as the source of all defilement of the flesh is self-gratification, so self-seeking is at the root of all defilement of the spirit. In relation to God, it manifests itself in idolatry, whether it is in the worship of other gods, the love of the world, or doing our will rather than His will. In relation to others, it shows itself in envy, hatred, a lack of love, cold neglect, or harsh judgment. In relation to ourselves, it is seen as pride, selfish ambition, and the disposition that makes self the center around which all must move and by which all must be judged.

We have often seen that what God has made holy, man must also make holy by accepting and appropriating the holiness God has given. So it is with the perfection the saints have in Christ. We must perfect holiness: holiness must be carried out into the whole of life, even to its end.

However deeply rooted the sin may appear, in constitution or in habit, we must cleanse ourselves of it if we would be holy. "If we walk in the light, as he is in the light . . . the blood of Jesus, his Son, purifies us from all sin" (1 John 1:7). Let us come into the light with our sins. The blood will prove its mighty power. Faith gives the courage and the power to cleanse from all defilement. As the Holy Spirit makes the promises of love and indwelling ours, we will share the victory that overcomes the world, even our faith.

The Path to Holiness

CHOOSING THE GOOD

But before the boy knows enough to reject the wrong and choose the right, the land of the two kings you dread will be laid waste.
ISAIAH 7:16

OF ALL THE WONDROUS powers with which God has endowed us, our will—the power that determines what we do and, therefore, what we are—is the most wonderful. To a large extent God gave us the power to decide what we will make of ourselves. The mind with all its marvelous capacities; the soul with all its wealth of feeling; the spirit, our moral and religious nature—all these have been given that we might be able to exercise the royal prerogative we have from God: to choose, and so to fashion our own being and destiny for eternity.

To the parent is given the solemn task of teaching his child how to use this power rightly. This delicate instrument of direction and choice is placed into the hands of parents to guard, strengthen, and train the child for the glory of God who gave it. Parents tend to shrink from the task, but if they will learn how wisdom can be gotten to train the child's will, they will likely count no sacrifice too great to secure it. To those who seek wisdom from God in faith, success is possible, even promised.

The problem is a delicate one: it is to combine the greatest degree of personal liberty with the fullest exercise of obedience. God's Word teaches that obedience is the child's first virtue—that in doing so, he must exercise his will. He is to obey not because he understands or approves of the command but because it comes from his parent. By voluntarily submitting to a higher authority, he really becomes the master of his own will. When this has been attained, a safe foundation has been laid for exercise of the free will, when the child is older and on his own, in the selection of what appears to be the best choice, even when he may be strongly influenced to choose otherwise.

Raising Your Child to Love God

THE SPIRIT IS GIVEN TO THE OBEDIENT

WHEN WE READ THESE words we might ask: How can this be? We need the Spirit to enable us to be obedient. We long for the Spirit's power because we regret the disobedience we find so common in ourselves and we desire to be otherwise. The Savior claims obedience as the condition of the Father's giving the Spirit and our receiving it.

It is a lesson we must learn. Even in God's own Son, by obedience alone could His relationship with the Father be maintained. Only by fully accepting and doing His divine will in our lives are we equipped to enter His presence. After a life of obedience and humility for thirty years the Son of God was baptized by John and then by the Holy Spirit for His ministry. The Spirit came upon Him because of His obedience. And then through His obedience unto death on the cross He received the Spirit to pour out upon His disciples (Acts 2:33). The fullness of the Spirit for His body, the church, was the reward of obedience. This law of the Spirit's coming, as revealed in the head, holds for every member of the body.

The promise to the obedient—the conscious, active indwelling of the Spirit—is a fact unknown to many Christians. The greater part of life is spent in regret over disobedience, regret over a lack of the Spirit's power in our lives. The meaning of the life of Jesus as our example is not always fully understood.

Let us cry fervently to God that He might awaken in His church the need for full obedience that the power of His Spirit might empower us.

> *"If you love Me, keep My commandments. And I will pray the Father, and He will give you another Helper, that He may abide with you forever—the Spirit of truth, whom the world cannot receive, because it neither sees Him nor knows Him; but you know Him, for He dwells with you and will be in you."*
> JOHN 14:15–17 (NKJV)

The Spirit of Christ

THE MODEL PRAYER

"In this manner, therefore, pray: Our Father in heaven, hallowed be Your name. Your kingdom come. Your will be done on earth as it is in heaven. Give us this day our daily bread. And forgive us our debts, as we forgive our debtors. And do not lead us into temptation, but deliver us from the evil one. For Yours is the kingdom and the power and the glory forever. Amen."
MATTHEW 6:9–13 (NKJV)

EVERY TEACHER KNOWS the power of example. He not only tells the pupil what to do and how to do it but also shows that it can be done. In condescension to our weakness, our heavenly Teacher gave us the very words to use as we draw near to our Father. We have in them a form of prayer that breathes the freshness and fullness of eternal life: so simple that a child can lisp it, so divinely rich that it covers all we need.

It is a form of prayer that becomes the model and inspiration for all other prayer and yet always draws us back to itself as the deepest utterance of our souls before our God. Remember that none of the saints in Scripture ever ventured to address God as their Father. The invocation places us at once in the center of the wonderful revelation that the Son came to make His Father our Father. It encompasses the mystery of redemption: Christ delivering us from the curse that we might become the children of God; the mystery of regeneration: the Spirit giving us new life by new birth; and the mystery of faith: even before their redemption is accomplished or understood, the word is given to the disciples in order to prepare them for the blessed experience yet to come.

The knowledge of God's Father-love is the first and simplest—but also the last and highest—lesson in the school of prayer. It is in personal relationship to the living God and fellowship with Him that prayer begins.

Teach Me to Pray

Our Prayer While We Wait

THE PRAYER OF OUR text is one of great importance in our spiritual life. If we draw near to God, it must be with a true heart. There must be perfect integrity and uprightness in our dealings with God. If it is to meet with the Holy One and receive His full blessing, it must be with a heart wholly given up to His will.

Let integrity and uprightness preserve me, for I wait for You.
PSALM 25:21 (NKJV)

And if in our first attempt to truly live a life of waiting on God we discover how much we are lacking in perfect integrity, this will be one of the blessings of our attempt. A soul cannot seek close fellowship with God or attain to a consciousness of waiting on Him without an honest and entire surrender to His will.

It is not only in connection with the prayer of our text but also with every prayer that surrender to His will is appropriate. And then it must be clear *what* we are waiting for, not simply that we are waiting. It may be that we long for a sense of His holy presence and nearness. Or we may have a special petition for which we need a precise answer. Perhaps our whole inner life thirsts for a manifestation of God's power. Beyond our own needs, we may pray for the state of the church, and God's people, or some part of His work. It is good that we sometimes take stock of exactly what we are waiting for and then renew our intention to wait only on *Him* for the answer.

This brings us to think about *who* we are waiting on—not an idol, a god we have conjured up by our poor concept of who He is. Let us acknowledge Him as the living God in His great glory, infinite holiness, power, wisdom, goodness, and love. Let us be still and wait and worship until we know He is near and then say, "It is on *you* that I wait."

Waiting on God

Continue in His Love

"As the Father loved Me,
I also have loved you;
abide in My love."
JOHN 15:9 (NKJV)

"AS THE FATHER loved me" . . . How can we rightly comprehend this love? Lord, teach us. God is love; love is His very being. Love is not an attribute, but the very essence of His nature, the center around which all His glorious attributes revolve.

As one of His redeemed ones you are His delight, and all His desire is to you, with the longing of a love that is stronger than death, and which many waters cannot quench. His heart yearns for you, seeking your fellowship and your love. If it were needed, He would die again to possess you. As the Father loved the Son, and could not live without Him—this is how Jesus loves you. His life is bound up in yours; you are to Him inexpressibly more indispensable and precious than you can ever know.

When it was needed, He sacrificed His throne and crown for you; He did not count His own life and blood too dear to give for you. His righteousness, His Spirit, His glory, even His throne—all are yours. This love holds nothing back, but, in a manner that no human mind can grasp, makes you one with itself. O wondrous love!

Love gives all, but also asks all. It does so not because it begrudges us what has been given, but because without this it cannot get possession of us to fill us with itself. In the love of the Father and the Son, it was so. In the love of Jesus to us, it was so. In our entering into His love to abide there, it must be so; our surrender to it must have no other measure than its surrender to us. If we could grasp even a part of its knowledge, all thought of sacrifice or surrender would pass away, and our souls would be filled with wonder at the unspeakable privilege of being loved with such love, of being allowed to come and abide in it forever.

Abiding in Christ

SET APART FOR THE HOLY SPIRIT

OUR PURPOSE HAS BEEN to discover the will of God concerning His work and to seek Him for the accompanying power. The story of our text includes some thoughts to guide us concerning this. The great lesson of the verses is: *The Holy Spirit is the director of the work of God on earth.* If we are to work for God, and if God is to bless our

The Holy Spirit said, "Set apart for me Barnabas and Saul for the work to which I have called them." So after they had fasted and prayed, they placed their hands on them and sent them off.
ACTS 13:2–3

work, we must stand in right relationship to the Holy Spirit. We must daily yield the place of honor that belongs to Him so that in all our work and in all our private life the Holy Spirit will always have the first place.

We are simply to be faithful in obedience, carrying out His orders. God has a plan for His church on the earth. Unfortunately, we too often make our own plans and think we know what should be done. We ask God to bless our meager efforts instead of refusing to go ahead unless God goes before us. God has planned for the work and the extension of His kingdom. The Holy Spirit is responsible for this. The work to be done by the church is really the Holy Spirit's work. May God teach us to be afraid of touching "the ark of God" except as we are led by the Holy Spirit.

If you wonder whether it is easy to receive these communications from the Spirit, I can tell you that it is easy to those who are in right fellowship with God and who understand the art of waiting upon Him. How often we ask how we can know the will of God. When people are troubled they pray that God would answer them at once. But God can reveal His will only to a heart that is humble, tender, and quiet, a heart that has learned to obey and honor Him in the small things of daily life.

Absolute Surrender

A MAN OF GOD

Then the LORD said to Moses, "Depart and go up from here, you and the people whom you have brought out of the land of Egypt. . . . And I will send My Angel before you, and I will drive out the Canaanite and the Amorite and the Hittite and the Perizzite. . . . Go up to a land flowing with milk and honey; for I will not go up in your midst, lest I consume you on the way, for you are a stiff-necked people."
EXODUS 33:1–4 (NKJV)

A MAN OF GOD. How much the name implies! It describes a man who comes from God, chosen and sent by Him; a man who walks with God, lives in fellowship with Him, and carries the mark of His presence; a man who lives for God and His will, whose being is pervaded and ruled by the glory of God, who involuntarily and unceasingly causes men to think of God; a man in whose heart God has taken His rightful place as All in All, who only desires that God should have that place throughout the world.

Such men of God are what the world needs; such men are what God seeks, that He may fill them with himself and send them out to teach others. Moses was such a man; others spoke of him as Moses the man of God. Every servant of God should aim at being such a person—a living witness and proof of what God is to him and what God himself claims to be.

Through sin, the world has fallen away from God. In Christ, the world has been redeemed. But God cannot show people what they ought to be except through the people of God in whom His life, spirit, and power are at work. When the redemption of Christ was completed by the descent of the Holy Spirit into the hearts of His people, this indwelling was restored and God regained possession of His home. Where we surrender ourselves wholly to the presence of the Holy Spirit, we may become, in the fullest meaning of the word, people of God!

The Believer's Daily Renewal

HEAVENLY JOY
THROUGH THE BLOOD

THE POWER OF the blood of Jesus not only opens the door of heaven for the sinner, but it also works in him in such a divine way that as he enters heaven its blessedness will appear to be perfectly suited to him.

Nearness to God and the Lamb and fellowship with them constitute the blessedness of heaven. To be before the throne of God and to see His face; to serve Him day and night in His temple; to be overshadowed by Him who sits upon the throne; to be fed and led by the Lamb; all these expressions point out how little the blessedness of heaven depends on anything else than on God and the Lamb. To see them, to have conversation with them, to be acknowledged, loved, and cared for by them—that is blessedness.

Therefore, "they are before the throne of God and serve him day and night in his temple; and he who sits on the throne will spread his tent over them. Never again will they hunger; never again will they thirst. The sun will not beat upon them, nor any scorching heat.

For the Lamb at the center of the throne will be their shepherd; he will lead them to springs of living water. And God will wipe away every tear from their eyes."
REVELATION 7:15–17

As the blood of reconciliation, it works out in the soul the full, living consciousness that belongs to those who are *at home in heaven*. It brings us into the Holy Place near to God. It makes us fit for heaven.

See that the blood, which always has a place at the throne of grace, manifests its power in your heart. Your life will become an unbroken fellowship with God and the Lamb: the foretaste of life in eternal glory. Let the thought enter deeply into your soul: The blood bestows in the heart here on earth the blessedness of heaven. The precious blood makes life on earth and life in heaven one.

The Blood of Christ

THE POWER OF PERSEVERING PRAYER

Then Jesus told his disciples a parable to show them that they should always pray and not give up. . . . "Listen to what the unjust judge says. And will not God bring about justice for his chosen ones, who cry out to him day and night? Will he keep putting them off? I tell you, he will see that they get justice."
LUKE 18:1, 6–8

ONE OF THE GREATEST mysteries of prayer is the need for perseverance. That our loving Lord, so longing to bless, should have to be sought time after time before the answer comes, is not easy to understand. It is also one of the greatest practical difficulties in the exercise of believing prayer. When even after persevering supplication our prayer remains unanswered, it is easy for our pampered flesh (with all the appearance of pious submission) to think that it must stop praying because God may have a reason for withholding the answer.

The difficulty is overcome by faith alone. When faith has taken its stand on God's Wor and has yielded itself to the leading of the Spirit to seek only God's will and honor in its prayer, it should not be discouraged by delay. We know from Scripture that the power of believing prayer is irresistible; *real faith can never be disappointed.* Just as the flow of a great amount of water creates accumulated pressure, there must often be a heaping up of prayer until God sees that the measure is full, and then the answer comes. Faith knows not a single believing prayer fails to have its effect in heaven; each has influence and is treasured up to work out an answer in due time to the one who perseveres to the end.

Even as Abraham through so many years in hope believed against hope and then through faith *and patience* inherited the promise, faith believes that the long-suffering of the Lord is salvation, *waiting* and *pressing on* until the coming of the Lord to fulfill His promise.

Believing Prayer

THE SEAL OF THE SPIRIT

THE FIRST CHAPTER of the letter to the Ephesians begins with the spiritual blessing with which God has blessed us in Christ, and then through the next ten verses shows us what we have in Him, closing these thoughts with the promise of the seal of the Holy Spirit in verse 13.

In Him you also trusted, after you heard the word of truth, the gospel of your salvation; in whom also, having believed, you were sealed with the Holy Spirit of promise.
EPHESIANS 1:13 (NKJV)

When a king appoints an ambassador or a governor, his commission is sealed with the king's seal, bearing his own likeness. The Holy Spirit is the seal of our redemption, but not in the sense of giving us the assurance of sonship apart from himself: He himself, *by His life in us*, is the seal of our sonship. His work is to reveal and glorify Christ in us, the image of the Father, and by focusing our heart and our faith on Him, to transform us into His likeness. The Spirit of the Father and the Son is the bond of our union with them, giving us the witness of the divine life within us and enabling us to live out that life on a daily basis. In the Christian life everything depends upon our knowing the presence of the Holy Spirit and understanding His work.

First, we must know that He comes to dwell in our whole person—spirit, soul, and body—and through that indwelling to reveal the life and the power of God as it works in our renewed personality. Just as Christ could not be glorified and receive the Spirit from the Father until He died on the cross—parting with the life in which He had borne our sin and weakness—so the coming of the Holy Spirit into our hearts in power implies that we have yielded ourselves to the fellowship of the Cross and consent to die entirely to our life of self and sin. Through the death of the self-life, the Holy Spirit is able to take complete control of our lives.

The Believer's Call to Commitment

Divine Ownership

You are not your own; you were bought at a price.
1 Corinthians 6:19–20

HERE IS THE ERROR that lies at the root of so much of our Christianity. A man thinks, "I have my business and family responsibilities and my duties as a citizen, and I cannot change this. Am I to take on more work and service in the church so that I can be kept from sin? God help me!"

No, it is not like that. When Christ came to earth, He bought us, sinners that we are, with His blood. If there were a slave market today, and I were to buy a slave, I would take that slave away to my own house from his old surroundings, and he would live at my house as my personal property. And if he were a faithful slave, he would live as having no will and no interests of his own, his one concern being to promote the well-being and honor of his master. And in like manner I, who have been bought with the precious blood of Christ, have been bought to live every day with one thought: *How can I please my Master?*

We find the Christian life difficult because we seek for God's blessing while we live according to our own will! We make our own plans and choose our own work, and then we ask the Lord Jesus to come in and see that sin doesn't overtake us too much and that we will not wander too far off the path. But our relationship to Jesus ought to be such that we are entirely at His disposal! Every day we should go to Him first, humbly and straightforwardly, and say, "Lord, is there anything in me that is not according to your will, that has not been ordered by you, or that is not entirely given up to you? What would you have me do today?" If we would daily wait patiently before Him, there would spring up a relationship between Christ and us so close and so tender that we would be amazed at how far we have fallen from fellowship with Him.

Divine Healing

IS IT POSSIBLE for someone who has the full blessing of Pentecost to lose it? God does not bestow this gift with such constraint that a man retains it whether he desires it or not. This blessing is entrusted to him as a talent that must be used; and only by use does it become secure. Just as the Lord Jesus after He was baptized with the Holy Spirit had to be perfected by obedience and submission to the Spirit, so the believer who has received the blessing of Pentecost must see that he guards safely what has been entrusted to him.

But you, dear friends, build yourselves up in your most holy faith and pray in the Holy Spirit. Keep yourselves in God's love as you wait for the mercy of our Lord Jesus Christ to bring you to eternal life.
JUDE 20–21

Scripture points us to the fact that our keeping the blessing depends on our entrusting it to the Lord to be kept by Him. Just as with the manna that fell in the wilderness, it must be renewed daily.

The fullness of the Spirit is not a gift that is bestowed once for all. It is rather a constantly flowing stream of the water of life that issues from the throne of God and of the Lamb. It is an uninterrupted communication of the life and love of Jesus, the most personal and intimate association of the Lord with His own upon the earth. It is by the faith that discerns this truth, assents to it, and holds to it with joy that Jesus will do His work of keeping.

Are you longing for this life and yet afraid to enter upon it because you do not know how you will continue? Just as Jesus Christ was daily with His disciples in physical presence, so He will be with you by His Spirit every day. Lay aside every burden and receive from Him the full blessing of Pentecost, a fountain that will spring up in you unto everlasting life.

The Fullness of the Spirit

HUMILITY AND HOLINESS

"All day long I have held out my hands to an obstinate people . . . who say, 'Keep away; don't come near me, for I am too sacred for you!'"
ISAIAH 65:2, 5

THE CHIEF MARK OF counterfeit holiness is its lack of humility. Every seeker after holiness needs to be on his guard lest unconsciously what was begun in the spirit is perfected in the flesh, and pride creep in where its presence is least expected.

Jesus the Holy One is the humble One: the holiest will always be the humblest. There is none holy but God: we have as much holiness as we have God. And according to what we have of God will be our real humility, because humility is nothing but the disappearance of self in the vision that God is all. The holiest will be the humblest. Let all teachers of holiness and all seekers after holiness take warning: There is no pride so dangerous, so subtle and insidious, as the pride of holiness. It is not that a man ever says, or even thinks, "Stay away. I am too sacred for you!" But unconsciously there can develop a private habit of soul that feels complacency in its attainments and cannot help but see how far it is ahead of others. It isn't always seen in self-assertion or self-praise, but in the absence of self-denial and modesty that reveals a lack of the mark of the soul that has seen the glory of God. It is a tone, a way of speaking of oneself or others, in which those who have the gift of discernment cannot but recognize the power of self. Even the world with its keen eye notices it, and points to it as proof that the profession of a spiritual life does not always bear spiritual fruits.

Beware, lest we make a profession of holiness, delighting in beautiful thoughts and feelings, in solemn acts of consecration and faith, while the mark of the presence of God—the disappearance of self—is obviously missing. Flee to Jesus and hide yourselves in Him until you are clothed with His humility. That alone is holiness.

Humility

"Follow Me"

THE LORD DID NOT say these words to all who believed on Him, or who hoped to be blessed by Him, but only to those whom He would make fishers of men. He said this not only when He first called the apostles but also later

"Come, follow me," Jesus said, "and I will make you fishers of men." At once they left their nets and followed him.
MATTHEW 4:19–20

on to Peter: "Don't be afraid; from now on you will catch men" (Luke 5:11). The holy art of winning souls, of loving and saving them, can be learned only in a close and consistent relationship with Christ. This intimate relationship was the great and particular privilege of His disciples. The Lord chose them that they might always be with Him and remain near Him.

Continuous fellowship with Christ is the only school for the training of students of the Holy Spirit. What a lesson for us all! Only he who, like Caleb, follows the Lord fully will have power to teach other souls the art of following Jesus. But what an amazing grace, that the Lord Jesus himself wants to train us to be like Him so that others may learn from us.

Never has a teacher taken such trouble with his scholars as Jesus Christ will with those who preach His Word. He will spare no pain; no time will be too limited or too long for Him. In the love that took Him to the cross, He wants to fellowship and converse with us, fashion us, sanctify us, and make us fit for His holy service. Will we not commit ourselves entirely to the love that gave up all for us and look upon it as our greatest joy to have daily fellowship with Him? All you who long for blessing in your ministry, He calls you to abide in Him. Let it be the greatest delight of your life to spend time with God; it will be the surest preparation for fruitful service.

Living a Prayerful Life

THE CUP OF THANKSGIVING

*Is not the cup of
thanksgiving for which
we give thanks a
participation in the
blood of Christ?*
1 CORINTHIANS 10:16

THE LORD'S SUPPER is a feast of thanksgiving: "And he took bread, *gave thanks* and broke it" (Luke 22:19). "Then he took the cup, *gave thanks* and offered it to them" (Matthew 26:27). After partaking of the Supper they sang a hymn. We learn from Jewish writers that the third cup of the Paschal feast was called the Cup of Thanksgiving, and that while it was being drunk, Psalms 116, 117, and 118 were sung.

The Supper is the feast of the redeemed, a joyful repast at which God himself says to us, "Let us eat and be merry"; a thanksgiving banquet at which is heard a prelude of the song of the Lamb.

When we offer praise, we glorify God. A joyful, thankful Christian shows that God can make those who serve Him truly happy. And he stirs up others to praise God along with him. Sadness cannot eat. It is a joyful heart that enjoys food. To be thankful for what we have received and for what our Lord has prepared is the surest way to receive more.

And so shall we be strengthened for conflict and for victory. If our Savior went singing from the Lord's Table to the conflict in Gethsemane, may we, in the joy of His redemption, follow Him with thanksgiving into every conflict to which He calls us.

The nearer we are to the throne of God the more thanksgiving we feel and offer. We see this in the book of Revelation: In heaven they praise God day and night. A Lord's Supper pervaded by the spirit of thanksgiving is a foretaste of it. And we have good reason to be thankful. Look at Jesus, His blood, His redemption, His love, His blessed fellowship, and let all that is within us praise Him. Drink abundantly of the Cup of Thanksgiving, giving thanks for the One who gave His life to offer it.

The Lord's Table

THE PLACE OF OBEDIENCE
IN SCRIPTURE

IN GENESIS 2:16 we read, "And the LORD God commanded the man . . . " And later (3:11), "Have you eaten from the tree that I commanded you not to eat from?" Note how obedience to the command is the one virtue of Paradise, the

"Does the LORD delight in burnt offerings and sacrifices as much as in obeying the voice of the LORD?"
1 SAMUEL 15:22

one condition of man's abiding there, the one thing his Creator asks of him. Nothing is said of faith or humility or love—obedience covers all.

Turn now from the beginning of the Bible to the end. In the last chapter we read, "Blessed are those who do His commandments, that they may have the right to the tree of life" (Revelation 22:14 NKJV). From beginning to end, from Paradise lost to Paradise regained, the law is unchanged: It is obedience that gives access to the tree of life and the favor of God.

How was the change effected? The cross of Christ. From disobedience at the beginning that closed the way to the tree of life, to obedience at the end that gained entrance to it again, that which stands midway between the beginning and the end is the cross of Christ. Romans 5:19 says, "For just as through the disobedience of the one man the many were made sinners, so also through the obedience of the one man the many will be made righteous." The whole redemption of Christ consists in restoring obedience to its place. The beauty of His salvation consists of this, that He brings us back to the life of obedience, through *which alone the creature can give the Creator the glory due to Him, or receive the glory of which his Creator desires him to partake.* Paradise, Calvary, heaven, all proclaim with one voice: Child of God, the first and the last thing your God asks of you is simple, universal, unchanging obedience.

A Life of Obedience

Is Prayerlessness Sin?

"Far be it from me that I should sin against the LORD by failing to pray for you."
1 SAMUEL 12:23

ANY DEEP QUICKENING of the spiritual life of the church will always be accompanied by a deeper sense of sin. Jesus is our Savior from sin. To see that our prayerlessness is sin is the first step toward a true and divine deliverance.

What we need is a revelation from God that our lack of prayer is an indication of unfaithfulness to our vow of consecration that gave God all our heart and life. We must see that prayerlessness, with the excuses we make for it, is a greater sin than we thought. It means that we have little taste or desire for fellowship with God. It shows that our faith rests more on our own work and efforts than on the power of God. It shows we have little sense of the heavenly blessing God waits to shower upon us. It means we are not ready to sacrifice the ease and confidence of the flesh for persistent pleading before God. It shows that the spirituality of our life and our abiding in Christ is too weak to allow us to prevail in prayer.

When the pressure of work for Christ becomes the excuse for our not finding time to seek and secure His presence and power, it proves we have no proper sense of our absolute dependence upon God. There is obviously no grasp of the divine work of God in which we are only His instruments.

God never speaks to His people of sin except with a view to saving them from it. The same power that condemns sin, if humbly yielded to, will give us the power to rise up and conquer.

Let us not be afraid, and let us not cling to the excuses and explanations that circumstances suggest. But rather let us confess, "We have sinned; we are sinning; we dare not sin any longer."

The Ministry of Intercessory Prayer

HOLINESS AND CREATION

IN THE WHOLE BOOK of Genesis the word *holy* occurs only once. But that one time is in such a connection as to open to us the secret spring from which flows all that the Bible has to teach or to give us of this heavenly blessing.

And God blessed the seventh day and made it holy, because on it he rested from all the work of creating that he had done.
GENESIS 2:3

When God blessed the seventh day and sanctified it, He lifted it above the other days and set it apart to a work and a revelation of himself excelling in glory all that preceded it. In this simple expression, Scripture reveals to us the character of God as the Holy One, who makes holy; the way in which He makes holy, by entering in and resting; and the power of blessing with which God's making us holy is always accompanied.

When God blessed the seventh day, He so filled it with the living power of His holiness that in it holiness might increase and reproduce itself in those who, like Him, seek to enter into its rest and sanctify it. The seventh day is that in which we are now living.

God's finished work of creation was marred by sin, and our fellowship with Him in the blessing of His holy rest was cut off. The finished work of redemption opened for us a truer rest and a surer entrance into the holiness of God. As He rested in His holy day, so He now rests in His holy Son. In Him we now can enter fully into the rest of God. "Made holy in Christ," let us rest in Him. Let us rest because we see that just as wonderfully as God by His mighty power finished His work of creation, so will He complete and perfect His work of sanctification. Let us yield ourselves to God in Christ, to rest where He rested, to be made holy with His own holiness, and to be blessed with God's own blessing.

The Path to Holiness

THE CERTAINTY OF AN ANSWER TO PRAYER

"Ask and it will be given to you; seek and you will find; knock and the door will be opened to you. For everyone who asks receives; he who seeks finds; and to him who knocks, the door will be opened."
MATTHEW 7:7–8

OUR LORD RETURNS to speak of prayer again in the Sermon on the Mount. The first time he told about the Father who is to be found in secret and rewards openly and gave us the pattern prayer (Matthew 6:5–15). Here He wants to teach us what all Scripture considers the most important thing in prayer: that it be heard and answered. He uses words that mean almost the same thing, and each time He repeats the promise distinctly: "It *will* be given to you; you *will* find; the door *will* be opened to you." In all this repetition, we can see that He wants to implant in our minds the truth that we may—and must—confidently expect an answer to our prayer. Next to the revelation of the Father's love, there is no more important lesson in the whole school of prayer than this: Everyone that asks receives.

A difference of meaning has been sought in the three words *ask, seek,* and *knock*. The first, ask, refers to the gifts we pray for. But I may ask for and receive a gift without the Giver. Seek is the word Scripture uses when speaking of looking for God himself. Christ assures me that I can find God. But it is not enough to find God in a time of need without also coming into an abiding fellowship with Him. Knock speaks of being admitted to dwell with Him and in Him. Asking and receiving the gift thus leads to seeking and finding the Giver. This again leads to the knocking and opening of the door to the Father's home and to His love. One thing is sure: The Lord wants us to believe with certainty that asking, seeking, and knocking will not be in vain.

Teach Me to Pray

SEEKING TO KNOW
HIS GOODNESS

DO YOU WANT TO know the goodness of God? Give yourself to a life of waiting on Him.

When we first enter the school of waiting on God, our hearts are chiefly set on His blessings. God graciously uses our

The LORD is good to those who wait for Him, to the soul who seeks Him.
LAMENTATIONS 3:25
(NKJV)

need and desire for help to educate us for something higher than we may have been thinking of. We were seeking gifts; He longs to give himself and to satisfy our soul with His goodness. It is for this reason that He often withholds the gifts and that the time of waiting seems long. He is always seeking to win the hearts of His children for himself. He hopes that we will not only say when He gives the gift, "How good God is!" but that long before it comes, and even if it never comes, we will always experience the fact that it is good to wait on God. *He* is worth the wait.

What a blessed life the life of waiting becomes: it is a continual worship of faith, adoring, and trusting His goodness. As your soul learns this secret, every act or exercise of waiting becomes a quiet entering into the goodness of God to let it do its blessed work. Instead of taking refuge only when we are in need, there will come a great longing to simply wait in His presence. And however our daily duties and responsibilities occupy our time and our minds, our souls will become more familiar with the secret art of waiting. It will become the habit and attitude of the soul.

What we need is *more of God*. We tend to be more occupied with our work than anything else. As with Martha, the very service we want to give to the Master separates us from Him. It is neither pleasing to Him nor profitable to us. The more we work, the more we need to wait on God. When we believe this truth, the doing of God's will, instead of exhausting us, will be our nourishment and refreshment and strength.

Waiting on God

OUR BOLDNESS IN PRAYER

This is the confidence we have in approaching God: that if we ask anything according to his will, he hears us. And if we know that he hears us—whatever we ask—we know that we have what we asked of him.
1 JOHN 5:14–15

UNDOUBTEDLY ONE OF the greatest hindrances to believing prayer is this: Many do not know if what they ask agrees with the will of God. As long as they are in doubt on this point, they cannot have the boldness to ask in the assurance that they will receive. And they soon begin to think that if they have made known their requests and receive no answer, it is best to leave it to God to do according to His good pleasure. The words of John, "If we ask anything *according to his will*, he hears us" (1 John 5:14), as they understand them, make answer to prayer impossible, because they cannot be sure what the will of God is. They think of God's will as His hidden counsel. How can man fathom what may be the purpose of the all-wise God?

However, this is the very opposite of what John was aiming at. He wanted to stir us to boldness, to full assurance of faith in prayer. He says, "*This is the confidence we have in approaching God*" (v. 14) that we can say, "Father, you know and I know that I ask according to your will. I know you hear me." "This is the confidence we have in approaching God: that if we ask anything according to his will, he hears us" (v. 14). But He adds at once, "If we know that he hears us—whatever we ask—we *know*," through this faith, "that we have what we asked of him" (v. 15).

John assumes that when we pray we first find out if our prayers are according to the will of God. They may be according to God's will, and yet not be answered at once, or they may not be answered without persevering prayer. To encourage us to persevere and be strong in faith, He tells us that if we ask anything according to His will, He hears us.

Teach Me to Pray

ENOUGH FOR THAT DAY: Such was the rule for God's giving and man's working in the gathering of the manna. It is still the law in all the dealings of

> *"The people are to go out each day and gather enough for that day."*
> EXODUS 16:4

God's grace with His children. A clear insight into the beauty and application of this arrangement is a wonderful help in understanding how one who feels himself utterly weak can have the confidence and the perseverance to hold on tightly through all his earthly years. A patient who had been in a serious accident once asked a doctor: "Doctor, how long will I have to lie here?" The answer, "Only a day at a time," taught the patient a precious lesson. It was the same lesson God recorded for His people: enough for that day.

That word completely takes away all care for tomorrow. Only today is yours; tomorrow is the Father's. The question "What security do you have that during all the years in which you have to battle the coldness, temptations, or trials of the world, you will always abide in Jesus?" is one you need not, may not ask. Manna, as your food and strength, is given only by the day; to faithfully fill the present is your only security for the future. Accept, enjoy, and fulfill with your whole heart the part you have to perform this day. His presence and grace enjoyed today will remove all doubt as to whether you can entrust tomorrow to Him, too.

As the Father, with each new morning, meets you with the promise of sufficient manna for the day, meet Him with the bright and loving renewal of your acceptance of the position He has given you in His beloved Son.

We begin to number our days not from the sun's rising over the world, or by the work we do or the food we eat, but by the daily renewal of the miracle of the manna—the blessing of daily fellowship with Him who is the Life and the Light of the world.

Abiding in Christ

PETER'S REPENTANCE

Then Peter remembered the word the Lord had spoken to him: "Before the rooster crows today, you will disown me three times." And he went outside and wept bitterly.
LUKE 22:61–62

THIS WAS THE TURNING point in Peter's life. Christ had said to him, "You cannot follow me now." Peter was not able to follow Christ because he had not come to the end of himself. But when he realized what he had done and how Christ's prophecy of his actions had come true, he wept. This is the point at which the great change came about. Jesus had previously said to him, "When you are converted, strengthen your brethren." At this new revelation of himself, Peter was converted from self to Christ.

I thank God for the story of Peter. I know of no other man in the Bible who gives greater comfort to the human frame. When we look at his character, so full of failures, and at what Christ made him by the power of the Holy Spirit, there is hope for every one of us. But remember that before Christ could fill Peter with the Holy Spirit and make him a new creation, Peter had to humble himself and admit his sin.

It is the story of every servant who will be truly used by God. Peter's story is a prophecy of what each of us can receive from God. We must not only pray for God's work and speak about it among ourselves, not only pray for an outpouring of the Spirit of love, but we must humbly come to God as individuals in repentance and faith. For it is only when individual servants are blessed of God that the work will prosper and the body of Christ will be strong and healthy.

The same Christ who led Peter to Pentecost is among us today and is waiting to take charge of every heart that is willing to surrender to Him. Are you at that place? Christ Jesus can free you; He can deliver you from the power of self. He only asks you to humble yourself before Him.

Absolute Surrender

THE POWER OF GOD'S WORD

And we also thank God continually because, when you received the word of God, which you heard from us, you accepted it not as the word of men, but as it actually is, the word of God, which is at work in you who believe.

1 THESSALONIANS 2:13

TO ME, THE VALUE of a person's words depends upon my knowledge of that person. What a difference between the words of those who promise "I will give you half of all I have" when one is a poor man and the other is a millionaire. One of the first prerequisites to fruitful Bible study is the knowledge of God the Omnipotent One and of the power of His Word.

The Word of the living God is a living word and it gives life. It not only calls into existence but it also makes alive that which was dead. All spiritual life comes through it.

One of the deepest secrets of receiving the blessing of God's Word is *faith*—faith that the Word will work in me the very thing it commands or promises. It effectually works in those who believe. Nothing can resist its power when received into the heart through the Holy Spirit.

By His Word God "calls things that are not as though they were" (Romans 4:17). As this is true of all God's mighty deeds from creation to the resurrection of the dead, it is true also of every word in His Book. Two things keep us from believing this as we should. The first is the experience of the world around us. The other is neglect of the teaching of Scripture that the Word is a seed. Seeds are small; they may long be dormant; they have to be hidden; and once they sprout, they grow slowly. Because the effect of God's Word is also hidden and unobserved, slow and weak by all appearances, we do not believe in its omnipotence. Let this be one of your first lessons: The Word I study is the power of God unto salvation; it will work in me all that I need and all that the Father requires.

The Believer's Daily Renewal

LIFE IN THE BLOOD

Jesus said to them, "I tell you the truth, unless you eat the flesh of the Son of Man and drink his blood, you have no life in you. Whoever eats my flesh and drinks my blood has eternal life, and I will raise him up at the last day. For my flesh is real food and my blood is real drink."
JOHN 6:53–56

WHEN WATER IS USED for washing it cleanses, but if we drink it we are refreshed and revived. The one who desires to know the full power of the blood of Jesus must be taught by Him what it means to drink the blood.

To many, there is something unpleasant about the phrase "drink the blood of the Son of Man," but it was more disagreeable to the Jews, for the use of blood was forbidden by the law of Moses, under severe penalty. When Jesus spoke of drinking His blood, it naturally annoyed them—but more than that, it was an *unspeakable offense* to their religious sensitivity. Our Lord, we may be sure, would not have used the phrase had He been able otherwise to make plain to them, and to us, the deepest and most glorious truths concerning salvation.

Our Lord distinguishes two kinds of life. The Jews who were there in His presence at the time had a natural life of body and soul. Many among them were devout, well-intentioned men, but He said they had no life in them unless they ate his flesh and drank his blood. They needed a new life, a heavenly one, which He had and could impart to them.

All creaturely life must obtain nourishment outside of itself. The natural life is naturally nourished by bread and water. The heavenly life must be nourished by heavenly food and drink, by Jesus himself. Our Lord said, "My flesh is food indeed, and My blood is drink indeed" (John 6:55 NKJV). Nourishment by His flesh and blood effects the most perfect union with Him. This is the reason that His flesh and blood have the power of eternal life.

The Blood of Christ

THE SPIRIT OF WISDOM

NO SOONER HAD PAUL mentioned the Holy Spirit as God's seal on believers, than he spoke of his unceasing prayer that God would give them a spirit of wisdom. It is not enough that the believer has the Holy Spirit; the Spirit can only do His work in answer to prayer. Paul prayed unceasingly, and taught believers to pray also for the wisdom of the Holy Spirit to enlighten the eyes of their hearts. The Christian life is supernatural, and it is such a divine mystery that without spiritual wisdom and understanding we cannot comprehend it.

That the God of our Lord Jesus Christ . . . may give to you the spirit of wisdom and revelation in the knowledge of Him, the eyes of your understanding being enlightened; that you may know what is the hope of His calling, what are the riches of the glory of His inheritance in the saints.
EPHESIANS 1:17–18 (NKJV)

We need to know three things. (1) What is "the hope of His calling": the high and holy heavenly calling of which we are to walk worthy; (2) "the riches of the glory of His inheritance in the saints"; what the unsearchable riches are of the heavenly treasure, which God has in His saints; and (3) "the power" by which we can fulfill our calling and possess our inheritance: "the exceeding greatness of His power toward us who believe" (Ephesians 1:19 NKJV).

The life of the Christian is the life of God in the human soul; we can do nothing to maintain it or renew it. It is a life that we have in Christ; it is a life we receive from Christ by faith daily and hourly; it is a life that the omnipotence of God alone begins and carries on. The work of the believer is to wait upon God for the Holy Spirit to show him "what are the riches of the glory of His inheritance in the saints." No mortal mind can grasp it; the Holy Spirit living in the heart reveals it and teaches us to believe it and expect it.

The Believer's Call to Commitment

Do Not Consider
Your Body

Against all hope,
Abraham in hope believed
and so became the father
of many nations. . . . He
did not waver through
unbelief regarding the
promise of God . . . being
fully persuaded that God
had power to do what
he had promised.
ROMANS 4:18, 20–21

WHEN GOD PROMISED to give Abraham a son, the patriarch would never have been able to believe in the promise if he had considered his own body, already aged and worn out. But Abraham would see nothing but God, who guaranteed him the fulfillment of His promise.

This enables us to lay hold of the difference between the healing that is expected from earthly remedies and the healing from God alone. When we have access to remedies for healing, all the attention of the sick one is upon the body, while divine healing calls us to turn our attention away from the body and to abandon ourselves, soul and body, to the Lord's care, occupying ourselves with Him alone.

This truth enables us to see the difference between the sickness retained for blessing and the healing received from the Lord. Some say sickness is more profitable to the soul than health. It is true that in the case of healing obtained by earthly remedies, many people would be more blessed in remaining ill than in recovering health, but it is quite the opposite when healing comes directly from the hand of God. In order to receive divine healing, sin must be truly confessed and renounced, one must be completely surrendered to the Lord, and the will of Jesus to take charge of the body must be firmly counted on. Healing then becomes the commencement of a new life of intimate communion with the Lord.

Divine Healing

How It Is to Be Received

THE SAME GOD WHO calls upon us to live in sobriety urges us with equal urgency to be filled with the Spirit. His command is the sure guarantee that He will give what He desires us to possess.

Do not get drunk on wine, which leads to debauchery. Instead, be filled with the Spirit.
EPHESIANS 5:18

In order to carry on her work in the world, the church absolutely requires the full blessing of the Spirit. To please God and to live a life of holiness, joy, and power, you need it, too.

The indwelling, the fullness of the Spirit, is nothing but the healthy state of the body of Christ. Be assured that the blessing is for you. A great distinction prevails in the matter of gifts, calling, and circumstances; but there can be no distinction in the love of the Father and His desire to see every one of His children in full health and in the full enjoyment of the Spirit of adoption.

The impartation of this heavenly blessing is as entirely an act of God as the resurrection of Christ from the dead was His divine work. As Jesus Christ had to entirely go down unto death and lay aside the life He had in order to receive new life from God, so must the believer abandon all hope of receiving this blessing on his own and take it as a free gift from God. The acknowledgment of our utter powerlessness, this descent into true self-denial, is indispensable if we would enjoy this supreme blessing.

Faith must lead me to the actual inheritance of the promise, to the experience and enjoyment of it. Do not rest content with a belief that does not lead to experience. God promises, He desires, to make you full of the Holy Spirit. He desires that your whole personality and life be under the power of the Holy Spirit. He asks if you on your part are willing, if you really desire to have it. Let this promise of God become the primary element in your life, the most precious, the only thing you seek.

The Fullness of the Spirit

HUMILITY AND SIN

Christ Jesus came into the world to save sinners—of whom I am the worst.

1 TIMOTHY 1:15

WE HAVE ONLY TO look at a man like the apostle Paul to see how throughout his life as a ransomed and a holy man, the deep consciousness of having been a sinner lived in him inextinguishably. We all know the passages in which he refers to his life as a persecutor and blasphemer: "I am *the least of the apostles* and *do not even deserve to be called an apostle*, because I persecuted the church of God. But by the grace of God I am what I am, and his grace to me was not without effect. No, I worked harder than all of them—yet not I, but the grace of God that was with me" (1 Corinthians 15:9–10, emphasis added). "Even though I was once *a blasphemer and a persecutor and a violent man*, I was shown mercy because I acted in ignorance and unbelief. . . . Christ Jesus came into the world to save *sinners—of whom I am the worst*" (1 Timothy 1:13, 15).

God's grace had saved Paul; God remembered his sins no more; but never could Paul forget how terribly he had sinned. The more he rejoiced in God's salvation, and the more his experience of God's grace filled him with joy unspeakable, the clearer was his consciousness that he was a saved sinner and that salvation had no meaning or sweetness except that his being a sinner made it precious and real to him personally.

It was the wonderful grace bestowed upon Paul, of which he felt the need every moment, that humbled him so deeply. The more abundant the experience of grace the more intense the consciousness of being a sinner. It is the revelation of God not only by the law condemning sin but also by His grace delivering from it that will make us humble. The law may break the heart with fear; it is only grace that works that sweet humility that becomes joy to the soul as its second nature.

Humility

THE LORD WHO
HEALS YOU

HOW OFTEN HAVE WE read these words without daring to take them for ourselves and without expectation that the Lord will fulfill them? We have believed that this promise applied only to the Old Testament and that we who live under the economy of the New Testament cannot expect to be kept from or healed of sickness by the direct intervention of the Lord!

"If you listen carefully to the voice of the LORD your God and do what is right in his eyes, if you pay attention to his commands and keep all his decrees, I will not bring on you any of the diseases I brought on the Egyptians, for I am the LORD, who heals you."
EXODUS 15:26

But today we see the church awakening and acknowledging her mistake. She sees that it is under the new covenant that the Lord Jesus acquired the title of Healer—by all His miraculous healings. It is not God or His Word that are to blame here; it is our unbelief that prevents the miraculous power of the Lord and holds Him back from healing as in former times.

His love is pleased to daily gift His beloved with His favors, to communicate himself with all His heart to all who desire to receive Him. Let us believe that He is ready to extend the treasure of blessing contained in the name "the Lord who heals you" to all who know and trust Him with their whole life.

God is ever seeking to make us true believers. Healing and health are of little value if they do not glorify God and serve to unite us more closely with Him. Therefore, in the matter of healing, our faith must always be put to the test. He who counts on the name of his God, who can hear Jesus saying to him, "Did I not tell you that if you believed, you would see the glory of God?" (John 11:40), will have the joy of receiving from God himself the healing of his body and of seeing it take place in a manner worthy of God.

Divine Healing

The Seed Is the Word

"A farmer went out to sow his seed. As he was scattering the seed, some fell along the path, and the birds came and ate it up. Some fell on rocky places, where it did not have much soil. It sprang up quickly. . . . But when the sun came up, the plants were scorched, and they withered because they had no root. Other seed fell among thorns, which grew up and choked the plants. Still other seed fell on good soil, where it produced a crop—a hundred, sixty or thirty times what was sown."

MATTHEW 13:3–8

I THINK IN ALL of nature there is no other illustration of the Word of God as true and full of meaning as that of the seed. The points of resemblance are obvious. There is the apparent insignificance of the seed: it is a small thing compared to the tree that springs from it. There is the life, enclosed and dormant within a husk. There is the need of suitable soil, without which growth is impossible. There is the slow growth, calling for the steady patience of the gardener. And there is the fruit, in which the seed reproduces and multiplies itself.

First, there is the lesson of *faith*. Faith does not look at appearances. By human judgment it looks improbable that a mere word from God could give life to the soul, could transform our character, or could fill us with strength.

Then there is the lesson of *labor*. The seed needs to be gathered, kept, and placed in prepared soil.

The seed also teaches the lesson of *patience*. The Word's effect on the heart, in most cases, is not immediate. It needs time to develop roots and grow up—Christ's words must *abide* in us.

Last, is the lesson of *fruitfulness*. However insignificant that little seed of a word of God appears, however feeble its life may seem, however deep its meaning may be hidden, and however slow its growth may be, you can be sure *the fruit will come*.

The Believer's Daily Renewal

PURCHASED FOR GOD BY THE BLOOD

BOUGHT IS A COMMON word understood by all. Buying and selling occupies a significant place in our lives. We are all at one time or another engaged in it, so that the ideas attached to it are understood by everyone: the right of the buyer over what he has purchased, the value he attaches to his possession after the price has been paid in full, the certainty that what he has bought will be his, and the use that he will make of his purchase.

"You are worthy to take the scroll and to open its seals, because you were slain, and with your blood you purchased men for God from every tribe and language and people and nation."
REVELATION 5:9

"With your blood you purchased men for God from every . . . nation" indicates to us the right He has obtained to us. As Creator, the Lord Jesus has a right to every soul on earth. Through Him God has bestowed life upon men that they might be His possession and inheritance.

It has often happened that someone has had to buy back what belonged to him in the first place but which had been taken from him by a hostile power. Many times people have had to buy back their land and their freedom with their blood. After such a buyback, land and liberty increase their value.

Thus the Son of God has ransomed us from the power of Satan. And now the message comes to us as from heaven: Jesus has bought us by His blood; He and no one else has a right to us: We belong to Him.

The fact that He has purchased us assures us that He will preserve and care for us. The man who has purchased something of value appreciates it and cares for it. This is so that he may have the utmost service and pleasure from his purchase. When Jesus Christ receives us—as glorious as that is—it is only the beginning. We can rely on Him who bought us by His blood to complete His work in us.

The Blood of Christ

FULL SALVATION, OUR HIGH PRIVILEGE

"'My son,' the father said, 'you are always with me, and everything I have is yours.'"
LUKE 15:31

THE ELDER SON, in the parable of the prodigal son, had always been with his father. Because of this, he had two privileges: unceasing fellowship and unlimited partnership. But he was worse off than the prodigal, because although he was always at home, he had never known or enjoyed, or even understood the privileges that were his. This full fellowship with his father had been offered him, but he had not received it. While the prodigal was away from home in a faraway country, his older brother was just as far from the enjoyment of his heritage, even though he was home.

Full salvation includes unceasing fellowship. An earthly father loves his child and delights to make him happy. God is love, and speaking with all reverence, He can't help but love us. We see His goodness toward the ungodly and His compassion on the erring, but His fatherly love is manifested toward all His children.

Full salvation includes unlimited partnership. "Everything I have is yours," the father told the elder son when he complained of his father's gracious reception of the brother who had gone astray. All the time He is saying to you, "All I have is yours; I have given it to you in Christ. All the Holy Spirit's power and wisdom, all the riches of Christ, all the love of the Father; there is nothing that I have that is not yours. I am God, and I love you."

My message is that the Lord your God desires that you live continually in the light of His presence. Your business, your temper, your circumstances, all of which you may complain of as being a hindrance, are not stronger than God. If you ask God to shine in you and upon you, you will see and prove that He can do it and that you as a believer may walk all day and every day in the light of His love. That is "full salvation."

Divine Healing

HOLINESS AND CRUCIFIXION

WE HAVE SEEN BEFORE that obedience is the path to holiness. In Christ we see that the path to perfect holiness is perfect obedience. That means obedience unto death, even the death of the cross. The sanctification that Christ wrought for us, offering His body, bears the death mark, and we cannot partake of it either except as we die to self and its will. Crucifixion is the path to sanctification.

Then he said, "Here I am, I have come to do your will." . . . And by that will, we have been made holy through the sacrifice of the body of Jesus Christ once for all. . . . Because by one sacrifice he has made perfect forever those who are being made holy.
HEBREWS 10:9–10, 14

Where is the place of death? How can the crucifixion that leads to holiness and to God be accomplished in us? Thank God! It is through no work of our own, no weary process of self-crucifixion. The crucifixion that is to sanctify us is an accomplished fact. The cross bears the banner "It is finished" (John 19:30). Our crucifixion, like our sanctification, is something that in Christ has been completely and perfectly finished. In that fullness, which it is the Father's good pleasure should dwell in Christ, the crucifixion of our old man, of the flesh, of the world, of ourselves, is all a spiritual reality. He who desires and knows and accepts Christ fully receives all this in Him.

Is this the holiness that you are seeking? Do you see that God alone is holy, that we are unholy, and that there is no way for us to be made holy except by our being crucified with Christ? "We always carry around in our body the death of Jesus, so that the life of Jesus may also be revealed in our body" (2 Corinthians 4:10). In a way and to a degree far beyond our comprehension, intensely divine and real, we are in Him who sanctified himself for us. Let us remain where God has placed us.

The Path to Holiness

The Indwelling Spirit

"And I will pray the Father, and He will give you another Helper, that He may abide with you forever; the Spirit of truth, whom the world cannot receive, because it neither sees Him nor knows Him; but you know Him, for He dwells with you and will be in you."
JOHN 14:16–17 (NKJV)

"HE . . . WILL BE in you." With these simple words, our Lord announces the wonderful mystery of the Spirit's indwelling, which is the fruit and the crown of His redeeming work. It was for this we were created. It was for this purpose Jesus lived and was about to die. Without this, the Father's purpose and His own work would fail to be accomplished. And for lack of the Spirit, the Master's work with the disciples had relatively small effect. He had hardly mentioned the Spirit's coming to them, knowing that they would not understand. But then on the last night, when time was running out, He disclosed the divine secret: When He left them, their loss would be compensated by a greater blessing than His bodily presence. Another would come in His place to abide with them forever.

The indwelling of the Spirit is to be recognized by faith. Even when I cannot see the least evidence of His working, I am quietly and expectantly to believe that He dwells in me. In faith, I am to restfully count upon His working and to wait for it. And in faith I must very decidedly deny my own wisdom and strength and in childlike self-abnegation depend upon Him to work everything in me.

He is a living person, who had descended into our weakness and hidden himself in our smallness. He fits us for becoming His dwelling place. Let your adoring worship of the glorified Lord seek to grasp the wondrous answer He gives to every prayer as the seal of our acceptance. It is the promise of deeper knowledge of our God, of closer fellowship and richer blessings. The Holy Spirit has come and He dwells in you.

The Spirit of Christ

THE INFINITE FATHERLINESS
OF GOD

OUR LORD CONFIRMS further what He said of the certainty of an answer to prayer. To remove all doubt and show us on what sure ground His promise rests, He appeals to a truth all have seen and experienced here on earth. We were all children, and know what we expected of our fathers. Any way we look at it, it is the most natural thing for a father to hear his child. And the Lord asks us to look up from our earthly parents—of whom the best are but evil—and to calculate *how much more* the heavenly

"Which of you, if his son asks for bread, will give him a stone? Or if he asks for a fish, will give him a snake? If you, then, though you are evil, know how to give good gifts to your children, how much more will your Father in heaven give good gifts to those who ask him!"
MATTHEW 7:9–11

Father will give good gifts to them that ask Him. Jesus shows us that to the degree that God is greater than sinful men, so should we base our assurance that God will grant our childlike petitions. As God is to be trusted more than men, *so much more certain* is it that our prayer will be heard of our Father in heaven.

This parable is simple and intelligible. Equally deep and spiritual is the teaching it contains. The Lord reminds us that the prayer of a child of God is influenced entirely by the relationship he has with his Parent. Prayer can exert that influence only when the child is living and walking in a loving relationship in the home and in the service of the Father. The power of the promise "Ask and it will be given to you" (Matthew 7:7) lies in that good relationship. Then the prayer of faith and its answer will be the natural result. Today the lesson is: Live as a child of God, and you may pray as a child with complete certainty of an answer.

Teach Me to Pray

THE ALMIGHTY ONE

But those who wait on the LORD shall renew their strength; they shall mount up with wings like eagles, they shall run and not be weary, they shall walk and not faint.

ISAIAH 40:31 (NKJV)

THE EAGLE is the king of birds and soars highest in the skies. Believers are to live a heavenly life in the presence and love and joy of God. They are to live where God lives and in His strength. To those who wait on Him, it shall be so.

Eagles are born with a potential power in their wings that surpasses all other birds. You are born of God. *You* have eagles' wings. God will teach you to use them.

Eagles are taught the use of their wings by their mothers. Imagine a cliff rising a thousand feet out of the sea. On a ledge high up on the rock the eagle builds her nest for her two young eaglets. When the time is right, the mother bird stirs up her nest, pushing the timid fledglings over the edge. They flutter and fall and sink toward the depths, but she swoops beneath them and bears them up on her own strong wings. And so they ride to a place of safety. Then she does it again, each time pushing them out over the edge and then swooping beneath them again until the eaglets become strong enough to fly on their own. The instinct of the mother eagle is God's gift, a picture of the love by which the Almighty trains His people to mount up as on eagles' wings.

He stirs up your nest. He prolongs your hopes. He tries your confidence. He makes you fear and tremble as all your strength fails and you feel utterly weary and helpless. And all the while He is spreading His strong wings beneath you to rest your weakness on and offering His everlasting strength to work in you. And all He asks is that you sink down in your weariness and *wait on Him* and allow Him in His Jehovah-strength to carry you as you ride on the wings of His omnipotence.

Waiting on God

EVERY MOMENT

THE VINEYARD WAS the symbol of the people of Israel, in whose midst the True Vine was to stand. The branch is the symbol of the individual believer, who stands in the Vine. The song of the vineyard is also the song of the Vine and its every branch.

In that day sing to her,
"A vineyard of red wine!
I, the LORD, keep it, I
water it every moment;
Lest any hurt it,
I keep it night and day."
ISAIAH 27:2–3 (NKJV)

Is a life of unbroken fellowship with the Son of God possible here in this earthly life? If abiding is our work, to be done in our strength, then the answer must be no. But thankfully the things that are impossible with men are possible with God. If the Lord himself will keep the soul night and day, and watch it and water it every moment, then surely uninterrupted communion with Jesus does become a blessed possibility to those who can trust God to mean and to do what He says.

Take from His own lips the watchword *"every moment."* In that, you have the law of His love and the law of your hope. Be content with nothing less. Do not allow your mind to think that the duties and cares, the sorrows and sins of this life, must succeed in hindering the abiding life of fellowship. Take rather the language of faith for the rule of your daily experience: I am persuaded that neither death with its fears, nor life with its cares, nor things present with their pressing claims, nor things to come with their dark shadows, nor height of joy, nor depth of sorrow, nor any other creature, shall be able, for one single moment, to separate us from the love of God which is in Christ Jesus our Lord (see Romans 8:38–39).

If we will only look to our God as our Keeper we will learn to believe that conscious abiding in Christ every moment, night and day, is indeed what God has prepared for them who love Him.

Abiding in Christ

ABSOLUTE SURRENDER

Now Ben-Hadad king of Aram mustered his entire army . . . and besieged Samaria. . . . He sent messengers into the city to Ahab king of Israel, saying . . . "Your silver and gold are mine, and the best of your wives and children. . . ." The king of Israel answered, "Just as you say, my lord the king. I and all I have are yours."
1 KINGS 20:1–4

WHAT BEN-HADAD ASKED for was absolute surrender, and that is what Ahab gave him. The words of the king of Israel are words that we might use to show our absolute surrender to our Lord. If our hearts are willing for this kind of commitment, there is no limit to what God will do for us or to the blessing that will follow in our lives.

Some time ago, in Scotland, I was discussing the condition of the church with a group of Christian workers. In our group there was a godly man whose ministry was training others in Christian service. I asked him what he thought was the greatest need of the church. He answered, "Absolute surrender to God is the main thing." The words struck me as never before. He went on to tell me that if the workers he trained were sound on that one point, even though they might be lacking in some areas, they proved teachable and able to improve; whereas those who were not totally surrendered very often went back on their commitment and left the work.

I desire by God's grace to make this point unquestionably clear: God answers your prayers for spiritual blessing with one requirement: the willingness to surrender yourself absolutely into His hands. God knows the hearts of those who have done so and of those who long to do it but still have doubts or fears. There are others who have said they surrendered, but have failed miserably and who feel condemned because they have not found the secret of the power to live a consecrated life. Surrender yourself to God. You will not be disappointed.

Absolute Surrender

How It May Be Increased

CAN THE FULL BLESSING of Pentecost be increased? Can anything that is already full become fuller? Absolutely. It can become so full that it overflows. This is especially true of the blessing of Pen-

"Whoever believes in me . . . streams of living water will flow from within him."
JOHN 7:38

tecost. Before a natural spring is opened up, it will seem weak, but when fully uncovered, the waters will rush up and overflow. Just so with the rivers of living water—as we draw on them they increase and overflow.

Be sure that you do not form any wrong conceptions of what the full blessing is. Do not imagine that the joy and power of Pentecost must be felt and seen immediately. Restoration takes time and often comes slowly. At first, one receives the full blessing only as a seed: the full life is wrapped up as if it were in a capsule. We tend to judge God and His work in us by sight and feeling. We forget that the whole process is the work of faith.

God is love. His whole being is a surrender of himself in love to be the life of His creatures, to enable them to participate in His holiness and blessedness. He blesses and serves all that lives. When a believer has the fullness of the Spirit, and desires to have it increased, let it be clear that he can enjoy this blessing to the degree that he is prepared to give himself to the service of love. The Spirit comes to expel the life of self and self-seeking. The fullness of the Spirit presupposes a willingness to consecrate ourselves to the blessing of others. The secret to having the blessing increased is to live as one who is left on earth that the love of God may work through him.

Let us believe that we are in Christ, that He surrounds us with His power, longing to make the rivers of His Spirit flow through us to the world. It is by the exercise of faith without ceasing that the blessing will flow without ceasing.

The Fullness of the Spirit

My God Will Hear Me

But as for me, I watch in hope for the LORD, I wait for God my Savior; my God will hear me.
MICAH 7:7

THE POWER OF PRAYER rests in the faith that God hears our prayers. It is this faith that gives us courage to pray; that gives us power to prevail with God. The moment I am assured that God hears *me*, I feel drawn to pray and to persevere in prayer. I feel strong to claim and to take by faith the answer God gives. One of the great reasons for lack of prayer is the lack of a living, joyous assurance that God hears us. If only we could get a vision of the living God waiting with open arms to grant our request. Wouldn't we then set aside everything to make time and space for the prayer of faith?

When a man can and does declare in living faith, "My God will hear me!" surely nothing will keep him from prayer. He knows that what he cannot do on earth can and will be done for him in heaven. Let us bow in quietness before God and wait on Him until He reveals himself as the God who hears.

Christ sits at the right hand of the Father making intercession for us. God *delights* in hearing our prayers. He has allowed us many times to be tried that we might be compelled to cry to Him and to know Him as the God who hears prayer.

Ordinary and insignificant though I am, filling a very small place in His kingdom, even I have access to this infinite God with the confidence that He hears me.

What a blessed prospect indeed—every earthly and spiritual anxiety exchanged for the peace of God, who cares for all and hears our prayer. What a blessed prospect in my work—to know that even when the answer is delayed and there is a call for patient, persevering prayer, the truth remains the same: Our God hears us.

The Ministry of Intercessory Prayer

How to Be Delivered From Prayerlessness

THE GREATEST STUMBLING block in the way of victory over prayerlessness is the secret feeling that we will never obtain the blessing of being delivered from it. Often we have tried, but in vain. The change needed in the entire

If we confess our sins, he is faithful and just and will forgive us our sins and purify us from all unrighteousness.
1 JOHN 1:9

life is too great and too difficult. If the question is put: "Is a change possible?" our sighing heart says, "For me it is entirely *im*possible!" Do you know why we answer like that? It is simply because we have heard the call to prayer as the voice of Moses and as a command of the law. Moses and his law have never given anyone the power to obey.

Do you really long for the courage to believe that deliverance from a prayerless life is possible for you and may become a reality? Then you must learn the great lesson that such a deliverance is included in the redemption that is in Christ Jesus, that it is one of the blessings of the new covenant that God himself will impart to you through Christ Jesus.

My prayer life must be brought entirely under the control of Christ and His love. Then for the first time prayer will become what it really is: the natural and joyous breathing of the spiritual life by which the heavenly atmosphere is inhaled and then exhaled in prayer.

Do you see that when this faith possesses us the call to a life of prayer that pleases God will be a welcome call? The cry "Repent of the sin of prayerlessness" will not be responded to by a sigh of helplessness or by the unwillingness of the flesh. The voice of the Father will be heard as He sets before us a widely opened door and receives us into blessed fellowship with himself.

In His blood and grace there is complete deliverance from all unrighteousness and from all prayerlessness. Praise His name forever!

Living a Prayerful Life

ONE BODY

Because there is one loaf, we, who are many, are one body, for we all partake of the one loaf. . . . "A new command I give you: Love one another. As I have loved you, so you must love one another. By this all men will know that you are my disciples, if you love one another."

1 CORINTHIANS 10:17;
JOHN 13:34–35

UNION WITH THE Lord Jesus, our Head, involves at the same time mutual union with the members of His body. He who partakes of the body and blood of Jesus is incorporated with His body, the church, and stands thenceforth in close relationship with all its members.

So deep and wonderful was this union of His believing disciples at the table of the new covenant that the Lord spoke of the love that must motivate them as a new commandment. In the new covenant there was present a new life, and thus also a new love: "By this all men will know that you are my disciples, if you love one another."

This thought is often forgotten at the Lord's Table to our great loss. How often have guests at Jesus' table sat next to each other for years without knowing or loving or having fellowship with one another? Many have sought a closer connection with the Lord and not found it because they would have the Head without the body! Jesus must be loved, honored, served, and known in His members. As by the circulation of the blood every member of our body is kept in the most vital connection with the others, so the body of Christ can increase and become strong only when, in the loving interchange of the fellowship of the Spirit and of love, the life of the Head can flow unhindered from member to member.

Not only must love to Him whose bread I eat be the object of my desire, promise, and prayer, but also love to all who eat that bread along with me.

The Lord's Table

PAUL, A MODEL OF PRAYER

OUR LORD TOOK PAUL, a man of like passions with ourselves, and made him a model of what Christ could do for one who called himself the chief of sinners. The words our Lord used of him at his conversion, "He is praying," may be taken as the keynote of Paul's life. The

The Lord told him, "Go to the house of Judas on Straight Street and ask for a man from Tarsus named Saul, for he is praying."
ACTS 9:11

heavenly vision that brought him to his knees ruled his life ever after. Christ at the right hand of God, in whom we are blessed with all spiritual blessings, was everything to Paul. Prayer and the expectation of heavenly power in his work and on his work was the simple outcome of Paul's faith in the Glorified One.

Paul had such a sense that everything must come from above, and such a faith that it would come in answer to prayer, that prayer was neither a duty nor a burden. It was the natural turning of the heart to the only place from where it could possibly obtain what it sought for others. This is the pattern Paul followed: First, come every day empty-handed and receive from God the supply of the Spirit in intercession. Then impart what has come to you to others.

Paul's requests for prayer are no less instructive than his own prayers for the saints. They show that he does not count prayer a special prerogative of an apostle; he invites the humblest and simplest believer to claim his right. They prove that he doesn't think only the new converts or weak Christians need prayer; he himself, as a member of the body, is dependent upon his brethren and their prayers.

We have the Holy Spirit, who brings the Christ-life into our hearts to prepare us for this work. As we set aside time each day for intercession, and count upon the Spirit's enabling power, confidence will grow that we can, in our own measure, follow Paul even as he followed Christ.

The Ministry of Intercessory Prayer

Holiness and Faith

"That they may receive forgiveness of sins and a place among those who are sanctified by faith in me."
Acts 26:18

BECAUSE GOD IS a spiritual and invisible being, every revelation of Him, whether in His works, His Word, or His Son, calls for faith. Faith is the spiritual sense of the soul, being to it what the physical senses are to the body. By faith alone we enter into communication and contact with God.

Faith is that meekness of soul that waits in stillness to hear, understand, and accept what God says, and to receive, retain, and possess what God gives or does. By faith we welcome God himself, the living person, to enter in to make His abode with us and become our very life. In the Christian life faith is the first thing—the one thing—that pleases God and brings blessing to us. And because holiness is God's highest glory and the highest blessing He has for us, it is especially in the life of holiness that we need to live by faith alone.

Our Lord himself is our sanctification just as He is our justification. God asks of us faith for each, and each is freely given. The participle used here is not the present, but the aorist, indicating an act done once for all. When we believe in Christ, we receive the whole Christ, our justification and our sanctification: We are all at once accepted by God as righteous and holy in Him.

As we are led to see what God sees and as our faith grasps that the holy life of Christ is ours in actual possession, to be accepted and appropriated for daily use, then we shall be able to live the life God calls us to—the life of holy ones in Christ Jesus. It will be the acceptance and application in daily life of the power of a holy life that has been prepared in Jesus, which has in the union with Him become our present and permanent possession and that works in us according to the measure of our faith.

The Path to Holiness

THE ALL-COMPREHENSIVE GIFT

IN THE SERMON on the Mount, the Lord uttered His wonderful "how much more?" (Matthew 7:9–11). Here in Luke, where He repeats the question, there is a difference. Instead of speaking of giving *good gifts*, He says, "How much more will your Father in heaven give *the Holy Spirit*." He thus teaches us that the best

"If you then, though you are evil, know how to give good gifts to your children, how much more will your Father in heaven give the Holy Spirit to those who ask him!"
LUKE 11:13

of these gifts is the Holy Spirit, that in this gift all others are comprised. The Holy Spirit is therefore the gift we ought to seek first.

Jesus spoke of the Spirit as "the gift my Father promised" (Acts 1:4)—the one promise in which God's fatherhood is revealed. The best gift a good and wise father can bestow on a child is his own spirit. To reproduce in his child his own disposition and character is the great objective of a father in education. If the child is to know and understand his father and enter into all his plans for him, if he is to have his highest joy in the father and the father in him, the child must be of one mind and spirit with his father. So it is impossible to conceive of God bestowing any higher gift on His child than His own Spirit. God is what He is through His Spirit. The Spirit is the very life of God. Think what it means for God to give His own Spirit to His child on earth.

Was not this the glory of Jesus as a Son upon earth—that the Spirit of the Father was in Him? At His baptism in Jordan the two things were united: the voice proclaiming Him the beloved Son and the Spirit descending upon Him. And so the apostle says of us, "Because you are sons, God sent the Spirit of his Son into our hearts, the Spirit who calls out, 'Abba, Father'" (Galatians 4:6).

Teach Me to Pray

THE CERTAINTY OF BLESSING

"Then you will know that I am the LORD, for they shall not be ashamed who wait for Me."
ISAIAH 49:23 (NKJV)

WHAT PROMISES! God seeks to get us to wait on Him by the most positive assurances. He says it will *never* be in vain: "'They shall not be ashamed who wait for Me.'" It is strange that though we should so often have experienced it we are still slow to learn that this waiting must and can be the very breath of our life, a continuous resting in God's presence and love, a constant yielding of ourselves to Him to perfect His work in us. Let us listen and meditate until our heart says with new conviction, "Blessed are all those who wait for Him!" We found in the prayer of Psalm 25 (NKJV), "Let no one who waits on You be ashamed," the fact that we fear we might be disappointed. Let us listen to God's answer until every fear is driven off and we send back to heaven the words God speaks.

In the same way that the sunshine enters with its light and warmth, its beauty and blessing, every little blade of grass that rises out of the cold earth, so the everlasting God meets, in the greatness and the tenderness of His love, each waiting child to shine in their heart "the light of the knowledge of the glory of God in the face of Jesus Christ" (2 Corinthians 4:6 NKJV). Read these words again until your heart learns to know what God waits to do for you. Who can measure the difference between the great sun and that little blade of grass? And yet the grass has all of the sun it needs or can hold. While waiting on God, believe that His greatness and your smallness suit each other wonderfully. Just bow in your emptiness and poverty, your powerlessness and humility, and surrender to His will. As you wait on Him, God will come near. He will reveal himself as the God who faithfully fulfills every one of His promises.

Waiting on God

Forsaking All for Him

WE ALL HAVE within us a natural life, with all the powers and gifts given to us by the Creator, which work with all the occupations and interests of the environment that surrounds us. Once you are truly converted, it is not enough that

> *I have suffered the loss of all things, and count them as rubbish, that I may gain Christ and be found in Him.*
> PHILIPPIANS 3:8–9 (NKJV)

you have a sincere desire to have all these devoted to the service of the Lord. The desire is good, but it cannot teach the way or give the strength to do it acceptably.

I must see how all my gifts and powers are, even though I am indeed a child of God, still defiled by sin, and under the power of the flesh. I must feel that I cannot proceed at once to use them for God's glory; I must first lay them at Christ's feet, to be accepted and cleansed by Him. *I must feel myself utterly powerless to use them correctly.* I must see that they are very dangerous to me because through them the flesh, the old nature, self, will so easily exert its power. In this conviction I must part with them, giving them entirely up to the Lord. When He has accepted them and set His stamp upon them, I can receive them back to hold as His property, to wait on Him for the grace to use them properly day by day and *to have them act only under His influence.*

Each blessed experience we receive as a gift of God must at once be returned back to Him from whom it came, in praise and love, in self-sacrifice and service; only in this way can it be restored to us again, fresh and beautiful with the bloom of heaven.

Nature shrinks back from such self-denial and crucifixion in its rigid application to our life. But what nature does not love and cannot perform, grace will accomplish, supplying you with a life full of joy and glory.

Abiding in Christ

CHRIST IS OUR LIFE

When Christ, who is your life, appears, then you also will appear with him in glory.
COLOSSIANS 3:4

I KNOW THAT MANY who have made an absolute surrender have felt as I have: How little I understand it! And they have prayed, "Lord God, if we are to know what it really means, you must take possession of us." By faith God does accept our surrender, although the experience and the power of it may not come at once. We are to hold fast our faith in God until the experience and power do come.

If absolute surrender is to be maintained and lived out, it can only be by having Christ enter our life in new power. *Christ is our life.* We often plead with God to work in the church and in the world that by the power of His Holy Spirit His people might be sanctified and sinners be converted. We must not neglect to pray also for ourselves, so that as Christ takes full possession of us, He will be able to work through us to the end that others might be helped.

Let us yield ourselves to God in prayer that He might search our hearts and reveal to us whether the life of Christ is the law of our life. Many people want eternal life but do not want to live the life here on earth that Christ lived.

Have you felt afraid to make a complete surrender because you felt unworthy? Consider this: Your worthiness is not in yourself or in the intensity of your consecration; *your worthiness is in Christ himself.*

Jesus Christ wants to be your companion so that you will never be alone. There is no trial or difficulty through which you pass without His promise: "I will be with you." No battle with sin or temptation, no weakness that makes you tremble at the consciousness of what you are in yourself, excludes the fact that Christ is at your side every moment.

Absolute Surrender

OBEDIENCE AND KNOWLEDGE

I ONCE RECEIVED a letter from an evidently earnest Christian, asking me for some tips to help him in his Bible study. My first thought was that there

"Blessed rather are those who hear the word of God and obey it."
LUKE 11:28

are so many sermons and books on the subject that he could surely find all I might say better said already. However, certain experiences in my own immediate circle soon showed me the need for instruction on this all-important subject.

The thing that comes before all else is this: In your Bible study, everything will depend upon *the spirit in which you approach it*—the objective you propose. If your aim is simply to know the Bible well, you will be disappointed. If you think that a thorough knowledge of the Bible in itself will be a blessing, you are mistaken.

God's Word is food, bread from heaven; the first prerequisite of Bible study is a great hunger after righteousness, a sincere desire to do all God's will. The Bible is a light; the first condition to its enjoyment is a hearty longing to walk in God's ways. The Word is nothing if it is not obeyed. All true knowledge of God's Word depends upon there being first a will to obey it. This is easily understood when we think of what *words* are meant to do. They stand between will and action. If someone decides to do something for you, before he does it, he will formulate his thoughts or purpose in words, either to himself or to you, and then he will do what he says he will do.

This is no less true of His commands, which He intends that we obey. If we do not obey them; if we seek to know them and admire their beauty and praise their wisdom, but do not obey them, we delude ourselves. *They are meant to be obeyed;* as we obey them, their real meaning and blessing can be revealed to us.

The Believer's Daily Renewal

RECONCILIATION THROUGH THE BLOOD

For all have sinned and fall short of the glory of God, and are justified freely by his grace through the redemption that came by Christ Jesus. God presented him as a sacrifice of atonement, through faith in his blood.
ROMANS 3:23–25

THE FACT THAT the blood has made reconciliation for sin and covered it and that as a result of this such a wonderful change has taken place in the heavenly realms, will avail us nothing unless we obtain a personal share in it.

God has offered a perfect acquittal from all our sin and guilt. Because reconciliation has been made for sin, we can now be reconciled to Him. "God was in Christ reconciling the world to Himself, not imputing their trespasses to them." Following this word of reconciliation is the invitation, "Be reconciled to God" (2 Corinthians 5:19–20). Whoever *receives* reconciliation for sin *is* reconciled to God. He knows that all his sins are forgiven.

So perfect is the reconciliation and so completely has sin been blotted out that he who believes in Christ is looked upon by God as entirely righteous. The acquittal that he has received from God is so complete that there is absolutely nothing to prevent him from approaching God with the utmost freedom. For the enjoyment of this blessedness nothing is necessary except faith in the blood. *The blood alone has done everything*.

The penitent sinner who turns from his sin to God needs only faith in the power of the blood—faith that it has atoned for sin and that it has atoned for him. Through that faith, he knows that he is fully reconciled to God and that there is now nothing to hinder God's pouring out on him the fullness of His love and blessing. If he looks toward heaven, which formerly was black with God's wrath and an awful coming judgment, that darkness will no longer be seen; everything is bright in the joyful light of God's love.

The Blood of Christ

THE SPIRIT OF ACCESS

IN VERSES 4–10 of Ephesians 2, we have the beautiful passage that leads up to the words of our text. And from this section we glean six qualities concerning Christian living and commitment.

For through Him we both have access by one Spirit to the Father.
EPHESIANS 2:18

In whom we have boldness and access with confidence through faith in Him.
EPHESIANS 3:12

It is a present reality: "[He] made us alive together with Christ . . . and raised us up together, and made us to sit together in the heavenly places."

It is by grace: "God, who is rich in mercy, because of His great love with which He loved us . . . that in the ages to come [that is, from the resurrection onward], He might show the exceeding riches of His grace in His kindness toward us in Christ Jesus."

It is through faith: "not of yourselves; it is the gift of God, not of works, lest anyone should boast."

It gives us access to the Father: In the tabernacle, the Holy of Holies was separated by a thick veil from the Holy Place, in which the priest came daily to serve. When Christ died, this veil was rent in two. The way was opened for every believer to enter into God's holy presence.

It is through the Son: This means more than our Advocate. Our High Priest lives and acts in the power of an endless, incorruptible life. He works in us by the power of His resurrection life.

It is in one Spirit: The Spirit has been given to us that we may be able to cry, "Abba, Father," even as Christ did. The Spirit dwells in us to reveal Christ; without Him, no one can truly call Jesus Lord.

The Spirit takes control of our whole life and being; where He is yielded to and trusted, He maintains fellowship with the Father through the Son, in the Holy of Holies, a divine reality in our life.

The Believer's Call to Commitment

GOD'S PRESCRIPTION
FOR THE SICK

Is any one of you sick? He should call the elders of the church to pray over him and anoint him with oil in the name of the Lord. And the prayer offered in faith will make the sick person well; the Lord will raise him up. If he has sinned, he will be forgiven.
JAMES 5:14–15

THIS SCRIPTURE clearly declares to the sick what they have to do in order to be healed. Sickness and its consequences abound in the world. What joy, then, for the believer to learn from the Word of God the way to healing! The Bible teaches us that it is the will of God to see His children in good health.

Suffering that may arise from various exterior causes is the portion of every Christian. There is a great difference between suffering and sickness. The Lord Jesus spoke of suffering as being necessary, as being willed and blessed of God, while He says of sickness that it ought to be cured. All other suffering comes to us from without, and will cease only when Jesus triumphs over the sin and evil that are in the world. Sickness is an evil that is in the body itself, in the body saved by Christ that it may become the temple of the Holy Spirit, and which, consequently, ought to be healed as soon as the sick believer receives by faith the very life of Jesus.

The direction given to the sick is to call for the elders of the church and to let them pray for him. The elders were the pastors and leaders of the churches, called to the ministry because they were filled with the Holy Spirit and were well known for their holiness and their faith. They were representatives of the church, the collective body of Christ, and it is the communion of believers that invites the Spirit to act with power. It is they, the servants of the God who forgives iniquities and heals diseases, who are called to transmit to others the Lord's graces for soul and body.

Divine Healing

HUMAN WISDOM OR THE POWER OF GOD?

WHEN THE PREACHING of the Cross is given only in the words of human wisdom, the faith of the hearers will be in the wisdom of men. When the preaching is in demonstration of the Spirit and of power, the faith of the believers will be in the power of God.

My message and my preaching were not with wise and persuasive words, but with a demonstration of the Spirit's power, so that your faith might not rest on men's wisdom, but on God's power.
1 CORINTHIANS 2:4–5

The Spirit of Pentecost is the Spirit of God's holiness. When He came upon the disciples in the Upper Room, their lives were transformed. Sin was cast out by the inflowing of the life of Jesus. It is because the full blessing of the Spirit is so little known or sought that believers still commit so much sin.

There is nothing that plagues pastors more than those believers who for a time are full of zeal and then fall away. As long as they have the benefit of enthusiastic and instructive preaching, they continue to push on, but when this ceases, they begin to backslide. The preaching, the Word itself, and the minister of the gospel can become hindrances instead of helps if they are not under the power of the Spirit.

The goal of Pentecost was to equip His servants for His work on the earth. The Spirit filled them with the desire and the impetus, the courage and the strength, to brave all hostility and danger, to endure all suffering and persecution, to succeed in making Jesus known as Lord.

Stop and consider the condition of the church, the Christian community around you, and your own heart. There will be neither healing nor restoration except by the fresh filling of the Spirit of God. All external means of grace inevitably change and fade. It is the Spirit alone that works the faith that stands in the power of God and so remains strong and unwavering.

The Fullness of the Spirit

HUMILITY IN DAILY LIFE

For anyone who does not love his brother, whom he has seen, cannot love God, whom he has not seen.
1 JOHN 4:20

IT IS A SOLEMN thought that our love for God is measured by our everyday relationships with others. It is easy to think that we humble ourselves before God, but our humility toward others is the only sufficient proof that our humility before God is real. To be genuine, humility must abide in us and become our very nature. True humility is to be made of no reputation—as was Christ.

In God's presence, humility is not a posture we assume for a time—when we think of Him or pray to Him—but the very spirit of our life. It will manifest itself in all our bearing toward others. A lesson of deepest importance is that the only humility that is really ours is not the kind we try to show before God in prayer, but the kind we carry with us, and carry out, in our ordinary conduct. The seemingly insignificant acts of daily life are the tests of eternity, because they prove what spirit possesses us. It is in our most unguarded moments that we truly show who we are and what we are made of.

The humble person seeks at all times to live up to the rule "Serve one another; consider others better than yourselves; submit to one another." The humble person feels no jealousy or envy. He can praise God when others are preferred and blessed before him. He can hear others praised and himself forgotten because in God's presence he has learned to say with Paul, "I am nothing." He has received the spirit of Jesus, who pleased not himself and sought not His own honor as the spirit of his life.

Let us look upon everyone who tries us as God's means of grace, God's instrument for our purification, for our exercise of the humility of Jesus. May we have true faith in the sufficiency of God and admit to the inefficiency of self, that by God's power we will serve one another in love.

Humility

LIFE AND PRAYER

They devoted themselves to the apostles' teaching and to the fellowship, to the breaking of bread and to prayer.
ACTS 2:42

OUR DAILY LIFE has a tremendous influence on our prayers, just as our prayers influence our daily life. In fact, our life is a continuous prayer. We are continually praising or thanking God by our actions and by the manner in which we treat others. At times God cannot hear the prayer of your lips, because the worldly desires of your heart cry out to Him much more strongly and loudly.

As we have said, life exercises a mighty influence over prayer. A worldly life or a self-seeking life makes prayer by that person powerless and an answer impossible. With many Christians there is conflict between their everyday life and their prayer life, and the everyday life holds the upper hand. But prayer can also exercise a strong influence over our everyday life. If I yield myself completely to God in prayer, prayer can overcome a life in the flesh and the practice of sin. The entire life may be brought under the control of prayer. Prayer can change and renew the life, because prayer calls upon and receives the Lord Jesus, and the Holy Spirit purifies and sanctifies us.

Because of their defective spiritual life, many people think they must make a supreme effort in order to pray more. They do not understand that only in proportion as the spiritual life is strengthened can the prayer life increase. Prayer and life are inseparably connected and the quality of each deeply related.

How sacred and powerful prayer is when it takes possession of the heart and life! It keeps one constantly in fellowship with God. Then we can literally say, *I wait on you, Lord, all day long.* Let us be careful to consider not only the length of time we spend with God in prayer but also the power prayer has to take possession of our whole life.

Living a Prayerful Life

FOR YOU

"This is my body given for you. . . . This cup is the new covenant in my blood, which is poured out for you."
LUKE 22:19–20

ALTHOUGH IT IS CLEAR that our Lord gave himself for all, "for many," it is important also to emphasize that He gave himself for me, "for you."

The secret of true blessedness lies in the phrase "for you." All knowledge of the truth and all acquaintance with the gospel are of no avail without personal appropriation. And the foundation of our confidence is our Lord's words: "given for you"; "poured out for you."

So it was at the Lord's Table. In speaking of His body and blood, the Savior addressed His disciples and said to them: "This is my body given for you. . . . This cup is the new covenant in my blood, which is poured out for you." Later the disciples would be strengthened by that very word. Peter, after his bitter denial; Thomas, in his grievous unbelief; and each of the others, in their various shortcomings and failings, could not fail to encourage themselves by remembering His words to them at that Last Supper.

By His Holy Spirit He is as near to us as He was to them. Unworthy as we may feel, He is faithful to His Word. His work of redemption was and is for each one of us. He only awaits our receiving what He has done, the application of His body and blood to our lives for healing, cleansing, forgiveness, and wholeness.

The Lord's Table

PRAY WITHOUT CEASING

WHO CAN DO THIS? Does praying without ceasing refer to continual physical acts of prayer in which we persevere until we obtain what we ask, or does it refer to the spirit of prayerfulness that animates and motivates us throughout

Pray without ceasing; in everything give thanks; for this is the will of God in Christ Jesus for you.
1 THESSALONIANS 5:17–18
(NKJV)

the day? It includes both. The example of our Lord Jesus shows us this. We should enter our place of private prayer for special seasons of prayer, and we are at times to persevere there in importunate prayer. We are also to walk all day in God's presence, with our whole heart focused on spiritual things. Without set times of prayer, the spirit of prayer will be lacking and weak. Without the continual attitude of prayerfulness, the set times of prayer will be ineffective.

Does this running prayer refer only to prayer for ourselves, or for others? Both. The death of Christ brought Him to the place of everlasting intercession. Your death with Him to sin and self sets you free from the care of self and elevates you to the dignity of intercessor—one who can receive life and blessing from God for others. Know your calling; begin your work. Give yourself wholly to it, and soon you will find something of this "prayer without ceasing" within you.

Take courage; it is in the intercession of Christ that you are called to take part. The burden and the agony, the triumph and the victory, are all His. Learn from Him, yield to His Spirit in you to know how to pray. "Our sufficiency is from God" (2 Corinthians 3:5 NKJV).

Let your faith rest boldly on His finished work. Let your heart wholly identify itself with Him in His death and His life. Like Him, give yourself to God as a sacrifice for others. It is your highest privilege, it is your true and full union with Him; it will be to you, as to Him, your power for intercessory prayer.

The Ministry of Intercessory Prayer

HOLINESS AND GLORY

"Who among the gods is like you, O LORD? Who is like you—majestic in holiness, awesome in glory, working wonders? . . . In your unfailing love you will lead the people you have redeemed. In your strength you will guide them to your holy dwelling . . . the sanctuary [holy place], O LORD, your hands established."

EXODUS 15:11, 13, 17

THE GLORY OF AN object, of a thing or person, is its intrinsic worth or excellence; to glorify is to remove everything that could hinder the full revelation of that excellence. In the holiness of God His glory is hidden; in the glory of God His holiness is manifested. Holiness is not so much an attribute of God as the comprehensive summary of all His perfections.

Only under the influence of high spiritual elevation and joy can God's holiness be fully apprehended or rightly worshiped. The sentiment that becomes us as we worship the Holy One, that fits us for knowing and worshiping Him aright, is the spirit of praise that sings and shouts for joy in the experience of His full salvation.

Praise God! The judgment is past. In Christ, the burning bush, the fire of the divine holiness has done its double work. In Him sin was condemned in the flesh, in Him we are free. In giving up His will to death and doing God's will, Christ sanctified himself, and in that will we are sanctified too. His crucifixion with its judgment of the flesh and His death with its entire putting off of what is natural are not only *for* us but are, in fact, *ours*—a life and power working within us by His Spirit.

Day by day we abide in Him. With fear and trembling but with rejoicing we take our stand in Him. The power of holiness as judgment against sin and flesh allows it to accomplish its glorious work. We give thanks at the remembrance of His holiness.

The Path to Holiness

THE BOLDNESS OF GOD'S FRIENDS

THE DISCIPLES ASKED Jesus to teach them to pray. In answer, He gave them the Lord's Prayer, so teaching them *what* to pray. He then speaks of *how* they ought to pray, and repeats what He said before about God's fatherliness and the certainty of an answer. Then He adds the beautiful parable of the friend who came at midnight to teach them the lesson that God wants us to pray not only for ourselves but also for the perishing around us and that in such intercession great boldness is often needed, is always lawful, and is even pleasing to God.

The parable is a perfect storehouse of instruction about true intercession. First, there is the *love* that seeks to help the needy: "My friend has come to me." Then the *need* that prompts the cry, "I have nothing to set before him." Then follows the *confidence* that help is to be had: "Friend, lend me three loaves of bread." An unexpected *refusal* comes: "I can't get up and give you anything." But his *perseverance* takes no refusal: "Because of the man's *boldness*. . . ." Last, there comes the reward of such prayer: "He will get up and give him *as much as he needs*." This wonderfully illustrates the way of prayer and faith in which the blessing of God has so often been sought and found.

"Suppose one of you has a friend, and he goes to him at midnight and says, 'Friend, lend me three loaves of bread, because a friend of mine on a journey has come to me, and I have nothing to set before him.' Then the one inside answers, 'Don't bother me. The door is already locked, and my children are with me in bed. I can't get up and give you anything.' I tell you, though he will not get up and give him the bread because he is his friend, yet because of the man's boldness he will get up and give him as much as he needs."
LUKE 11:5–8

Teach Me to Pray

THE GOD OF JUDGMENT

Therefore the LORD will wait, that He may be gracious to you; and therefore He will be exalted, that He may have mercy on you. For the LORD is a God of justice; blessed are all those who wait for Him.
ISAIAH 30:18 (NKJV)

GOD IS A GOD of mercy and of judgment. All His dealings involve these two. We see mercy in the midst of judgment in the time of the Flood, in the deliverance of Israel out of Egypt, and in the overthrow of the Canaanites. We see it, too, in the inner circle of His people. Judgment punishes sin, while mercy saves the sinner. In waiting on God, we must beware of forgetting this. Though He is merciful, He is also a God of judgment. If we are honest in our longing for holiness, in our prayer to be wholly the Lord's, His holy presence will stir up and uncover hidden sin. It will bring us conviction of our sinful nature, its opposition to God's law, and its resistance to fulfill that law.

In great mercy God executes within the soul His judgments on sin, making the soul feel its guilt. Many try to flee these judgments. The soul that longs for God and for deliverance from sin bows under them in humility and in hope. In silence it says, "Rise up, O LORD! Let Your enemies be scattered" (Numbers 10:35 NKJV).

No one who seeks to learn the blessed art of waiting on God should be surprised if at first the attempt to wait on Him only reveals more sin and darkness. Let no one despair because unconquered sin, evil thoughts, or discouragement appear to hide God's face. Even when His beloved Son, the gift and bearer of His mercy, was at Calvary, mercy was hidden for a time because of the sin He bore for us. Submit to the judgment of sin. Judgment prepares the way for mercy.

Wait on God in faith that His tender mercy is working out His redemption. He will be gracious to you.

Waiting on God

GOD HIMSELF WILL
ESTABLISH YOU IN HIM

THESE WORDS OF PAUL teach us a much-needed and most blessed truth— that just as our first being united with Christ was the work of divine omnipotence, so we may also look to the

He who establishes us with you in Christ and has anointed us is God.
2 CORINTHIANS 1:21
(NKJV)

Father for being kept and being established more firmly in Him.

What peace and rest to know that there is a Vinedresser who cares for the branch, to see that it grows stronger, and that its union with the Vine becomes more perfect, who watches over every hindrance and danger and supplies every need! What peace and rest to fully and finally give up our abiding into the care of God, and never to have a wish or thought, never offer a prayer or engage in an exercise connected with it, without first gladly remembering that what we do is only the manifestation of what God is doing in us! But this He can do with power only as we stop interrupting Him by our self-working, as we accept by faith the dependent posture that honors Him and opens the heart to let Him work.

Listen to what the Word teaches you: "The Lord *will establish* you as a holy people to Himself" (Deuteronomy 28:9 NKJV); "Now to Him who is able *to establish you* . . . be glory through Jesus Christ forever" (Romans 16:25, 27 NKJV); "The Lord is faithful, who will establish you and guard you from the evil one" (2 Thessalonians 3:3 NKJV). Can you take these words to mean anything less than that you, too—however spasmodic your spiritual life has been up to now, however unfavorable your natural character or your circumstances may appear—can be established in Christ Jesus?

If we take the time to listen, in simple childlike humility, to these words as the truth of God, the confidence will come: As surely as I am in Christ, I will also, day by day, be established in Him.

Abiding in Christ

THE BLESSEDNESS OF THE DOER

Do not merely listen to the word, and so deceive yourselves.
JAMES 1:22

IT IS A TERRIBLE delusion to be content, even delighted, at hearing the Word and yet not being willing to do it. Actually, it is quite common for many Christians to listen to the Word of God regularly, even eagerly, and yet not obey it. If their own employee were to listen to their instructions but not do what was asked of him, they would be very displeased. And yet so complete is the delusion, they seldom realize that they are not living consistent Christian lives.

For one thing, people mistake the pleasure they have in hearing the Word for spirituality and worship. The mind delights in having the truth clearly presented; the imagination is gratified by its illustration; the emotions are stirred by its application. To an active mind, knowledge gives pleasure. And so many people go to church and enjoy the preaching—but they have no intention of doing what God asks. The unconverted and the converted man alike may remain content to continue sinning, confessing, and sinning again.

Another cause of this delusion is the pervasive doctrine that we are incapable of doing any good. The grace of Christ that can enable us to obey, keep us from sinning, and make us a holy people is rarely embraced. Most Christians think that sinning is inevitable, and God cannot expect exact obedience when we are helpless to render it. This error cuts at the very root of a determination to do all God has said. It closes the heart to any desire to believe and experience all that God's grace can do in us, and keeps us self-contented in the midst of sin. Hearing and not doing is a terrible self-delusion.

The Believer's Daily Renewal

REDEMPTION BY THE BLOOD

THE SHEDDING OF His blood was the culmination of the sufferings of our Lord. The atoning efficacy of those sufferings was in that shed blood. It is, therefore, of great importance that the believer not rest satisfied with the mere acceptance of the truth that he is redeemed by that blood, but should press on to a fuller knowledge of what is meant by the fact and to learn what the blood is intended to do in a surrendered soul.

For you know that it was not with perishable things such as silver or gold that you were redeemed from the empty way of life handed down to you from your forefathers, but with the precious blood of Christ, a lamb without blemish or defect.
1 PETER 1:18–19

Who can tell the value or the power of the blood of Jesus? In that blood dwells the soul of the holy Son of God. The eternal life of the Godhead was carried in that blood (Acts 20:28). The blood has a marvelous power for removing sin and for opening heaven for the sinner whom it cleanses, sanctifies, and equips for heaven.

The power of that blood in its diverse effects is nothing less than the eternal power of God himself. It is because of the wonderful Person whose blood was shed and because of the wonderful way in which it was shed—fulfilling the law of God while satisfying its just demands—that the blood of Jesus has such wonderful power. It is the blood of Atonement, and hence has such efficacy to redeem—accomplishing everything for, and in, the sinner that is necessary for salvation.

Our faith may be strengthened by noticing what the blood has already accomplished. Heaven and hell bear witness to that. Let us fully expect that as we enter more deeply into the fountain, its cleansing, quickening, life-giving power will be more fully revealed.

The Blood of Christ

The Temple of the Spirit

Jesus Christ Himself being the chief cornerstone, in whom the whole building, being fitted together, grows into a holy temple in the Lord, in whom you also are being built together for a dwelling place of God in the Spirit.

Ephesians 2:20–22 (nkjv)

OUR TEXT SPEAKS of the holy Trinity: the Father, God, for whom the dwelling place is built; the Son, Jesus Christ, the chief cornerstone, in whom the holy temple grows; the Spirit, the Builder, through whom all the living stones are united with one another and with the chief cornerstone, and are thus in perfect fellowship with God. The triune God is the God of our salvation. The primary focus of the passage is fellowship. It is first spoken of as the fellowship of believers, built up into one holy temple. Paul spoke of the Gentiles as strangers to the covenant of promise, brought near by the blood of Christ; of the enmity being abolished and nailed to the cross that we both might have access in one Spirit to the Father.

The Cross ended all separation among men: Jews and Gentiles, Greeks and barbarians, wise and foolish—all are become one in Christ Jesus. National and social distinctions are nothing compared to the unity the Spirit gives in Christ. The catalyst that holds the living stones together is nothing less than the Spirit and the life and love of God.

Fellowship with God, with Christ the chief cornerstone, and with other Christians is the blessing of our being built as a dwelling place of God in the Spirit. In the Cross of Christ all selfishness has been destroyed so that the love that only seeks to give itself for others has been made possible. Close fellowship with one another is as sacred and indispensable as fellowship with God. There is no way of proving to the world our love for God and the reality of God's love for us except through our love for our fellow Christians; our spiritual life depends on it.

The Believer's Call to Commitment

HEALTH AND OBEDIENCE

ISRAEL HAD JUST been released from the yoke of Egypt when their faith was put to the test in the desert by the waters of Marah. It was after He had sweetened the bitter waters that the Lord promised He would not put upon the children of Israel any of the diseases that He had brought upon the Egyptians as long as they obeyed Him. They would be exposed to other trials; they might sometimes suffer the need of bread and water; they would have to contend with their enemies and encounter other dangers; all these things might come upon them in spite of their obedience, but sickness would not touch them.

"If you listen carefully to the voice of the LORD your God and do what is right in his eyes, if you pay attention to his commands and keep all his decrees, I will not bring on you any of the diseases I brought on the Egyptians, for I am the LORD, who heals you."
EXODUS 15:26

Give thanks to the LORD, for he is good; his love endures forever.
PSALM 107:1

This calls our attention to a great truth; that is, the intimate relationship that exists between obedience and health; between sanctification that is the health of the soul and divine healing that ensures health for the body. Both are comprised in the salvation that comes from God. It is noteworthy that in several languages these three words—*salvation, healing,* and *sanctification*—are derived from the same root and present the same fundamental thought. Thus it is in giving health to the body and sanctification to the soul that Jesus is the Savior of His people.

If you are looking for healing from the Lord, receive it with joy. God asks of us a childlike abandonment, the attention that listens and consents to be led. This is what God expects of us, and the healing of the body is the reward for childlike faith. The Lord will reveal himself as the mighty Savior who heals the body and sanctifies the soul.

Divine Healing

HUMILITY IN THE DISCIPLES OF JESUS

"The greatest among you should be like the youngest, and the one who rules like the one who serves."
LUKE 22:26

WE HAVE SEEN the occasions on which the disciples proved how much they lacked the grace of humility. Once they were disputing about who should be the greatest. Another time the sons of Zebedee, with their mother, had asked for the first places—the seats on the right hand and the left of Jesus in glory. And later on, at the Last Supper, there was a contention again about who should be counted the greatest. This is not to say that there were not moments when they did humble themselves before the Lord. Peter cried out, "Go away from me, Lord; I am a sinful man!" (Luke 5:8). But such infrequent expressions of humility only emphasize the general habit of their minds, as shown in the natural and spontaneous revelations of the place and power of self.

The disciples had a fervent attachment to Jesus. They had forsaken all to follow Him. They believed in Him, they loved Him, and they obeyed His commandments. When others fell away, they remained faithful to Him. They were ready to die with Him. But deeper than all of this devotion was the existence of an inner power of sin and selfishness. This power had to be dealt with before they could be witnesses of the power of Jesus to save. It is so with all of us.

All Christ's teaching of His disciples, and all their vain efforts, were the needful preparation for His entering into them in divine power, to give and be in them what He had taught them to desire. On Pentecost He came and took possession of the church. The lives and the epistles of James and Peter and John bear witness that all was changed, and that the spirit of the meek and suffering Jesus had taken possession of them.

It is only where we, like the Son, truly know and show that we can do nothing of ourselves that God will do everything.

Humility

THINK OF GOD, His greatness, His holiness, His unspeakable glory, and then imagine the inestimable privilege to which He invites His children, that each one of them, no matter how sinful or frail, may have access to God anytime

Let the hearts of those who seek the LORD rejoice. Look to the LORD and his strength; seek his face always.
1 CHRONICLES 16:10–11

and may talk with Him as long as he wishes. God is ready to meet His child anytime he enters his prayer room; He is ready to have fellowship with him, to give him the joy and strength that he needs along with the assurance that God is with him and will undertake for him in everything. In addition, God promises that He will enrich His child in his outward life and work with those things he has asked for in secret. We ought to cry out with joy. What an honor! What a salvation!

We might well imagine that no place on earth would be so attractive to the child of God as the prayer room, where the presence of God is promised and unhindered fellowship with the Father awaits. But what is the response? From everywhere the conclusion is reached that private, personal prayer is as a general rule neglected by those who call themselves believers.

Is there no hope of change? Must it always be so? The man through whom God has made known the message of the inner room is none other than our Lord Jesus Christ, who saves us from our sins. He is able and willing to deliver us from this sin, and He will deliver us. In your sin and weakness come into your prayer room, and begin to thank God, as you have never thanked Him before, that the grace of the Lord Jesus will make it possible for you to converse with your Father as a child ought to.

Even though your heart may be cold and dead, persevere in the exercise of faith that Christ is an almighty and faithful Savior. You may be sure that deliverance will come. Expect it.

Living a Prayerful Life

For the Many

"This is my blood of the covenant, which is poured out for many for the forgiveness of sins."
MATTHEW 26:28

THE WORD WE WANT to emphasize in our text is *many*. Jesus has a large heart. At the Supper table, He not only forgot himself in order to think of His own who were gathered there around Him, but His loving eye looked forward to all who would be redeemed by His blood. He taught His disciples to maintain fellowship not merely with those with whom they sat at table, but with the entire host of the redeemed—the multitude that no man can number. This truth binds all the celebrations of the Supper into one single communion, in immediate contact with Him who first instituted it. It unites also the separate circles of Christ's disciples into one universal church, and all distinction and all separation vanish in the joyful truth that every member shares equally in the love and life of the one Head from whom also he received the bread.

The observance of the Supper accordingly must renew our sense of unity not only with the Head but also the body of which we are members. The Supper will enlarge our heart until it is as wide as the heart of Jesus. Next to our love of the Lord Jesus, our love for the body of Christ must fill our souls.

Some Christians are satisfied when all goes well in their own little circle: they think of going to heaven only in company of those that belong to them. This is wrong thinking. The Supper must enlarge the heart in love and prayer for all that belong to Jesus so as to make us rejoice with them or weep with them. We must not stop even at this point. The true disciple of Jesus thinks of all who may yet be in their sins and who do not know about the blood that was shed for them. He that partakes of the cup becomes a partaker of the life and love poured forth in that blood. All selfishness and narrow-mindedness will be swept away.

The Lord's Table

THE COMING REVIVAL

REVIVAL IS GOD'S work. He alone can give it; it must come from above. We may be looking to all the signs of life and good around us and congratulating our-

Will you not revive us again, that your people may rejoice in you?
PSALM 85:6

selves on all the organizations and support groups that are being created, while the need of God's direct intervention is not significantly felt and entire dependence upon Him is not cultivated.

Regeneration, the giving of divine life, we all acknowledge to be God's act, a miracle of His power. The restoring or reviving of the divine life in a soul or a church is equally a supernatural work. It is God who gives revival; it is absolute dependence upon God, giving Him the honor and the glory, that will prepare us for it.

Those who know anything of the history of revivals will remember how often both widespread and local revivals have been distinctly traced to specific prayer. An extraordinary spirit of prayer, urging believers to private as well as united prayer, motivating them to labor fervently in their supplications, will be one of the surest signs of approaching showers and floods of blessing.

"I live in a high and holy place, but also with him who is contrite and lowly in spirit, to revive the spirit of the lowly and to revive the heart of the contrite" (Isaiah 57:15). Revival is promised to the humble and contrite. Every true revival among God's people must have at its root a deep sense and confession of sin. Until those who would lead the church in the path of revival bear faithful testimony against the sins of the church, it is likely that it will find people unprepared. Most would prefer to have a revival as the result of their programs and efforts. God's way is the opposite. Out of death, acknowledged as the wage of sin, and confession of utter helplessness, God revives.

The Ministry of Intercessory Prayer

Prayer Supplies Laborers

Then He said to His disciples, "The harvest truly is plentiful but the laborers are few. Therefore pray the Lord of the harvest to send out laborers into His harvest."
MATTHEW 9:37–38

OUR LORD FREQUENTLY taught His disciples that they must pray, and how they should pray, but seldom *what* to pray. This He left to their sense of need and the leading of the Spirit. But in this text we have one thing He expressly commands them to remember. In view of the abundant harvest and the need of reapers, he tells them to call on the Lord of the harvest to send forth laborers. Just as in the parable of the friend who comes at midnight, He wants them to understand that prayer is not to be selfish. It is the power through which blessing can come to others. The Father is Lord of the harvest, so when we pray for the Holy Spirit, we are to pray that He will prepare and send out laborers for His work.

Is it not strange that He should ask His disciples to pray for this? Could He not call out laborers? Would not one prayer of His accomplish more than a thousand of theirs? Did not God, the Lord of the harvest, see the need, and would He not in His own good time send forth laborers—even without the disciples' prayers? Such questions lead us to the deepest mysteries of prayer and its power in the kingdom of God. Answers to such questions convince us that prayer is indeed a power on which the gathering of the harvest and the coming of the kingdom truly depend.

Prayer is not meant to be an empty form or show. It calls upon the power of God. He called on the disciples to pray for laborers to be sent among the lost because He believed their prayer would accomplish the needed result. The success of the work would actually depend on them, whether they were faithful or unfaithful in prayer.

Teach Me to Pray

THE GOD OF OUR SALVATION

IF SALVATION INDEED comes from God, and is entirely His work, just as our creation was, it follows that our first and highest duty is to wait on Him

Truly my soul silently waits for God; from Him comes my salvation.
PSALM 62:1 (NKJV)

to do the work that pleases Him. Waiting then becomes the only way to experience full salvation, the only way to truly know God as the God of our salvation. All the difficulties that are brought forward, keeping us back from full salvation, have their cause in this one thing: our lack of knowledge and practice of waiting on God. All that the church and its members need for the manifestation of the mighty power of God in the world is the return to our true place, the place that belongs to us, both in creation and redemption, the place of absolute and unceasing dependence on God.

God, as Creator, formed man to be a vessel in which He could show forth His power and goodness. Man was not to have in himself a fountain of life or strength or happiness. The ever-living and only living One was intended each moment to be the communicator to man of all that he needed.

Because believers do not know their relationship to God of absolute poverty and helplessness, they have no sense of the need of absolute and unceasing dependence or the blessedness of continual waiting on God. But once a believer begins to see it and consent to it, he by the Holy Spirit begins each moment to receive what God each moment works. Waiting on God becomes his brightest hope and joy.

First we wait on God for salvation. Then we learn that salvation is only to bring us to God and teach us to wait on Him. Then we find what is better still: that waiting on God is itself the highest salvation. It is ascribing to Him the glory of being all; it is experiencing that He is all to us. May God teach us the blessedness of waiting on Him!

Waiting on God

HE IS YOUR REDEMPTION

*Of Him [God] you are in
Christ Jesus, who became
for us wisdom from
God—and righteousness
and sanctification
and redemption.*
1 CORINTHIANS 1:30
(NKJV)

HERE WE REACH the top of the ladder as it ascends into heaven—the blessed end to which Christ and life in Him is to lead. The word *redemption*, though sometimes applied to our deliverance from the guilt of sin, here refers to our complete and final deliverance from all the consequences of sin, when the Redeemer's work will be fully displayed, even to the redemption of the body itself (Ephesians 1:14; 4:30). The expression points us to the highest glory to be hoped for in the future, and therefore also to the highest blessing to be enjoyed in the present in Christ.

The blessings flowing from abiding in Christ as our redemption are great. The soul is delivered from all fear of death. There was a time when even the Savior feared death. But no longer. He has triumphed over death; even His body has entered into God's glory. The believer who abides in Christ as his full redemption realizes even now his spiritual victory over death. It becomes to him the servant that removes the last rags of the old carnal robe before he is clothed with the new body of glory. The resurrection of the body is no longer an empty doctrine but a living expectation, because the Spirit of Him who raised Jesus from the dead dwells in the body as the pledge that even our mortal bodies will be made alive (Romans 8:11–23).

God's purpose will not be accomplished and Christ's glory will not be fully exhibited until the body, which includes the whole of nature, has been transformed by the power of the spiritual life. It will then become the transparent garment that will shine forth with radiance as it reflects the glory of the Infinite Spirit.

Abiding in Christ

KEEPING CHRIST'S COMMANDMENTS

THE BLESSING OF God's Word is only to be known and enjoyed by obeying it: "If you love me, you will obey what I command" (John 14:15). Keeping

"Now that you know these things, you will be blessed if you do them."
JOHN 13:17

His Word is the only proof of a genuine saving knowledge of God, of not being self-deceived in our faith, of God's love being experientially known and not merely imagined. Those who obey his commands live in Him, and He in them. Keeping the commandments is the secret of confidence toward God and intimate fellowship with Him.

Our profession of love is worthless until it is proven true by the keeping of His commandments in the power of a life born of God. Knowing God, being born of Him, having the love of God perfected in us, having boldness with God, and abiding in Him—all these depend on one thing: our keeping the commandments.

When we realize the prominence Christ and Scripture give to this truth, we will desire to give it the same prominence in our life. It will become one of the keys to successful Bible study. The person who reads his Bible with longing and determination to learn and to obey every commandment of God is on the right path to receiving all the blessing the Word is meant to bring. He will learn two things in particular: the need to wait for the Holy Spirit to lead him into all God's will, and the blessedness of performing daily responsibilities not only because they are right but also because they are the will of God.

Make a determined effort to grasp what this life of full obedience means. Embrace Christ's clearest commands: "Love one another as I have loved you"; "Wash one another's feet"; "Do as I have done to you," and practice Christlike love and humility as the law of the supernatural life you are called to live.

The Believer's Daily Renewal

SANCTIFICATION THROUGH THE BLOOD

And so Jesus also suffered outside the city gate to make the people holy through his own blood.
HEBREWS 13:12

THE FIRST AND SIMPLEST meaning of the word *sanctification* is "separation." That which is taken out of its surroundings by God's command and is set aside or separated as His own possession and for His service is holy. This does not mean separation from sin only but from all that is in the world, even from what may be permissible.

Sanctification can become ours only when it sends down its roots into and takes up its abode in the depths of our personal life, in our will, and in our love. God sanctifies no man against his will; therefore, the personal, wholehearted surrender to God is an indispensable part of sanctification. It is for this reason that the Scriptures not only speak of *God* sanctifying us but also that *we* must sanctify ourselves.

Partaking of the divine nature is the blessing that is promised to believers in sanctification. "That we may share in his holiness" (Hebrews 12:10)—that is the glorious aim of God's work in those whom He separates for himself. But this impartation of His holiness is not a gift of something that is apart from God himself. True sanctification is fellowship with God and His dwelling in us. So it was necessary that God in Christ should take up His abode in the flesh and that the Holy Spirit should come to dwell in us.

How glorious are the results of such sanctification! Through the Holy Spirit, the soul's fellowship is in the living experience of God's abiding nearness, accompanied by the awakening of the most tender carefulness against sin, and guarded by caution and the fear of God.

Christians, let us follow Jesus in His example of separation, and let us trust Him to make known to us the power of the blood. Let us yield ourselves wholly to its blessed efficacy.

The Blood of Christ

THE SPIRIT OF MISSIONS

A STUDY OF THE EPISTLE to the Ephesians reveals that the New Testament standard of Christian commitment is barely realized in the church today. Its whole tone is intensely supernatural. Christian commitment and devotion involves a life totally identified with the life of Christ. It must be a life in the continual presence and under the guidance of the Holy Spirit.

In the first chapter of our epistle, Paul sets before us the source of the divine life, followed by the prayer that such a life might be revealed by the Holy Spirit in the hearts of his readers. In chapter 2 we have the communication of that life, God himself making us alive in Christ and making us His workmanship, created in Christ Jesus for good works. Now in chapter 3 we are taught that the proclamation of that divine life is equally the work of God and His Spirit. As surely as the origin and communication of His life is a supernatural one, so the provision for its being proclaimed in the world is entirely supernatural.

He made known to me . . . the mystery of Christ . . . which in other ages was not made known to the sons of men, as it has now been revealed by the Spirit to His holy apostles and prophets: that the Gentiles should be fellow heirs, of the same body, and partakers of His promise in Christ through the gospel.
EPHESIANS 3:3–6 (NKJV)

As it was through the Spirit that the revelation of what had been hid in God through the ages was revealed, so it was under the presence and direction of the Holy Spirit that the work of bringing the Gospel to every creature was begun and was to be carried out.

All mission work has been placed under the direction of the Holy Spirit; in every department of that work His guidance is to be sought for and counted upon.

The Believer's Call to Commitment

HEALTH AND SALVATION BY THE NAME OF JESUS

"By faith in the name of Jesus, this man whom you see and know was made strong. It is Jesus' name and the faith that comes through him that has given this complete healing to him. . . . It is by the name of Jesus Christ of Nazareth, whom you crucified but whom God raised from the dead, that this man stands before you . . . healed. . . . Salvation is found in no one else, for there is no other name under heaven given to men by which we must be saved."

ACTS 3:16; 4:10, 12

WHEN, AFTER PENTECOST, the paralytic was healed through Peter and John at the gate of the temple, it was "by the name of Jesus Christ of Nazareth" that they said to him, "Get up, take your mat and go home," and as soon as the people in their amazement ran toward them, Peter declared that it was the name of Jesus that had completely healed the man.

We see that healing and health form part of Christ's salvation. Peter clearly states this in his discourse to the Sanhedrin, where, having spoken of healing, he immediately goes on to speak of salvation through Christ. In heaven even our bodies will have their part in salvation; salvation will not be complete until our bodies enjoy the full redemption of Christ. Why shouldn't we believe in this work of redemption here and now?

The one who comes to understand that it is the will of God to heal, to manifest the power of Jesus, and to reveal to us His fatherly love, is greatly blessed. The body is part of our being; even the body has been saved by Christ. Therefore, it is through our body that our Father wills to manifest the power of redemption and to let men see that Jesus lives. Let us believe in the name of Jesus for salvation and for healing.

Divine Healing

MINISTERS OF THE SPIRIT

MANY PRAY FOR the Spirit that they may make use of Him and His power for their work. This is an entirely wrong concept. It is He who must use you. Your relationship toward Him must be one of deep dependence and utter submission. The Spirit must have you under His power.

There are many who think they must only preach the Word, and that the Spirit will make the Word fruitful. They do not understand that it is the Spirit, in and through the preacher, who will bring the Word to the heart of the listeners. I must not be satisfied with praying to God to bless through the operation of His Spirit the Word that I preach. The Lord wants me to be filled with the Spirit; then I will speak as I should and my preaching will be in the manifestation of the Spirit and power. We see this occurring on the day of Pentecost. They were filled with the Spirit and began to speak, and spoke with power through the Spirit who was in them.

When the Lord promised the apostles that they would receive power when the Holy Spirit came upon them it was as though He said: "Do not dare to preach without this power. It is the indispensable preparation for your work. Everything depends on it."

Every manifestation of the power of the flesh in us and the weakness of our spiritual life must drive us to the conviction that God, through the powerful operation of His Holy Spirit, will work out a new and strong life in us. He will cause the Word to become joy and light in our souls. He will also help us in prayer to know the mind and will of God and to find in it our delight.

He has made us competent as ministers of a new covenant—not of the letter but of the Spirit; for the letter kills, but the Spirit gives life. . . . If the ministry that condemns men is glorious, how much more glorious is the ministry that brings righteousness!
2 CORINTHIANS 3:6, 9

Living a Prayerful Life

THE NEW COVENANT

*In the same way, after the
supper he took the cup,
saying, "This cup is the
new covenant in my blood,
which is poured
out for you."*
LUKE 22:20

THE LORD'S SUPPER is a covenant meal—the feast of the new covenant. It is of great importance that we understand what the new covenant means. It is something quite different from the old covenant, infinitely better and more glorious. God gave His people His perfect law with the glorious promise of His help and guidance and blessing if they continued to observe it. But man's inner life was still under the power of sin, lacking the strength needed for abiding in the covenant.

God promised to make a new covenant. In it He promised to bestow complete forgiveness of sins and to take man altogether into His favor. He further promised to communicate to him His law, not externally, as written on tables, but inwardly and in his heart so that he would have strength to fulfill its precepts. He would give him a new heart and a new spirit—His own Holy Spirit. God took the initiative and promised that He would enable man to keep His commandments: "And I will put my Spirit in you and move you to follow my decrees and be careful to keep my laws" (Ezekiel 36:27).

In the new covenant Jesus is the Mediator and our Guarantor (Hebrews 12:22–24; 8:6). As Guarantor, He stands pledged to us to secure that God will fulfill all of His promises. God fully relied on His Son to see to it that His honor was respected. And in Jesus we too may bravely enter this covenant without fear that we will not be able to fulfill it. We can rely upon Jesus to see to it that He will bring everything to completion. Jesus has not only discharged our old debt but also undertaken the responsibility for whatever else may be required.

The Lord's Table

A LACK OF PRAYER

WE ALL SEE THE contrast between a man whose income barely maintains his family and keeps up his business and a man whose income enables him to

No one calls on your name or strives to lay hold of you.
ISAIAH 64:7

expand his business and also help others. There may be an earnest Christian who prays just enough to maintain his position but without further spiritual growth in Christlikeness. The former is more of a defensive attitude, seeking to fight off temptation, rather than an aggressive one that reaches after higher attainment. If we desire to grow from strength to strength and to experience God's power in sanctification and blessing on others, we must be more persevering in prayer.

The law of God is unchangeable; as on earth, so in our communication with heaven, we only get as we give. Unless we are willing to pay the price, to sacrifice time and attention and seemingly legitimate or necessary tasks for the sake of the spiritual gifts, we need not look for much power from above in our work.

God's call to much prayer need not be a burden or cause for continual self-condemnation. He intends it to be a joyful task. He can make it an inspiration. Through it He can give us strength for all our work and bring blessing to others by His power that works in us.

Without hesitation, let us confess our sin of neglect and confront it in the name of our Mighty Redeemer. *The same light that shows us our sin and condemns us for it will show us the way out of it, into a life of liberty that pleases God.* Let our lack of prayer convict us of the coolness in our Christian life that lies at the root of it. God will use the discovery to bring us not only the power to pray that we long for but also the joy of a new and healthy life of which prayer is the spontaneous expression.

The Ministry of Intercessory Prayer

HOLINESS AND HEAVEN

Since everything will be destroyed in this way, what kind of people ought you to be? You ought to live holy and godly lives.
2 PETER 3:11

WE ARE ON our way to see God. We have been invited to meet the Holy One face to face. The infinite mystery of holiness, the glory of the invisible God, before whom the seraphim veil their faces, is to be unveiled, revealed, to us. This is not something that we will merely look into or study. No, we will actually see the Trinity, the living God himself. God, the Holy One, will show himself to us.

All our schooling here in the life of holiness is simply the preparation for that meeting and that vision. "Blessed are the pure in heart, for they will see God" (Matthew 5:8). "Make every effort . . . to be holy; without holiness no one will see the Lord" (Hebrews 12:14).

In his second epistle, Peter reminds believers that the coming of the day of the Lord is to be preceded and accompanied by the most tremendous catastrophe—the dissolution of the heavens and the earth. He asks them to think seriously about what that coming day of the Lord will be and what it will bring, to consider what the life of those who look for such things ought to be. Holiness must be the one universal characteristic.

There must not be a moment of the day or a relationship in life, nothing in the outer conduct or in the inmost recesses of the heart, that is not holy. It must be as Peter said when he spoke of God's call—holy in all manner of living.

Remembering the love of our Lord Jesus and the coming glory, in view of the coming end, of the need of the church and of the world, shall we not give ourselves to Him that we may have the power to bless each one we meet with the message of what God will do? Then it is possible that we might be a light and a blessing to this perishing world.

The Path to Holiness

PRAYER MUST BE SPECIFIC

THE BLIND MAN had been crying out over and over, "Jesus, Son of David, have mercy on me!" The cry reached the ear of the Lord, who knew what the man

"What do you want me to do for you?" Jesus asked him.
MARK 10:51

wanted, and Jesus was ready to give it to him. But first Jesus asks, "What do you want me to do for you?" Jesus wants to hear from the man's own lips not only the general petition for mercy but also the distinct expression of his desire. Until he declares it, he is not healed.

There are still many to whom the Lord puts the same question and who cannot, until it has been answered, get the help they seek. Our prayers must not be vague appeals to His mercy or indefinite cries for blessing, but the distinct expression of a specific need. It is not that Jesus' loving heart does not understand our cry or is not ready to hear, but He desires that we be specific for our own good. Prayer that is specific teaches us to better know our own needs. To find out what our greatest need is demands time, thought, and self-scrutiny. To find out whether our desires are honest and real, and whether we are ready to persevere in them, we are put to the test. It leads us also to discern whether our desires conform to God's Word and whether we really believe that we will receive the things we ask. It helps us to wait for a definite answer and to be aware of it when it comes.

And yet how much of our prayer is vague and pointless. Some cry for mercy without saying why they need mercy. Others ask to be delivered from sin but do not begin by naming any sin from which deliverance may be claimed. Still others pray for God's blessing on those around them, for the outpouring of God's Spirit on their land or the world, and yet do not pinpoint a particular spot where they will wait and expect to see God answer. To all of us, the Lord asks, "What is it you really want and expect me to do?"

Teach Me to Pray

THE GOD WHO WAITS ON US

Therefore the LORD will wait, that He may be gracious to you. . . . For the LORD is a God of justice; blessed are all those who wait for Him.
ISAIAH 30:18 (NKJV)

WE MUST THINK not only of *our* waiting on God but also of God's waiting on us. Let us seek in the spirit of humble waiting on God to find out something of what it means that the Lord waits to be gracious unto us.

Look up and see our great God on His throne. He is Love—He longs and delights to bless. He has inconceivably glorious plans concerning each of His children to reveal in them His love and power by the power of His Holy Spirit. He waits with all the anticipation of a father's heart. He waits to be gracious to you.

You may ask, "How is it, if He waits to be gracious, that when I come and wait on Him, He does not always give the help I seek?" There is a twofold answer. The first is that God is a farmer. He waits for the precious fruit of the earth and has patience. He cannot gather the crop until it is ripe. He knows when we are spiritually ready to receive the blessing to our profit and His glory. Waiting in the sunshine of His love is what will ripen the soul for His blessing. Waiting under the cloud of trial that breaks in showers of blessing is essential. Be assured that if God waits longer to answer than you anticipated, it is only to make the blessing all the more precious.

The second answer points to what has been said before. The Giver is more than the gift; God is more than the blessing; and our time spent waiting on Him is the only way to learn to find our life and joy in *Him*. It is a blessing when a waiting soul and a waiting God meet each other.

Waiting on God

THE WAY INTO THE MOST HOLY PLACE

IN THE PASSOVER we saw how redemption and holiness were dependent on the blood. In the sanctuary we know how the sprinkling of blood was what alone secured access to God. And now that the blood of Jesus has been shed what divine power, what everlasting efficacy we have in gaining access into the holiest of all.

The way in which Christ walked when He shed His blood is the very same in which we must walk. That way is the way of the cross. There must not only be faith in Christ's sacrifice but also fellowship with Him in it.

Therefore, brothers, since we have confidence to enter the Most Holy Place by the blood of Jesus, by a new and living way opened for us through the curtain, that is, his body, and since we have a great priest over the house of God, let us draw near to God with a sincere heart in full assurance of faith.
HEBREWS 10:19–22

Here we find the solution of a great mystery—why so many Christians stand far off and the holiness of God's presence is so little seen in them. They thought that it was only in Christ that the flesh needed to be rent and not in themselves. They didn't know that the way into true and full holiness was only to be reached through conformity to the death of Jesus. Into His self-denial, His self-sacrifice, His crucifixion, He takes up all who long to be holy as He is holy.

Do you see what holiness is and how it is to be found? It is not something formed in you. It is not something put on you from without. Holiness is the presence of God resting on you. Holiness comes as you consciously abide in that presence, doing all as a sacrifice to Him.

Having a Great High Priest over the house of God, let us draw near. In the power of the blood, in the power of the new and living way, in the power of the living Jesus, let the holiest of all, the presence of God, be the home of your soul.

The Path to Holiness

The Faith That Appropriates

"Therefore I tell you, whatever you ask for in prayer, believe that you have received it, and it will be yours."
MARK 11:24

WHAT A PROMISE—so large, so divine, that our limited understanding cannot take it in. In every possible way we seek to limit it to what we think safe or probable instead of allowing it to remain as He gave it in all its quickening power and energy. Faith is very far from being a mere conviction of the truth of God's Word or a conclusion drawn from certain premises. It is the ear that has heard God say what He will do, the eye that has seen Him doing it.

Therefore, where there is true faith, the answer *must* come. If we only do the one thing that He asks of us as we pray: "Believe that you have received it," He will do what He has promised: "It *will be yours*." In this spirit let us listen to the promise Jesus gives; each part of it has its divine message.

"Whatever you ask for . . ." When we hear this, our human wisdom begins to doubt and say, "Surely this cannot be literally true." But if it is not, why did the Master say it, using the strongest expression He could find: "*Whatever* you ask." It is not as if this were the only time He spoke this way. He also said, "*Everything* is possible for him who believes" (Mark 9:23). Faith is so wholly the work of God's Spirit through His Word in the prepared heart of the believing disciple that it is impossible that the fulfillment should not come. The tendency of human reasoning is to interpose here certain qualifying clauses—"if expedient"; "if according to God's will"—to break the force of a statement that appears presumptuous. Beware of dealing this way with the Master's words. His promise is literally true. He wants His "whatever" to penetrate our hearts and reveal how mighty the power of faith is and how our Father shares His power, placing it at the disposal of the child who fully trusts Him.

Teach Me to Pray

GOD'S HOLINESS IS His condescending love. It is a consuming fire against all who exalt themselves before Him, but to the spirit of the humble it is like the shining of the sun, heart-reviving and life-giving.

For this is what the high and lofty One says—he who lives forever, whose name is holy: "I live in a high and holy place, but also with him who is contrite and lowly in spirit, to revive the spirit of the lowly and to revive the heart of the contrite."
ISAIAH 57:15

The deep significance of this promise comes out clearly when we connect it with the other promises of New Testament times. The great feature of the new covenant, in its superiority to the old, is that whereas in the law and its institution all was external, in the new the kingdom of God would be within. God's laws are given and written on the heart, a new spirit is put within us, God's own Spirit is given to dwell within our spirit, and so the heart and the inner life are fitted to be the temple and home of God. Our text is perhaps the only one in the Old Testament in which this indwelling of the Holy One—not only among the people but also in the heart of the individual believer—is clearly brought out.

Just when we see that there is nothing in us to admire or rest in, God sees in us everything to admire and to rest in because there is room for himself. The lowly one is the home of the Holy One. Faith allows the contrite to believe—even in his deepest consciousness of unholiness and fear that he never can be holy—that God, the Holy One who makes holy, is near to him as his Redeemer and Savior.

Happy the soul who is willing to learn the lesson early that we will always have the simultaneous experience of weakness and power, of emptiness and filling, of deep humiliation as well as the most wonderful indwelling of the Holy One.

The Path to Holiness

Our Lord's Prayer Life

Very early in the morning, while it was still dark, Jesus got up, left the house and went off to a solitary place, where he prayed.
MARK 1:35

THE CONNECTION BETWEEN the prayer life and the Spirit life is close and indissoluble. This was very evident in the life of our Lord. A study of His life will give us a picture of the power of prayer. While others slept, He went away to pray and to renew His strength in communion with His Father. He needed this time with God—otherwise He would not have been ready for the new day.

Think of the calling of the apostles as recorded in Luke 6:12–13: "One of those days Jesus went out to a mountainside to pray, and spent the night praying to God. When morning came, he called his disciples to him and chose twelve of them." Read Luke 11:1: "One day Jesus was praying in a certain place. When he finished, one of his disciples said to him, 'Lord, teach us to pray.'" And then He gave them that inexhaustible prayer: "Father, hallowed be your name. . . ." Read John 17, the high-priestly, most holy prayer! This prayer gives us a glimpse into the remarkable relationship between the Father and the Son.

Now look at the most stunning instance of all: In Gethsemane, according to His habit, our Lord consulted and arranged with the Father the work He had to do on earth. First, He besought Him in agony to allow the cup to pass from Him. When He understood that this could not be, He prayed for strength to drink the cup and surrendered himself with the words "Your will be done." He was able to meet the Enemy full of courage, and in the power of God gave himself over to death on the cross.

Learn from our Lord Jesus how impossible it is to walk with God, obtain God's blessing or leading, or do His work joyously and fruitfully apart from close, unbroken fellowship with the One who is our living fountain of spiritual life and power.

Living a Prayerful Life

INTERCESSORY PRAYER

JAMES BEGINS BY speaking to us of the prayers of the elders of the church; but here he addresses all believers by saying, "Pray for each other so that you may be healed." Having already spoken of confession and of pardon, he still adds, "Confess your sins to each other."

Therefore confess your sins to each other and pray for each other so that you may be healed. The prayer of a righteous man is powerful and effective.
JAMES 5:16

This shows us that the prayer of faith that asks for healing is not the prayer of an isolated believer but of members of the body of Christ united in the Spirit. God certainly hears the prayer of each one of His children as soon as it is presented to Him with living faith, but the sick one does not always have this faith, so there must be several members of the body of Christ united in claiming His presence before the Holy Spirit can act with power.

This dependence on the body of Christ should be exercised in two ways: First, we must confess our faults to any whom we may have wronged and receive pardon from them. Apart from this, if the one who is sick sees that a sin he has committed is the cause of his sickness and recognizes his illness as a chastening from God, he ought to acknowledge his sin before the elders or other members of the body of Christ who are able to pray for him with more light and faith. The result will be a closer communion between the sick and those who intercede for him, and their faith will be quickened, as well.

James notes another essential condition to successful prayer: it must be the prayer of the righteous. Whether an elder or a simple believer, it is only after one is wholly surrendered to God and living in obedience to His will, that one can pray effectually for the brethren. May the Lord raise up in His church many righteous men, alive with faith, whom He can use to glorify Jesus as the divine healer!

Divine Healing

THE SPIRIT OF POWER

For this reason I bow my knees to the Father of our Lord Jesus Christ, from whom the whole family in heaven and earth is named, that He would grant you, according to the riches of His glory, to be strengthened with might through His Spirit in the inner man, that Christ may dwell in your hearts through faith.

EPHESIANS 3:14–17 (NKJV)

SPEAKING OF HIS CONVERSION, Paul said it was the good pleasure of God to reveal his Son in him that he might preach Him among the Gentiles. When he preached the unsearchable riches of Christ, he preached Him as dwelling in the heart. He desired that none of his readers be without that experience.

The night before His betrayal our Lord spoke of the gift of the Holy Spirit. He went on to add that if a man loved Him, he would keep His Word; and then His Father would love him; He would love him, and manifest himself to him. Together they would come and make their home with him. At the close of His High Priestly prayer He asked that the love wherewith He was loved would be in them and He in them. It is obvious that our Lord here speaks of something beyond the initial grace of pardon and regeneration. He speaks of what would be given to those who love Him and keep His commandments; of the special gift of the Holy Spirit dwelling and working in them. Paul prayed that God would do something special and mightily strengthen their inner man. In his doxology he gives glory to God as able to do something abundantly above all that we can ask or think.

Paul would have us take time to think of God's glory and His inconceivable riches. By faith Paul would have us expect that God will do nothing less for us than the standard of the riches of that glory. What is to be done in our inner man is of the same essence as the glory of God.

The Believer's Call to Commitment

"When I See the Blood"

WE KNOW WHY GOD established the blood as the sign of safety. Although Israel was God's people, they were also a sinful people. If their sins were treated as was deserved, the Israelites would also be judged. But the blood was a sign of redemption. A slain lamb was considered a scapegoat, taking the place of the one

"The blood will be a sign for you on the houses where you are; and when I see the blood, I will pass over you. No destructive plague will touch you when I strike Egypt."
EXODUS 12:13

who deserved death because of his sin. The redemption of Israel was not to take place simply by the exercise of power, but according to law and righteousness. Therefore, the punishment of the sin in each Israelite home had to be warded off by the blood of the paschal lamb.

In the New Testament, we read, "Christ, our Passover, was sacrificed for us." The significant name that He bears in heaven, the Lamb of God, refers chiefly to what He has done to secure our redemption.

The blood delivered the Israelites immediately and completely from the threatened danger of that awful night. From the moment you are sprinkled with (Christ's) precious blood, you are justified from your sins and the judgment of God is averted.

The God who delivered Israel from Egypt by the blood was not satisfied until He had brought Israel into Canaan. God bestows upon you not only the blood of Christ but also Christ himself. Each moment of your life He will care for you. He undertakes to provide for every weakness and need. He will, here in this life, lead you into the full blessedness of God's love. He becomes surety for your arrival in eternal glory. His blood is the eternal and undeniable proof that God the Father and Christ will do for you all that is needed, and that they will not forsake you until they have accomplished their work in you from beginning to end.

The Blood of Christ

THE POWER OF INTERCESSION

Therefore I will give him a portion among the great, and he will divide the spoils with the strong, because he poured out his life unto death, and was numbered with the transgressors. For he bore the sin of many, and made intercession for the transgressors.
ISAIAH 53:12

TELL ME WHERE your strength comes from. This is something we might ask an intercessor who has had power with God and been successful. More than one who has desired to give himself or herself to this ministry has wondered why it was so difficult to rejoice in it, to persevere, and to succeed. If we study the lives of the heroes of prayer, we might discover their secrets.

A true intercessor is one who knows that his or her heart and life are completely given over to God. This is the only condition on which an officer of the court of an earthly ruler could expect to exert much influence. Moses, Elijah, Daniel, and Paul all proved this to be true in the spiritual realm. In fact, our Lord himself proved it, because He did not save us by intercession but by the sacrifice of His own life. His power in intercession was established by His sacrifice; intercession claims what the sacrifice has already won. He first gave himself over to the will of God, winning the power to influence that will. He gave himself for sinners in all-consuming love, earning the power to intercede for them. And there is no other way for us. Wholehearted devotion and obedience to God are the first characteristics of an intercessor.

You may say that you don't know how to pray like this and ask how you might be equipped to do so. You feel that you are weak in faith, lacking in love for souls and delight in prayer. The one who would have power in intercession must lay aside these complaints and accept that his or her nature is perfectly adapted to the work. You are created in Christ to pray; it is your very nature as a child of God to do so.

The Believer's Daily Renewal

HE IS YOUR RIGHTEOUSNESS

Of Him [God] you are in Christ Jesus, who became for us wisdom from God—and righteousness and sanctification and redemption.
1 CORINTHIANS 1:30
(NKJV)

JESUS CHRIST CAME to restore peace on earth and peace in the soul by restoring righteousness. Because He is Melchizedek, king of righteousness, He reigns as king of Salem, king of peace (Hebrews 7:2). In this He fulfills the promise the prophets held out: "A king will reign in righteousness . . . the fruit of righteousness will be peace; the effect of righteousness will be quietness and confidence forever" (Isaiah 32:1, 17). God has made Christ to be righteousness for us; because of God we are in Him as our righteousness. In fact, we are made the righteousness of God in Him (2 Corinthians 5:21).

The union to Jesus has changed not only our relationship to God but also our personal state before God. And as this intimate fellowship is maintained, the growing renewal of the whole being makes righteousness our very nature.

Live your daily life in full consciousness of being righteous in God's sight, an object of delight and pleasure in Christ. Connect every view you have of Christ in His other graces with this first one: Christ Jesus—our righteousness from God. This will keep you in perfect peace.

You will enter into, and dwell in, the rest of God. And your inmost being will be transformed into being righteous and doing righteousness. In your heart and life it will become obvious where you dwell; abiding in Jesus Christ, the Righteous One, you will share His position, His character, and His blessedness. It is said of Him: "You have loved righteousness and hated wickedness; therefore God, your God, has set you above your companions by anointing you with the oil of joy" (Hebrews 1:9). This joy and gladness will be your portion, too, as you abide in Him.

Abiding in Christ

LIFE AND KNOWLEDGE

And the LORD God made all kinds of trees grow out of the ground—trees that were pleasing to the eye and good for food. In the middle of the garden were the tree of life and the tree of the knowledge of good and evil.
GENESIS 2:9

THERE ARE TWO WAYS of knowing things. One is in the mind: I know *about* something. The other is in the life: I know this by experience. An intelligent blind man may know all that science teaches about light simply by having books read to him. Yet a child, or even an uneducated person, who has never thought about what light is, knows it far better than the blind scholar. The former knows all the facts about light; the latter knows it by experience.

It is the same in faith and Christian practice. The mind can think about God and know all the doctrines of salvation, while the inner life may not know the saving power of God. We may know all about God and even about love; we may even be able to think beautiful thoughts and say compassionate things, but unless we actually love deeply from the heart, we do not truly know God. Only true love can know God, and the knowledge of God is life eternal.

Only the life that experiences God and His goodness is quickened in the inner man. The knowledge of the intellect cannot quicken. "If I have the gift of prophecy and can fathom all mysteries and all knowledge, and if I have a faith that can move mountains, but have not love, I am nothing" (1 Corinthians 13:2). The danger of pursuing knowledge shows itself in our daily Bible reading; there it must be identified and reckoned with. We need the intellect to hear and understand God's Word in its literal sense. But the possession of truth in this way cannot benefit us unless the Holy Spirit makes it life and truth in the heart.

Believer's Daily Renewal

THE UNITY OF THE SPIRIT

THESE WORDS bring us to the very roots of the Christian life. As we have said repeatedly, the first sign of the call of Christ upon a believer is *humility*. In verse 4 we have mention of "one body and one Spirit" and the further unveiling of what the Spirit does to maintain unity. In the midst of diversity of character and the temptations arising from the imperfections of those around us, the mark of true commitment remains a life wholly devoted and given over to God.

I therefore, the prisoner of the Lord, beseech you to walk worthy of the calling with which you were called, with all lowliness and gentleness, with longsuffering, bearing with one another in love, endeavoring to keep the unity of the Spirit in the bond of peace.
EPHESIANS 4:1–3 (NKJV)

If you would understand more deeply the meaning of the words, remember that this lowliness and gentleness do not only comprise your disposition and attitude toward God but also toward others: We bear with one another in love. There is no clearer proof that God's spiritual blessings in Christ Jesus have truly reached and conquered a person than lowliness and gentleness in his relationships with others. The greatness of God's power in us who believe makes us like Christ, who was willing to wear a servant's garments and to do a servant's work.

The same Christlike disposition is seen in Paul's words to the Philippians: "Let nothing be done through selfish ambition or conceit, but in lowliness of mind let each esteem others better than himself" (2:3 NKJV). The Master, the meek and lowly Lamb of God, said, "Learn from Me, for I am gentle and lowly in heart" (Matthew 11:29 NKJV). The Master emptied himself, taking the form of a servant, becoming obedient unto death, even the death of the cross. Our salvation is rooted in this; it is in the spirit and practice of a life like this that Christ will be magnified and our hearts sanctified.

The Believer's Call to Commitment

IS SICKNESS A PUNISHMENT?

For anyone who eats and drinks without recognizing the body of the Lord eats and drinks judgment on himself. That is why many among you are weak and sick, and a number of you have fallen asleep.
But if we judged ourselves, we would not come under judgment. When we are judged by the Lord, we are being disciplined so that we will not be condemned with the world.
1 CORINTHIANS 11:29–32

THE APOSTLE PAUL reproved the Corinthians for the way they observed the Lord's Supper, bringing upon themselves the chastisement of God. Here, therefore, we see sickness as a punishment for sin. Paul tells them that if by self-examination they judged themselves, discovered the cause of their sickness, and condemned their own sins, the Lord would not need to punish them.

God "does not willingly bring affliction or grief to the children of men" (Lamentations 3:33). It is not without a reason that He deprives us of health. Perhaps it may be to call our attention to some sin that we will recognize; perhaps it is because God's child has become entangled in pride and worldliness; or it may be that over-confidence or carelessness have been mixed with one's service for God. It is quite possible that the chastisement may not be directed against any particular sin, but may be the result of the sin that weighs upon the entire human race. In the case of the man born blind (John 9:2–3) Jesus does not say that there is no connection between sin and sickness, but He also teaches us not to accuse every sick person of sin.

Our Father chastens His child only when it is necessary. It is with joy that He will deliver you from chastisement, reveal himself to you as your healer, and bring you closer to Him than ever before. If as a wise and faithful Father He has been obliged to chasten you, it is also as a Father that He wills your healing and desires to bless and keep you.

Divine Healing

HUMILITY IN THE
LIFE OF JESUS

THOUGH THE WORD *humble* does not occur in Scripture, the humility of Christ is clearly revealed. In Jesus we see

> *"I am among you as one who serves."*
> LUKE 22:27

how both as the Son of God in heaven and the Son of Man on earth, He took the place of entire subordination and gave God the Father the honor and glory due Him.

He was nothing that God might be all. He resigned himself to the Father's will and power that He might work through Him. Of His own power, His own will, His own glory, His whole mission with its works and teaching—of all this, He said, I am nothing. I have given myself to the Father to work; He is all.

This life of entire self-abnegation, of absolute submission and dependence upon the Father's will, Christ found to be the source of perfect peace and joy. He lost nothing by giving all to God. God honored His trust and did all for Him, and then exalted Him to His own right hand in glory.

His humility was simply the surrender of himself to God, to allow Him to do in Him what He pleased, regardless of what men might say of Him or do to Him. It is to bring us to this disposition that we are made partakers of Christ.

We must learn of Jesus, how He is meek and lowly of heart. He teaches us where true humility begins and finds its strength—in the knowledge that it is God who works all in all, that our place is to yield to Him in perfect resignation and dependence, in full consent to be and to do nothing of ourselves. If we feel that this life is too high for us and beyond our reach, it must all the more urge us to seek it in Him. It is the indwelling Christ who will live this life in us.

Humility

RECOGNIZING PRAYERLESSNESS FOR WHAT IT IS

"Who is the Almighty, that we should serve him? What would we gain by praying to him?"
JOB 21:15

THE HOLY AND MOST glorious God invites us to come to Him, to converse with Him, to ask Him for the things we need, and to experience the depth of blessing there is in fellowship with Him. He has created us in His own image and has redeemed us by His own Son, so that in conversation with Him we should find our greatest delight.

What use do we make of this heavenly privilege? How many of us admit to taking a mere five minutes for prayer! The claim is that there is no time. The reality is that a heart desire for prayer is lacking. Many do not know how to spend half an hour with God! It is not that they absolutely do not pray; they may pray every day—but they have no joy in prayer. Joy is the sign that God is everything to you.

If a friend comes to visit, there is time. We make time—even at the cost of something else—for the sake of enjoying pleasant conversation with our friend. Yes, there is time for everything that truly interests us, but time is scarce to practice fellowship with God and to enjoy being with Him! We find time for someone who can be of service to us; but day after day, month after month passes, and for many there is no time to spend even one hour with God. We must acknowledge that we disrespect and dishonor God when we say we cannot find time for fellowship with Him.

If conscience is to do its work and the contrite heart is to feel its proper remorse, it is necessary for each individual to confess his sins by name. May the Lord lay the burden of the sin of prayerlessness so heavy on our hearts that we may not rest until it is taken far from us through the name and power of Jesus.

Living a Prayerful Life

THE CUP

LEVITICUS 17:11 SAYS, "For the life of a creature is in the blood, and I have given it to you to make atonement for yourselves on the altar; it is the blood that makes atonement for one's life." For the blood is the life, the living spirit; and therefore atonement is linked with the shedding of blood. Under the old covenant, it was the life of an innocent animal that was given in the place of a guilty man. And so under the new covenant, the shedding of Jesus' blood meant the surrender of His life for our sins. The worth and power of that blood are the worth and power of the life of Jesus. Every drop of His blood has in it the power of an endless life.

Then he took the cup, gave thanks and offered it to them, saying, "Drink from it, all of you. This is my blood of the covenant, which is poured out for many for the forgiveness of sins." . . . Is not the cup of thanksgiving for which we give thanks a participation in the blood of Christ? And is not the bread that we break a participation in the body of Christ?
MATTHEW 26:27–28;
1 CORINTHIANS 10:16

When I partake of that blood, I have a part in the Atonement that it established, the forgiveness it secured. I have a part in the life of Jesus, surrendered on the cross, raised from the grave, and now glorified in heaven. The spirit of Jesus' life is the spirit of my life. How powerful, how heavenly must be that life that is nourished by the new wine of the kingdom and communion with the Son.

My prayer is that Jesus would unfold to you the secret of His life in you that He gave when He shed His precious blood on Calvary. May He renew afresh this life in you as you partake of the Supper and drink the cup of remembrance of His great sacrifice.

The Lord's Table

THE LIFE THAT CAN PRAY

"If you remain in me and my words remain in you, ask whatever you wish, and it will be given you."
JOHN 15:7

HERE ON EARTH, the influence of one who asks a favor for someone else depends entirely on his character and the relationship he has to him with whom he is interceding. *It is who he is that gives weight to what he asks*. It is no different with God. Our power in prayer depends upon our life. When our life is right, we will know how to pray so as to please God, and prayer will secure the answer.

Think for a moment of the people of prayer in Scripture and see in them what kind of person could pray in such power. We spoke of Abraham as an intercessor. What gave him such boldness? He knew that God had chosen and called him away from his home and people to walk before Him so that all nations might be blessed through him. He knew that he had obeyed and forsaken all for God. Implicit obedience, to the very sacrifice of his son, was the law of his life. He did what God asked so that he dared trust God to do what he asked.

We pray only as we live. It is our manner of life that enables us to pray. The life that with wholehearted devotion gives up all for God and to God can also claim all from God. Our God longs to prove himself the faithful God and mighty helper of His people. He only waits for hearts wholly turned from the world to himself and open to receive His gifts. The one who loses all will find all and will dare to ask and to receive it.

The branch that truly abides in Christ, the Heavenly Vine, is entirely given up like Christ to bear fruit unto salvation. Christ's words become part of that one's life so that he may dare ask whatever he wishes—and it will be done.

The Ministry of Intercessory Prayer

HOLINESS AND INDWELLING

BECAUSE GOD IS HOLY, the house in which He dwells is holy. Holiness is the only attribute of God that He can and does communicate to His house. Among men there is a very close link between the character of a house and its occupants. When there is no obstacle to prevent it, the house naturally reflects the master's likeness.

"Then have them make a sanctuary [holy place] for me, and I will dwell among them."
EXODUS 25:8

Holiness expresses not so much an attribute as the essential being of God in His infinite perfection, and His house testifies to this truth: He is holy, where He dwells He must have holiness, and His indwelling makes a place holy.

No union is so intimate, so real, or so perfect, as that of an indwelling life. Think of the life that circulates through a large and fruitful tree. How it penetrates and fills every portion; how inseparably it unites the whole as long as it exists—in wood and leaf, in flower and fruit, everywhere the indwelling life flows and fills. Not less intimate, but far more wonderful and real, is the indwelling of the Spirit in the heart of the believer.

As the Indwelling One God revealed himself in the Son, whom He sanctified and sent into the world. More than once our Lord insisted, "Don't you believe that I am in the Father, and that the Father is in me? The words I say to you are not just my own. Rather, it is the Father, living in me, who is doing his work" (John 14:10). It is especially as the temple of God that believers are more than once called holy in the New Testament: "The whole building is joined together and rises to become a holy temple in the Lord" (Ephesians 2:21). It is through the Spirit that the heart is prepared for the indwelling of the Holy Spirit. The measure of His indwelling and His revelation of Christ is the measure of holiness.

The Path to Holiness

HOLINESS AND TRUTH

"Sanctify them by the truth; your word is truth."
JOHN 17:17

JESUS HAD JUST SAID, "For I gave them the words you gave me" (John 17:8). Do we realize what that means? Think of that great transaction in eternity: the Infinite Being whom we call God giving His words to His Son; in His words opening up His heart, communicating His mind and will, revealing himself and all His purpose and love. In the same living power Christ gave His disciples those words—full of divine life and energy to work in their hearts as they were able to receive them.

But people can be familiar with these words, study and speak them, and still be complete strangers to their holiness or their power to make holy. God himself, the Holy One, must be the one to produce holiness through the Word. Every seed in which the life of a tree is contained is encircled by a husk or shell that protects and hides the inner life. Only where the seed finds congenial soil and the husk is burst and removed can the seed germinate and grow. And only where there is a heart in harmony with God's holiness, longing for it, yielding itself to it, will the Word make one holy.

Just as the words that God gave Him were all in the power of eternal life, the love and will of God, revealing and communicating the Father's purpose, and just as God's Word was truth to Him and in Him, so it can be in us. When we thus receive it, we are made holy in the truth.

Beware of trying to study or understand or even to take possession of God's Word without that Spirit through whom the Word was spoken of old. Without it we shall find only the husk. The truth or thought and sentiment may be very beautiful perhaps but have no power to make us holy. To the simple, humble, childlike spirit, the truth of the Word will be unsealed and revealed. In such the Spirit of truth comes to dwell.

The Path to Holiness

KNOWING THE SPIRIT

THE VALUE OF KNOWLEDGE, that is, true spiritual knowledge, in the life of faith cannot be overemphasized. Just as a person is none the richer though an inheritance come to him, if he does not know about it or is not aware

Do you not know that you are the temple of God and that the Spirit of God dwells in you?
1 CORINTHIANS 3:16
(NKJV)

how he may acquire it, so the gifts of God's grace cannot bring their full blessing unless we know about them and then appropriate them. In Christ are hidden all the treasures of wisdom and knowledge. The Father has given each one of His children not only Christ, who is the truth, the reality of life and grace, but the Holy Spirit, who is the very Spirit of Christ and the truth. We receive the Spirit of God that we might know the things that are freely given us by God.

How do we know when it is the Spirit who is teaching us? If our knowledge of divine things is to be of use to us, we must know the Teacher. It is only in knowing Him that we can be sure our spiritual knowledge is not a deception. It is the Spirit who bears witness because the Spirit is truth. As we allow Him to dwell in us, we give Him full liberty to testify of Jesus as Lord. He will bring his own credentials. He will prove himself to be the Spirit of God. As the truth and experience of the indwelling of the Spirit are restored among God's people, and the Spirit is free again to work in power among us, His blessed presence will be His own sufficient proof: we shall indeed know Him.

There is no way of knowing a fruit unless we taste it. There is no way of knowing the light unless we are in it. We know a person by close fellowship with that person, and we know the Spirit when we possess Him and He possesses us. To live in the Spirit is the only way to know the Spirit.

The Spirit of Christ

THE SECRET OF
BELIEVING PRAYER

"Have faith in God,"
Jesus answered. "I tell
you the truth, if anyone
says to this mountain,
'Go, throw yourself into
the sea,' and does not
doubt in his heart but
believes that what he says
will happen, it will be
done for him. Therefore I
tell you, whatever you ask
for in prayer, believe that
you have received it,
and it will be yours."
MARK 11:22–24

THE PROMISE OF ANSWERS to prayer is one of the most wonderful lessons in all of Scripture. But in how many hearts has it raised the question "How can I attain to the faith that knows that it will receive what it asks?" Our Lord answers the question. Before He gave that wonderful promise to His disciples, He told where faith in the answer to prayer begins and where it receives its strength. Have faith in God: This word precedes the other, where He said to have faith in the promise of an answer to prayer. The power to believe a *promise* depends entirely on faith in *the one who made the promise*. Trust in a person generates trust in his word. Only when we live in a personal, loving relationship with God in which He is everything to us, only when our whole being is open to the mighty working of His holy presence within, is a capacity developed to believe that He gives whatsoever we ask.

This connection between faith in God and faith in His promises becomes clear to us if we think about what faith really is. Often it is compared to the hand or the mouth by which we take and appropriate what is offered to us. But it is important to understand that faith is also the ear by which I hear what is promised, the eye by which I see what is offered to me. On this the power to receive depends. I must *hear* the person who gives me the promise. The very tone of his voice gives me courage to believe. I must *see* him. In the light of his eye and the expression of his face, all fear as to my right to receive fades away.

Teach Me to Pray

THE KEYNOTE OF LIFE

I have waited for your salvation, O Lord!
GENESIS 49:18 (NKJV)

IT IS NOT EASY to say in exactly what sense Jacob used these words that appear right in the middle of his prophecies regarding the future of his sons. But they do certainly indicate that both for himself and for them his expectation was from God alone. It was God's salvation Jacob waited for, a salvation God had promised and that God alone could work out. Jacob knew he and his sons were under God's charge. Jehovah, the everlasting God, would show them what His saving power was and what it could do. The words point forward to that wonderful story of redemption that is not yet finished and to the glorious future in eternity where our redemption leads. They suggest to us that there is no salvation but God's salvation, and waiting on God for it, whether for our personal experience or for the world around us, is our first responsibility.

Let us meditate on the divine glory of the salvation God purposes to work out in us until we know the truths it implies. Our heart is the scene of a divine operation more wonderful than Creation. We can do as little toward the work as we could toward creating the world, except as God works in us to will and to do. God only asks us to yield, to consent, to wait on Him, and He will do it all.

The application of the truth to wider circles, to those we labor among or intercede for, to the church of Christ around us, or throughout the world, is not difficult. There can be no good except what God works; to wait on God and to have the heart filled with faith in His working, and in that faith to pray for His mighty power to come down, is our only wisdom. Oh, for the eyes of our heart to be opened to see God working in us and in others, and to see how blessed it is to worship and simply to wait for His salvation!

Waiting on God

HE IS YOUR SANCTIFICATION

*Of Him [God] you are in
Christ Jesus, who became
for us wisdom from
God—and righteousness
and sanctification
and redemption.*
1 CORINTHIANS 1:30
(NKJV)

A SUPERFICIAL acquaintance with God's plan leads to the view that while justification is God's work, by faith in Christ, sanctification is our work, to be performed under the influence of the gratitude we feel for the deliverance we have experienced, and by the aid of the Holy Spirit. But the sincere Christian soon finds how little gratitude can supply the power. When he thinks that more prayer will bring it, he finds that indispensable as prayer is, it is not enough. Often the believer struggles hopelessly for years, until he listens to the teaching of the Spirit as He glorifies Christ again, and reveals Christ, our sanctification, to be appropriated by faith alone.

Christ is made sanctification to us by God. Holiness is the very nature of God, and *that alone is holy which God takes possession of and fills with himself.*

There is no other way for us to become holy but by becoming partakers of the holiness of Christ. And there is no other way of this taking place than by our personal spiritual union with Him, so that through His Holy Spirit His holy life flows into us. Don't listen to the suggestion that the corruption of your old nature renders holiness an impossibility. In your flesh dwells no good thing, that is true, and that flesh, though crucified with Christ, is not yet dead but continually seeks to rise up and lead you to evil. But the Father is your Vinedresser. He has grafted the life of Christ onto your life. That holy life is stronger than your evil life; under the watchful care of the Vinedresser, that new life can keep down the workings of the evil life within you, and you will be able to bear fruit to the glory of the Father.

Abiding in Christ

THE HEART AND THE
UNDERSTANDING

THE PRIMARY OBJECTIVE of the book of Proverbs is to teach knowledge and discretion and to guide us in the path of wisdom and understanding. Proverbs guides us into righteousness,

Trust in the LORD with all your heart and lean not on your own understanding.
PROVERBS 3:5

the fear of the Lord, and a proper understanding of life and its pitfalls. But it also warns us to distinguish between trusting our own understanding and seeking spiritual understanding, which only God can give.

One of the main reasons why so much of our Bible teaching and Bible knowledge is comparatively fruitless, and why there is such a lack of holiness, devotion, and power is because we tend to rely on our own understanding when it comes to spiritual matters.

Learn to question your own understanding. It can only give you an idea of divine things without the reality. It will lead you to believe that truth, if received into the mind, will somehow enter the heart as well. It will blind you to the universal experience that people daily read and weekly delight to hear God's Word and yet are made neither humble, nor holy, nor heavenly-minded by it.

Instead of trusting your understanding, come with your *heart* to the Word. Instead of trusting your understanding, trust in the Lord with all your heart. Set your heart upon the living God as your Teacher when you enter the quiet place. Only then will you find true understanding. God will give you a heart to understand spiritual truth.

When your natural understanding grasps a truth from the Word, go before God in dependence and trust. Believe that God can and will make the truth clear and applicable to your life. Persevere in this, and the Holy Spirit will come to your aid and shine His light of understanding into your heart and make the Word the strength of your life.

The Believer's Daily Renewal

JESUS AND THE DOCTORS

"Daughter, your faith has healed you. Go in peace and be freed from your suffering."
MARK 5:34

A WOMAN WAS THERE who had been subject to bleeding for twelve years. She had suffered a great deal under the care of many doctors and had spent all she had, yet instead of getting better she grew worse. When she heard about Jesus, she came up behind him in the crowd and touched his cloak, because she thought, *If I just touch his clothes, I will be healed.* Immediately her bleeding stopped and she felt in her body that she was freed from her suffering. At once Jesus realized that power had gone out from him. He turned around in the crowd and asked, "Who touched my clothes?" Then the woman, knowing what had happened to her, came and fell at His feet and told Him the whole truth.

We can be thankful to God for doctors. Their vocation is one of the most noble, for a large number of them seek to do all they are able to alleviate the sufferings that burden humanity. Nevertheless, it is Jesus himself who is the greatest physician.

Jesus' method is quite different from that of doctors. They serve God in making use of remedies that are found in the natural world, and God makes use of these according to the properties of each, but the healing from Jesus is by the power of the Holy Spirit. His healing brings with it more real blessing than the healing obtained through doctors. When the woman who touched the hem of Christ's garment was healed, she learned what divine love means.

If you are suffering from some sickness, know that Jesus, the sovereign healer, is still in our midst, and He is giving His church proof of His presence through healing. It may take some time to break the chains of your unbelief, but remember that none who wait on Him will be put to shame.

Divine Healing

PREACHING AND PRAYER

WE ARE FAMILIAR with the vision of the valley of dry bones. There was a noise, and bone came together to bone, and flesh came up, and skin covered them—but there was no breath in them. The prophesying to the bones—the preaching of the Word of God—had a powerful influence. It was the beginning of the great miracle that was about to happen, and there lay an entire army of men newly made. It was the beginning of the work of life in them, but there was no spirit there.

"Prophesy to these bones and say to them, 'Dry bones, hear the word of the LORD!' This is what the Sovereign LORD says to these bones: I will make breath enter you, and you will come to life."
EZEKIEL 37:4–5

Then he said to me, "Prophesy to the breath; prophesy, son of man, and say to it, 'This is what the Sovereign Lord says: Come from the four winds, O breath, and breathe into these slain, that they may live'" (v. 9). When the prophet had done this, the Spirit came upon them, and they lived and stood on their feet, a very great army. Prophesying to the bones, that is, preaching, has accomplished a great work. There lay the beautiful new bodies. But prophesying to the Spirit: "Come, O Spirit," that is prayer, and that has accomplished a far more wonderful thing. The power of the Spirit was revealed through prayer.

Preaching must always be followed up by prayer. The preacher must come to see that his preaching is comparatively powerless to bring new life until he begins to take time for prayer, and according to the teaching of God's Word, he strives and labors and continues in prayer; and he takes no rest and gives God no rest until He bestows the Spirit in overflowing power.

We must with all our strength, and as consistently as Paul did, pray unceasingly. For the prayer: "Come, breathe into these slain," the answer is certain.

Living a Prayerful Life

THE OBEDIENCE BORN OF FAITH

By faith Abraham obeyed when he was called to go out to the place which he would receive as an inheritance. And he went out, not knowing where he was going.
HEBREWS 11:8 (NKJV)

THE LAND OF PROMISE that has been set before us is *the blessed life of obedience*. We have heard God's call to us to go out and to dwell there. We have heard the promise of Christ to bring us there and to give us possession of the land. But do we desire that all our life and work be lifted to the level of a holy and joyful obedience? If so, our aim is high. It can only be reached by an inflow of the power of the Holy Spirit.

Five simple declarations are expressive of the disposition of a believing heart, the one who enters into the good land: *I see it, I desire it, I expect it, I accept it, and I trust Christ for it.*

Think about Abraham's faith. It rested in God, in His omnipotence and His faithfulness. Abraham was strong in faith, giving glory to God, being fully persuaded that what He had promised He was able to perform.

There can be no strong faith without strong desire. It is the desire for God and the closest possible fellowship with Him, the desire to be what He would have us to be and to have as much of His will as possible that will make the Promised Land attractive to us.

It is a great step forward when desire becomes expectation. Look to His power and His love and say, "Surely this life is for me!" Then wholeheartedly expect it.

To accept is more than to expect. Many wait and hope and never possess because they do not accept God's gifts.

All the promises of God are in Christ Jesus, and in Him they are sure and firm to the glory of God. Trust Him for the faith to make the vow, for the heart to keep it, and for the strength to carry it out.

A Life of Obedience

THE BREAD

WHEN THE LORD SAID this, He was pointing out the fact that His body is not so much His as it is ours; He received his human body and allowed it to be broken on the cross not for His own sake but for ours. He now desires that we should look upon it and appropriate it as

While they were eating, Jesus took bread, gave thanks and broke it, and gave it to his disciples, saying, "Take and eat; this is my body."
MATTHEW 26:26

our own possession. With His body He gives himself to us and desires that we should take Him. The fellowship of the Lord's Supper is a fellowship of giving and receiving.

The giver gives value to the gift. The One who gives His body for us is our Creator, who alone can give us what our soul needs. He is our Redeemer, who at the table will give us what He has purchased for us. He gives the greatest and the best that He can bestow—His own body and blood.

Why does He give this? Because He loves us. He wants to redeem us from death and bestow upon us eternal life. He gives himself in order to be to us the food, the joy, the living power of our soul.

No less blessed is the receiving, and it is so simple. Just as I take with my hand the bread that is passed at the meal, so by faith in the Word I take Him for myself, and I know that He is truly mine. The power of the Atonement is mine; and the gift is free! I think of my unworthiness, and then remember that the Righteous One died for the unrighteous. My misery is the poverty and hunger for which the feast is prepared. What Jesus gave so heartily and willingly, we must receive in the same manner.

The Lord's Table

HOLINESS AND LIBERTY

It is for freedom that Christ has set us free. Stand firm, then, and do not let yourselves be burdened again by a yoke of slavery.
GALATIANS 5:1

NO POSSESSION IS more precious or priceless than liberty. On the other hand, nothing is more depressing and degrading than slavery. It robs a man of the power of self-decision, self-action, of being and doing what he would like.

Sin is slavery—the bondage to a foreign power that has obtained control over us and often compels a most reluctant service. The redemption of Christ restores our liberty and sets us free from the power of sin. If we are to live as redeemed ones, we need not only to look at the work Christ did to accomplish our redemption but also to accept how complete and absolute is the liberty with which He has made us free.

In the past when Turks or Moors made slaves of Christians, large sums were frequently paid to ransom those who were in bondage. But it happened more than once that the ransomed ones, deep in the interior of the slave country, never received the news. Others received the word, but had grown too accustomed to their bondage to stir themselves to try to reach the coast and freedom.

Satan always tries to lay on us again either the yoke of sin or the law and to create again the spirit of bondage, as if sin or the law with their demands somehow had power over us. Do not let him ensnare you. Stand fast in the liberty with which Christ has made you free.

The more deeply we enter by faith into our liberty in Christ, the more joyfully and confidently we present our members to God as instruments of righteousness. Doing God's will leads to fellowship—wholehearted agreement with God himself—out of which comes the reflection of the divine presence, which is holiness.

The Path to Holiness

THE CURE OF UNBELIEF

WHEN THE DISCIPLES saw Jesus cast the evil spirit out of the epileptic whom they could not cure, they asked the Master for the reason for their failure. He had given them power and authority over all demons and the power to cure all diseases. They had often exercised that power and joyfully told how the demons were subject to them. But now, while He was on the Mount, they had utterly failed. It had been proven that there was nothing in the will of God or in the nature of the case to render deliverance impossible. At Christ's bidding, the evil spirit had left the man.

Then the disciples came to Jesus privately and said, "Why could we not cast it out?" So Jesus said to them, "Because of your unbelief; for assuredly, I say to you, if you have faith as a mustard seed . . . nothing will be impossible for you. However, this kind does not go out except by prayer and fasting."
MATTHEW 17:19–21
(NKJV)

From their question "Why could we not cast it out?" it is evident that they had tried to do so. They had no doubt invoked the Master's name and called upon the evil spirit to leave, but their efforts had been in vain.

Christ's answer was plain: "Because of your unbelief." The cause of His success and their failure was not due to His having a special power to which they had no access. He had taught them that there is one power to which everything must bow: faith.

Though the simplest, faith is the highest exercise of the spiritual life, where our spirit yields itself in perfect receptivity to God's Spirit and so is strengthened to its highest activity. This faith depends entirely upon the state of our spiritual life. Only when this is strong and in full health, when the Spirit of God has full sway in our life, is there the power of faith to do its work.

Teach Me to Pray

HOLINESS AND OBEDIENCE

*"You yourselves have seen
what I did to Egypt, and
how I carried you on
eagles' wings and brought
you to myself. Now if you
obey me fully and keep my
covenant, then out of all
nations you will be my
treasured possession. . . .
You will be for me . . .
a holy nation."*
EXODUS 19:4–6

ISRAEL HAS REACHED Horeb. The law is to be given and the covenant made. Here are God's first words to the people; He speaks of redemption and its blessing, fellowship with himself: "You yourselves have seen . . . how I . . . brought you to myself." He speaks of holiness as His purpose in redemption: "You will be for me . . . a holy nation." As the link between the two, He places obedience: "If you obey me fully and keep my covenant." God's will is the expression of His holiness; as we do His will, we come into contact with His holiness. The link between redemption and holiness is obedience.

Holiness is a moral attribute; it is that which a free will chooses and determines for itself. What man wills to have of God and His will, and truly appropriates, has moral worth and leads to holiness. Obedience is the path to holiness because it is the path to union with God's holy will. Obedience itself is not holiness, but as the will opens itself to accept and to do the will of God, God communicates himself and His holiness.

Obedience is not knowledge of the will of God, it is not even approval; it is not the will to do it but the doing of it. *Action alone* proves whether the object of my interest has complete mastery over me. God wants His will done. This alone is obedience. Only in this way is it seen whether the whole heart has fully yielded to the will of God; whether we live His will and are ready by any sacrifice to make it our own by doing it. God has no other way of making us holy. "Keep my decrees and follow them. I am the LORD, who makes you holy" (Leviticus 20:8).

The Path to Holiness

THESE WORDS FOLLOW the promise "If you believe, you will receive whatever you ask for in prayer" (Matthew 21:22). Before that, "Have faith in God" (Mark 11:22) taught us that effective prayer depends upon our clear relationship to God. Now these words

"And when you stand praying, if you hold anything against anyone, forgive him, so that your Father in heaven may forgive you your sins."
MARK 11:25

remind us that our relationship with others must be clear too. Prayer from a heart that is not right—either with God or with others—cannot prevail. Faith and love are essential to each other.

Our Lord frequently emphasized this thought. When speaking about the sixth commandment, He taught His disciples that acceptable worship of the Father was impossible if everything was not right with our fellow-man. "If you are offering your gift at the altar and there remember that your brother has something against you, leave your gift there in front of the altar. First go and be reconciled to your brother; then come and offer your gift" (Matthew 5:23–24). Later He taught us to pray, "Forgive us our debts, as we also have forgiven our debtors" (Matthew 6:12). Then at the close of the prayer, He added, "If you do not forgive men their sins, your Father will not forgive your sins" (Matthew 6:15). At the close of the parable of the unmerciful servant, He applies His teaching: "This is how my heavenly Father will treat each of you unless you forgive your brother from your heart" (Matthew 18:35).

Throughout His life, the Lord learned that disobedience to the law of love was a common sin, even among praying people, and a cause of the weakness of their prayer. He now wants to lead us into His own blessed experience that nothing gives such liberty of access and such power in believing as the consciousness that we have given ourselves in love and compassion for those whom God loves.

Teach Me to Pray

YOUR BODY IS THE TEMPLE OF THE HOLY SPIRIT

Do you not know that your bodies are members of Christ himself? Shall I then take the members of Christ and unite them with a prostitute? Never! . . . Do you not know that your body is a temple of the Holy Spirit, who is in you, whom you have received from God? You are not your own; you were bought at a price. Therefore honor God with your body.

1 CORINTHIANS 6:15, 19–20

WHEN THE CHURCH understands that the body also has a part in the redemption of Christ by which it ought to be brought back to its original destiny, to be the dwelling place of the Holy Spirit, to serve as His instrument, and to be sanctified by His presence, she will also recognize the place that divine healing has in the Bible and in the counsel of God.

The account of Creation tells us that man is composed of three parts: body, soul, and spirit. God first formed the body from the dust of the earth, after which He breathed into it "the breath of life." He caused His own life, His Spirit, to enter into it. By this union of Spirit with matter, the man became a "living soul." This union of spirit and body forms a combination that is unique in creation; it makes man the jewel of God's work.

We know what sin and Satan have done. We know also what God has done to destroy the work of Satan. Faith puts us in possession of all that the death of Christ and His resurrection have procured for us, and it is not only in our spirit and our soul that the life of the risen Jesus manifests its presence here below but it is also in the body that it would act according to the measure of our faith.

In the same way in which the Holy Spirit brings to our soul and spirit the life of Jesus, He comes also to impart to the sick body all the vigorous vitality of Christ as soon as the hand of faith stretches out to receive it.

Divine Healing

UNTO HIM BE GLORY

IT IS REMARKABLE what prominence Paul gives to the idea of our entire salvation being under the working of God's almighty power. In Ephesians 1:11 he speaks of "the purpose of Him who works all things according to the counsel of His will." God does this not only regarding the great work of deliverance through Christ, but equally in every detail of the daily life of the Christian.

Now to Him who is able to do exceedingly abundantly above all that we ask or think, according to the power that works in us, to Him be glory in the church by Christ Jesus to all generations, forever and ever. Amen.

EPHESIANS 3:20–21 (NKJV)

We too often think of Him as the omnipotent One, able to work mightily where He sees the need. But the words suggest something far greater; He is the God who works without ceasing not only in nature with its every leaf and flower but in His children as well. He works all that they need to carry out His blessed will.

The normal pattern in the Christian life is to strive after the standard that the Word sets before us, with the prayer that God will help us in our weakness. This pattern completely misses the exceeding greatness of God's power that alone can do the work in us. The weakness of God is stronger than our strength. And the strength of God is found only in the consciousness of our own weakness. This was the sign of the working of His power in Christ. Our Lord set aside His power and authority to rescue himself when He died on the cross, yielding himself utterly to the Father. Then God's power raised Him out of that place of weakness to the place of power on the throne. Only the teaching of the Holy Spirit can enable us to know the greatness of God's power working in us.

If we would understand the standard of life that Paul puts before us, we must allow God to work in us the courage to see and to accept a life that pleases Him in everything.

The Believer's Call to Commitment

SOUL-WINNING

The fruit of the righteous is a tree of life, and he who wins souls is wise.
PROVERBS 11:30

SOUL-WINNING IS the first great requisite to being a missionary. Going to a mission field will not make a person a soul-winner. It is at home, before one enters the foreign field, that the spirit of self-sacrifice and soul-winning must be gained and exercised. The danger continually threatens of our lapsing into traditional and mechanical methods. Continual, fervent, united and private prayer ought to be made for more love of souls so that our companions may be won for Christ.

Where is the passionate longing to help people to know Christ? Where is the urgent prayer for souls that will not be denied? At the very heart of the whole matter is a lack of interest. It is only what genuinely interests us that will influence others. It is only when deep down among the eternal interests of the soul there flames the passionate desire to lead others to Christ that we will meet those who need our help and who will welcome it. It is only words and deeds that come from a burning passion of desire to help others that find opportunities to influence lives. It is only where there is such a desire that the Holy Spirit is a fellow worker with us. And without Him we are powerless either to find those who are needy or, having found them, to give them any help.

The great characteristic of the divine life, whether in God the Father or in Christ or in us is *love seeking to save the lost*. May this be the Christian life we seek: a love that finds its happiness in saving souls. This life can be cultivated only by close personal fellowship with Jesus. It is in the quiet place that this fellowship with the Father and the Son is to be maintained. Here the Father who sees in secret will reward us openly.

The Believer's Daily Renewal

YOU WILL FIND REST FOR YOUR SOULS

REST FOR THE SOUL: Such was the first promise extended by the Savior to win the burdened sinner. Simple though it appears, the promise is as large and comprehensive as can be found. Rest for the soul—does it not imply deliverance from every fear, the supply of every want, the fulfillment of every desire? And now this is the prize with which the Savior woos back the wandering one, the

> *"Come to Me, all you who labor and are heavy laden, and I will give you rest. Take My yoke upon you and learn from Me, for I am gentle and lowly in heart, and you will find rest for your souls."*
> MATTHEW 11:28–29
> (NKJV)

one who is mourning that his rest has not been so abiding or so full as he had hoped, to return and abide in Him. This was the reason that rest either has not been found or, if found, has been disturbed or lost again: You did not abide in Him.

These words of the Savior uncover what you have perhaps often wondered: How is it that the rest you at times enjoy is so often lost? This must have been the reason: You did not understand how *entire surrender to Jesus is the secret of perfect rest.* Giving up one's whole life to Him to rule and order, taking up His yoke, and allowing ourselves to be led and taught of Him, abiding in Him, to be and do only what He wills—these are the conditions of discipleship without which there can be no thought of maintaining the rest that was bestowed on first coming to Christ. This rest is in Christ, not something He gives apart from himself, and so it is only in having Him that the rest can really be kept and enjoyed.

It is the peace of God, the great calm of the eternal world, that passes all understanding and that keeps the heart and mind. With this grace secured, we have strength for every duty, courage for every struggle, a blessing in every cross, and the joy of life eternal in death itself.

Abiding in Christ

GOD'S THOUGHTS AND OUR THOUGHTS

As the heavens are higher than the earth, so are my ways higher than your ways and my thoughts than your thoughts.
ISAIAH 55:9

THE WORDS OF A WISE man often mean something different than what a casual hearer understands. It is easy to see, then, how the words of God mean something infinitely higher than we initially comprehend. Remembering this will prevent us from being content with our knowledge and thoughts concerning the Word of God. Instead, we will wait on God to know His mind. Our prayer for the Holy Spirit's teaching will reveal to us what has not yet entered into our heart to conceive. It will fortify the hope that there is even in this life a fulfillment beyond our highest thoughts.

Faith in the Word should teach us two lessons: one of ignorance, the other of expectation. We should learn to come to the Word as little children. Jesus said, "'I praise you, Father, Lord of heaven and earth, because you have hidden these things from the wise and learned, and revealed them to little children'" (Matthew 11:25).

The deeper our distrust of our own understanding of the thoughts of God, the greater our expectancy will be. God wants to make His Word true in us: "You yourselves have been taught by God to love each other" (1 Thessalonians 4:9). The Holy Spirit is *already* in us to reveal the things of God. In answer to our humble believing prayer God will, through Him, give ever-increasing insight into the mystery of God—our wonderful union and resemblance to Christ, His living in us, and our being as He was in this world.

In fact, if our hearts thirst after it and wait for it, a time may come when, by a special communication of His Spirit, all our yearnings will be satisfied; Christ will so take possession of the heart that the phrase "as the heavens are higher than the earth so are his thoughts higher than our thoughts" will no longer be a matter of faith but of experience.

The Believer's Daily Renewal

HE IS YOUR STRENGTH

NO TRUTH IS MORE generally admitted among sincere Christians than that they are utterly weak. Yet there is no truth more generally misunderstood and abused than this. Here, as elsewhere, God's thoughts are high above ours (Isaiah 55:8).

"All authority has been given to Me in heaven and on earth."
MATTHEW 28:18 (NKJV)

"My strength is made perfect in weakness."
2 CORINTHIANS 12:9 (NKJV)

The Christian often tries to forget his weakness, but God wants us to remember it, and to feel it deeply. Christians want to conquer their weakness and to be freed from it; God wants us to rest and even rejoice in it. Christians think their weakness is the greatest hindrance in their life and service to God; but God tells us that our weakness is actually the secret of strength and success. It is our weakness, heartily accepted and continually realized, that gives us our claim and access to the strength of Him who said, *"My strength is made* perfect *in weakness."*

It is in the power of the omnipotent Savior that the believer must find his strength for life and for work. The disciples found this principle to be true. During ten days in the Upper Room they worshiped and waited at the footstool of His throne. Jesus Christ was their sole object of thought, of love, of delight. In such worship and devotion their souls grew up into intense communion with Him upon the throne, and when they were prepared, the baptism of power came. It was power within and power around them.

All power in heaven and earth was indeed given to Him, and by Him imparted to His people just as they needed it, whether for a holy life or effective service. And what Jesus was to these first disciples, He is to us, too. Our one care must therefore be to abide in Christ as our strength. Our one duty is to be strong in the Lord and in the power of *His* might.

Abiding in Christ

MEDITATION

Blessed is the man who does not walk in the counsel of the wicked or stand in the way of sinners or sit in the seat of mockers. But his delight is in the law of the LORD, and on his law he meditates day and night.
PSALM 1:1–2

THROUGH MEDITATION the heart holds and appropriates the Word. The "meditation of the heart" implies desire, acceptance, surrender, love. Out of the heart flow the issues of life; whatever the heart truly believes, it receives with love and joy and allows it to influence the life. The intellect gathers and prepares the "food" by which you will be nourished. In meditation the heart digests the food and makes it a part of your life.

The art of meditation needs to be cultivated. Just as a man is trained to concentrate his mental powers to think clearly and accurately, so a Christian needs to diligently consider and meditate until the holy habit of yielding up the whole heart to every word of God is established. The very first requirement is to present yourself before God. It is *His* Word; it has no power of blessing apart from Him. The Word is intended to bring you into His presence and fellowship. Practice His presence and receive the Word as from His hand, confident that He will make it effective in your heart.

The second requirement of true meditation is quiet restfulness. As we study Scripture and try to grasp an argument or master a difficulty, our mind often expends considerable effort. This is not true of meditation. In meditation we take a truth we have found or some mystery for which we await divine interpretation and hide the Word in the depth of our heart, believing that by the Holy Spirit its meaning and power will be revealed to us. Meditation leads to prayer and by its nature provides subjects for prayer. It motivates us to ask and receive what we have seen in the Word. Meditation is deliberate and wholehearted preparation for prayer.

The Believer's Daily Renewal

THE ALTAR SANCTIFIED BY THE BLOOD

"For seven days make atonement for the altar and consecrate it. Then the altar will be most holy, and whatever touches it will be holy."
EXODUS 29:37

WHY DID THE ALTAR occupy such an important position? The Hebrew word for altar gives us the answer. It means the place of death. Even the place of incense—where no slain victim was offered—bore the name "altar," because gifts offered in sacrifice to God were laid upon it. The altar, then, is the place of sacrifice, of consecration, and of fellowship with God.

In our text we learn that the altar itself had to be sanctified by blood if it was to possess the power of sanctifying whatever touched it. Through the blood of Jesus, through the perfect reconciliation and the power of an eternal life that His blood revealed, the cross of Jesus has been sanctified forever as an altar on which everything that is presented to God must be offered. And the cross is not merely that cross on which we are to believe that Jesus died for our sins but also the cross on which we must die. The cross has been sanctified by the blood of Jesus as the altar on which we may become a sacrifice, holy and acceptable to God.

The altar is sanctified by blood that in time it may sanctify the gift that is laid upon it. What is the gift that we have to lay on the altar? We find the answer in a word Paul wrote to the Romans: "Therefore, I urge you, brothers, in view of God's mercy, to offer your bodies as living sacrifices, holy and pleasing to God—this is your spiritual act of worship" (Romans 12:1).

Are you willing to ascend the altar, the place of death? Are you willing to make the cross your abode, the place where you will pass every hour of your life in fellowship with the crucified Jesus? It is the only way to close fellowship with Jesus, and through Him a free entrance to the eternal Father and His love.

The Blood of Christ

THE SPIRIT OF UNITY

There is one body and one Spirit, just as you were called in one hope of your calling; one Lord, one faith, one baptism; one God and Father of all, who is above all, and through all, and in you all.

EPHESIANS 4:4–6 (NKJV)

THE KNOWLEDGE OF what the body of Christ means, insight into its glory and purpose, and the fulfilling of the place and ministry to which God has called us in the body have a deeper connection with our spiritual life than is generally recognized. To receive the Holy Spirit and the love of Christ into our hearts means death to every area of selfishness. It means a complete surrender of our own interests as a member of the body for the sake of Christ and His body. It means that the welfare of every member within our circle becomes of supreme interest to us. We must realize what the body of Christ is in reality: it is the vessel through which the Spirit of God seeks to manifest himself.

We know what a masterpiece of divine workmanship a human body is; though made from dust, it is the dwelling place and instrument through which the human soul can unfold and express itself. This is but an image or a shadow of that body of which Christ is the head. In regard to it our epistle tells us (1:22–23 NKJV) that God "gave Him to be head over all things to the church, which is His body, the fullness of Him who fills all in all." The body of Christ is to contain and to exhibit the divine fullness as it dwells in Christ. It tells us that we "are being built together for a dwelling place of God in the Spirit" (2:22 NKJV). It reminds us that "Christ also loved the church and gave Himself for her, that He might sanctify and cleanse her with the washing of water by the word, that He might present her to Himself a glorious church, not having spot or wrinkle or any such thing, but that she should be holy and without blemish" (5:25–27 NKJV).

The Believer's Call to Commitment

JESUS BORE OUR SICKNESS

ARE YOU FAMILIAR with the beautiful fifty-third chapter of Isaiah? It has been called the fifth gospel. In the light of the Spirit of God, Isaiah describes beforehand the sufferings of the Lamb of God as well as the divine graces that should result from those sufferings.

The Lamb of God bore our sins, even the iniquity of us all. Sin was not found in Him, but it was put upon Him, and He took it voluntarily. In bearing it, He put an end to it, and because of this He has the power to save us. Because our sins have been borne by Jesus Christ, we are delivered from them as soon as we confess them and believe this truth.

He took up our infirmities and carried our sorrows. . . . He was pierced for our transgressions, he was crushed for our iniquities; the punishment that brought us peace was upon him, and by his wounds we are healed. . . . For he bore the sin of many, and made intercession for the transgressors.
ISAIAH 53:4–5, 12

In this chapter of Isaiah we see that what Christ bore for us relates to two different things. He not only bore our sins (v. 12) but He also bore our sicknesses (v. 4). The human nature of Jesus could not be touched by sickness because it remained holy. We never find in the account of His life any mention of sickness. Participating in all the weaknesses of our human nature: hunger, thirst, fatigue, and sorrow, He still had no trace of sickness. He was without sin, and sickness had no hold on Him.

Sin had attacked and ruined equally the soul and the body. Jesus came to save both. Having taken upon Him sickness as well as sin, He is in a position to set us free from the one as well as the other, and that He may accomplish this double deliverance, He expects from us only one thing: our faith. Jesus longs to reveal himself as the perfect Savior to all those who will trust themselves unreservedly to Him.

Divine Healing

It Is Poured Out From Heaven

"If you love me, you will obey what I command. And I will ask the Father, and he will give you another Counselor to be with you forever—the Spirit of truth. The world cannot accept him, because it neither sees him nor knows him. But you know him, for he lives with you and will be in you."

JOHN 14:15–17

EVERY LIVING BEING is governed by the nature it received at birth. The same holds true in the church. She received the law of her existence by that which was bestowed upon her in the Holy Spirit on the day of her birth. This is why it is so important for us to understand the Day of Pentecost and not to rest until we experience what God did for His people on that day. The first disciples serve as forerunners on the way to the fullness of the Spirit.

They were deeply attached to the Lord Jesus. A personal relationship to Him is the first condition for the reception of the full gift of the Comforter.

They left all for Jesus. The parables of the pearl of great price and the treasure hid in a field teach us that in order to gain possession of the kingdom within us, we must sell all that we have.

They despaired of themselves and all that man alone can accomplish. There is nothing that hampers us more than a secret reliance on something in ourselves or in the church that we imagine can help us.

They received and held fast the promise of the Spirit given by the Lord Jesus. They all had only one thought: Something has been promised to us by our Lord; it will surely give us a share in His heavenly power and glory; we are confident of its coming.

He has said that those who believe in Him will know rivers of living water flowing from their hearts. We need to hold fast to His Word as the disciples did, to set our hearts upon the fulfillment of it, and to lay aside all else until we inherit the promise.

The Fullness of the Spirit

Suggestions for Private Prayer

AS YOU ENTER A TIME of private prayer, let your first focus be to give thanks to God for the unspeakable love that invites you to come to Him and to converse freely with Him.

"When you pray, go into your room, close the door and pray to your Father, who is unseen. Then your Father, who sees what is done in secret, will reward you."
MATTHEW 6:6

You must prepare yourself for prayer by Bible study. Read a few verses from the Bible. Take what you do understand, apply it to yourself, and ask the Father to make His Word light and power in your heart.

When you have thus received the Word into your heart, turn to serious prayer. Take time to present yourself reverently and in quietness before God. Remember His greatness, holiness, and love. Think over what you want to ask of Him. Do not be satisfied with going over the same things every day. Let your prayer be something definite, originating either from the Word that you have read or from the real spiritual needs that you long to have satisfied.

What has been said is in reference to your own needs. But you know that we are encouraged to pray for the needs of others. Remember your family; your church with its many interests and endeavors; your own neighborhood; your friends. Let your heart be enlarged, and take up the interests of missions and the church throughout the world. Become an intercessor, and you will experience for the first time the blessedness of being used of God to bless others through prayer.

Do not forget the close bond between the inner room and the outside world. The attitude of the inner prayer room must remain with us all day. The inner room is intended to bind us to God, to supply us with power from God, and to enable us to live for God alone.

Living a Prayerful Life

In Remembrance of Me

And he took bread, gave thanks and broke it, and gave it to them, saying, "This is my body given for you, do this in remembrance of me."
LUKE 22:19

IS THIS INJUNCTION really necessary? Is it possible for us to forget Him? Jesus, who thought of us in eternity, who indeed forgot His own sorrows on the cross but never forgets ours; who says that a mother will sooner forget her nursing child than He will forget us—He without whose love I cannot live: Can I ever forget Jesus?

Although we are reminded afresh of Him at the Lord's Table, we do often forget Him. It may be at the time of some particular worry or sin or grief that we forget, or it may be in times of prosperity and joy that we momentarily forget where everything that is good comes from.

But Jesus will not be forgotten. He will see to it that this does not happen. He loves us so dearly that He sets great value on our love for Him. Our love is His greatest joy. He requires it of us. So truly has He chosen us that He longs to live in our remembrance every day.

Jesus yearns to be always with us and beside us that we may taste of His crucified love and power and heavenly life. Jesus desires that we should always remember Him.

I thank God that Jesus gives himself to me at the table. He will satisfy me with His love. He will so unite himself with me and so give His life to me that by the power of His indwelling it will not be a duty to remember Him but impossible to forget Him.

The Lord's Table

HOLINESS AND REDEMPTION

AS SOON AS THE PEOPLE had been redeemed from Egypt, God's very first word to them was "Consecrate to me every firstborn male. The first offspring belongs to me." The Word reveals how ownership is one of the central thoughts both in redemption and sanctification, the link that binds them together. And though the word here speaks only of the firstborn, they are a type of the whole people.

"Consecrate to me every firstborn male."
Exodus 13:2

"I have redeemed you . . . you are mine."
Isaiah 43:1

If holiness in the human race is to be true and real, it must be the result of a self-appropriation. And so the firstborn are sanctified, and afterward the priests in their place, as the type of what the whole people are to be as God's firstborn among the nations, "a holy nation."

After centuries of needed preparation, He revealed himself as the Redeemer. The people whom He had chosen and formed for himself, He gave up to oppression and slavery that their hearts might be prepared to long for and welcome a deliverer. He taught them that redemption is not only deliverance from an unjust oppressor here on earth but also from the righteous judgment their sins deserved. During their stay at Sinai and in the wilderness, the thought was continually pressed upon them that they were the Lord's people, whom He had made His own by the strength of His arm that He might make them holy for himself. The purpose of redemption is possession, and the purpose of possession is likeness to Him.

When Isaiah announced the second redemption, it was given to him even more clearly than to Moses: "A highway will be there; it will be called the Way of Holiness. Only the redeemed will walk there" (Isaiah 35:8–9). Just as the Redeemer is the Holy One, the redeemed are holy, too.

The Path to Holiness

THE POWER OF
UNITED PRAYER

"Again, I tell you that if two of you on earth agree about anything you ask for, it will be done for you by my Father in heaven. For where two or three come together in my name, there am I with them."
MATTHEW 18:19–20

ONE OF THE FIRST lessons our Lord taught about prayer was that the pray-er was not to be seen of men. He was to enter an inner room and be alone with the Father. The second lesson would be that we need not only secret and solitary prayer but also public, united prayer. He gives a very special promise for the united prayer of two or three who agree on what they ask.

For its full development, a tree has its roots hidden in the ground and its stem growing up into the sunlight. In the same way, prayer needs both the hidden secrecy in which the soul meets God alone and the public fellowship with those who find in the name of Jesus their common meeting place.

The reason for this is quite plain. The bond that unites a Christian to fellow believers is no less real or close than that which unites him to God: He is one with them. Grace renews our relationship not only to God but also to others. Nothing would be more unnatural than for each child of a family to regularly meet with his or her father separately but never in the company of the whole family. Believers are members not only of one family but also of one body. Just as each member of the body depends on the others, and the full action of the spirit dwelling in the body depends on the union and cooperation of all, so Christians cannot attain the full blessing God wants to give through His Spirit unless they seek and receive it in fellowship with one another. In the union of believers, the Spirit is free to manifest His full power. It was to the one hundred and twenty continuing in one place together and praying with one accord that the Spirit of the glorified Lord came down at Pentecost.

Teach Me to Pray

SELF-SURRENDER

LET US EXAMINE our hearts to see whether we have demonstrated genuine thankfulness toward God. Have we dedicated ourselves to the Lord as a living thank-offering? I am not talking about our possessions only or an activity here or there, but our whole life. This is what Jesus desires. Every redeemed soul consecrated to God, entirely separated unto

For Christ's love compels us, because we are convinced that one died for all . . . that those who live should no longer live for themselves but for him who died for them and was raised again.
2 CORINTHIANS 5:14–15

Him—His will, His work, His honor. This is what the believer confesses and renews in the Lord's Supper.

The Lord's Supper is a sacrificial meal in a double sense. Under the old covenant there were special sacrifices. The sin-offering, by which atonement was made, was a type of the sacrifice of Christ: He was made sin for us. The burnt-offering, which had to be wholly consumed by fire on the altar as a symbol of entire devotion to the service of God, was a type both of the sacrifice of Christ and the sacrifice of believers in which they surrender themselves to the Lord. Then lastly, the idea of a thank-offering was exhibited in the participation of the feast itself and the ensuing fellowship around the table.

Jesus offers himself to me, and I offer myself to Him. My sacrifice is the reflection of His. Let everyone examine his heart. The observance of the Lord's Supper is a glorious opportunity for renewed dedication to the Lord. Let the Holy Spirit reveal to you what it is to be a committed Christian: undividedly, unceasingly surrendered to Jesus in heart and hand, at home and in society; living for Jesus, working zealously for Him, a burnt-offering given entirely for God and consumed by the fire of the Spirit.

The Lord's Table

Jesus Heals the Sick

When evening came, many who were demon-possessed were brought to him, and he drove out the spirits with a word and healed all the sick. This was to fulfill what was spoken through the prophet Isaiah: "He took up our infirmities and carried our diseases."
MATTHEW 8:16–17

IT WAS BECAUSE JESUS had taken on His own body all our sicknesses that He could heal them. If He had not done so, one part of His work of redemption would have remained powerless and fruitless.

This text of the Word of God is not generally understood in this way. It is a widely accepted view that the miraculous healings done by the Lord Jesus are to be looked upon only as proof of His mercy or as a symbol of spiritual grace. They are not seen to be a necessary consequence of redemption, although that is what the Bible declares. The body and the soul have been created to serve together as a habitation of God; the sickly condition of the body, as well as that of the soul, is a consequence of sin, and that is what Jesus came to bear, to expiate, and to conquer.

"Jesus went throughout Galilee, teaching in their synagogues, preaching the good news of the kingdom, and healing every disease and sickness among the people" (Matthew 4:23). Matthew adds, "Great crowds came to him, bringing the lame, the blind, the crippled, the mute and many others, and laid them at his feet; and he healed them" (15:30).

If Jesus bore our sicknesses as an integral part of redemption, if He has healed the sick that it might be fulfilled which was spoken through the prophet Isaiah, and if His Savior-heart is always full of mercy and love, we can believe with certainty that to this very day it is the will of Jesus to heal the sick in answer to the prayer of faith.

Divine Healing

THE WAY TO THE NEW SONG

LISTEN TO THE testimony of one who can speak from experience of the sure and blessed outcome of patient waiting on God. True patience is so foreign to our self-confident nature, yet so indispensable to our waiting on God. It is an essential element of true faith, and we will once again meditate on what the Word has to teach us concerning it.

I waited patiently for the LORD; and He inclined to me, and heard my cry. . . .
He has put a new song in my mouth—praise to our God; many will see it and fear, and will trust in the LORD.
PSALM 40:1, 3 (NKJV)

The word *patience* is derived from the Latin word for suffering. It suggests the thought of being under the constraint of some power from which we are eager to be free. At first we submit against our will. Then experience teaches us that when it is useless to resist, patient endurance is our wisest alternative. In waiting on God, it is important that we submit not because we are forced to, but because we want to be in the hands of our blessed Father. Patience becomes our highest blessing and our highest grace. It honors God and gives Him time to work His will in us. It is the highest expression of our faith in His goodness and faithfulness. It brings the soul perfect rest in the assurance that God is carrying on His work. It is the evidence of our consent that God deal with us in the way and time that He thinks best. True patience loses self-will to His perfect will.

Patient waiting on God brings a rich reward; the deliverance is sure; God himself will put a new song in your mouth. And if you sometimes feel patience is not your gift, remember it *is* God's gift. Take the prayer from 2 Thessalonians 3:5 (NKJV): "Now may the Lord direct your hearts into the love of God and into the patience of Christ."

Waiting on God

IN AFFLICTION AND TRIAL

"Every branch that bears fruit He prunes, that it may bear more fruit."
JOHN 15:2 (NKJV)

IN THE WHOLE PLANT world there is not a tree to be found that so suits the image of man in his relationship to God as the vine. No other plant has fruit and juice that are so full of spirit, so alive and stimulating. But there is also none that has such a natural tendency toward evil, growth that loves to run into wood that is utterly worthless except for the fire. Of all plants, the vine most needs the pruning knife to be used unsparingly and unceasingly. But even with all these problems, no other plant yields a richer reward to the vinedresser.

In His wonderful parable, the Savior refers to this need of pruning the vine, and the blessing it brings. In this dark world, often full of suffering and sorrow for believers, we can take comfort in His words about pruning, knowing that He means it for our good. Abide in Christ! This is *the Father's object* in sending the trial. In a storm the tree puts down deeper roots into the soil; through suffering the Father leads us to enter more deeply into the love of Christ.

Our hearts are continually prone to wander from Him; prosperity and enjoyment all too easily satisfy us, dull our spiritual perception, and make us unfit for full communion with God. It is an unspeakable mercy that the Father comes with His affliction and makes the world around us dark and unattractive. This leads us to feel more deeply our sinfulness, and for a time we lose our joy in what was becoming so threatening to our spiritual life. He does this in the hope that when we have found our rest in Christ in time of trouble, we will learn to choose abiding in Him as our best option. Then when the affliction is removed, His hope for us is that we will have grown more firmly in Him, so that in prosperity He will still be our true joy.

Abiding in Christ

Revealed Unto Children

THE "WISE AND LEARNED" are those who are conscious and confident of their power of mind and reason to aid them in their pursuit of divine knowledge. The "children" are those whose primary concern is not the mind and its power but the heart and its disposition. Humility, reverence, dependence, meekness, teachableness, trust, and love are the attitudes God seeks in those whom He teaches.

"I praise you, Father, Lord of heaven and earth, because you have hidden these things from the wise and learned, and revealed them to little children."
MATTHEW 11:25

One of the most important elements of the quiet time is the study of God's Word. But we must remember to wait for the Father to reveal its truth to us. We must seek to have the childlike disposition to which our Father loves to impart the secrets of His love. To the wise and learned, head knowledge is the most important thing, and God obscures from them the spiritual meaning of the very thing they think they understand. To children, heart and feeling, humility, love, and trust are important, and God reveals to them the very thing they know they cannot understand by themselves.

In the secret place of prayer and study, we must be our own teacher and preacher. We must train ourselves in the habit of childlike simplicity and openness of mind and heart. Our first concern must be to wait on the Father to reveal to us the hidden mystery of its power in the inner life. With this disposition, we exercise the childlike spirit that receives the kingdom without doubt or question.

The first mark of being a child of God, of being like Jesus Christ, is an absolute dependence upon God for every blessing, and especially for any real knowledge of spiritual things. Put aside everything else to obtain it. God will reveal to you His hidden wisdom.

The Believer's Daily Renewal

THE BLOOD-BOUGHT MULTITUDE

And they sang a new song: "You are worthy to take the scroll and to open its seals, because you were slain, and with your blood you purchased men for God from every tribe and language and people and nation."
REVELATION 5:9

THE MEN WHO IN all ages have stood at the head of great missionary undertakings have received from heaven, by the Word and Spirit of God, the light and power needed for their work. It was the eye of faith fixed on Jesus as King that opened their hearts to receive His command and His promise, in which they found both the motivation and the courage to go to a foreign land and labor there for Him without thought for their own comfort or convenience.

Our text tells us of a vision of things in heaven that sheds the light of eternity upon the work of missions. We hear the song of the redeemed, who praise the Lamb that He has redeemed them for God by His blood. There is no people or nation that will not have its representatives among those redeemed by the blood of the Lamb; there is no division of language or nationality of which the breach has not been healed. All will be united in one spirit of love and in one body before the throne.

What else is that vision but a heavenly revelation of the high calling and glorious result of mission work? Without missions, that vision could not have become fact, nor could that song be sung. In the song is set forth the divine right of missionary endeavor and the heavenly supply that empowers it.

He who does not love Jesus cannot understand missions, for he knows nothing about its secret blessing or the redemption of souls. If you are a Christian, you must be a friend of missions. Live for missions: Give financial support to it, pray for it, speak for it, and give yourself to it. He who knows the power of the blood in his own heart cannot be anything less than an advocate of God's method of reaching the lost around the world.

The Blood of Christ

Job's Sickness and Healing

THE VEIL THAT HIDES the unseen world from us is lifted for a moment in the mysterious story of Job; it reveals to us heaven and hell occupied with God's servants on earth. We see in it the temptations that are particular to sickness and how Satan makes use of them to dispute

So Satan went out from the presence of the LORD and afflicted Job with painful sores from the soles of his feet to the top of his head.
JOB 2:7

with God. Satan seeks the perdition of the soul, while God seeks to sanctify it by the same trial.

Satan is the prince of the kingdom of darkness and of sin; sickness is a consequence of sin. Herein is constituted the right of Satan over the body of sinful man. It is he who torments men with sickness and seeks to turn them from God and destroy their lives. But we would be quick to say that the power of Satan is far from being almighty; it can do nothing without God's authorization. God permits him to do all he does in tempting men, even believers, but it is in order that the trial may bring forth in them the fruit of holiness.

How are we to be delivered from sickness? A father never prolongs the punishment of his child beyond the time necessary. God, who has His purpose in permitting sickness, will not prolong the chastisement longer than is necessary to attain His end. As soon as Job understood Him, from the time he condemned himself and repented in dust and ashes through to hearkening to what God had revealed to him of himself, the discipline was over. God delivered him from Satan's hand and healed him of his sickness.

God uses Satan like a wise government uses the prison system. He leaves His children in his power for a given period only, after which time His will is to connect us with the redemption of Him who has conquered Satan.

Divine Healing

HUMILITY IN THE TEACHING OF JESUS

"Whoever wants to be first must be your slave— just as the Son of Man did not come to be served, but to serve."
MATTHEW 20:27–28

OH THAT GOD would convince us that Jesus means this! We all know what the character of a faithful servant or slave implies. Devotion to the master's interests, thoughtful study and care to please him, delight in his prosperity and honor and happiness. There are servants on earth in whom these dispositions have been seen and to whom the name of servant has never been more applicable. To how many of us has it been a new joy in the Christian life to know that we may yield ourselves as servants, as slaves to God, and to find that His service gives us the greatest liberty—freedom from sin and self?

We need to learn another lesson—that Jesus calls us to be servants of one another, and that as we accept it heartily, this service will be a most blessed one, a new and fuller deliverance from sin and self. At first it may appear hard—this is because of the pride that still asserts itself.

Here is the path to the higher life. It is the lowest path! This was what Jesus said to the disciples who were thinking of being great in the kingdom and of sitting on His right hand and His left. Ask not for exaltation. That is God's work. See that you humble yourselves and take no place before God or man but that of a servant. That is your work; let that be your one purpose and prayer. God is faithful. Just as water seeks and fills the lowest place, so the moment God finds the creature empty, His glory and power flow in to exalt and to bless. He that humbles himself—that must be our chief aim—shall be exalted; that is God's aim. By His mighty power and in His great love He will do it.

Humility

TRUSTING HIM TO KEEP YOU

"ABIDE IN ME": These words are no law of Moses, demanding from the sinful what they cannot perform. They are the command of love, which is only a promise in a different shape. Think of this

I press on to take hold of that for which Christ Jesus took hold of me.
PHILIPPIANS 3:12

until all feeling of burden, fear, and despair pass away, and the first thought that comes as you hear of abiding in Jesus is one of bright and joyous hope: It is for me; I know I will enjoy it. You are not under the law with its demanding *Do*, but under grace, with its blessed *Believe* what Christ will do for you. And if the question is asked, "But surely there is something for us to do," the answer is, "Our doing and working are but the fruit of Christ's work in us." It is when the soul becomes utterly passive, looking for and resting on what Christ will do, that its energies are stirred to their highest activity, and we work most effectively because we know that He works in us. It is as we see in the words "Remain in me" (John 15:4) the mighty energies of love reaching out after us to have us and to hold us, that all the strength of our will is awakened to abide in Him.

This connection between Christ's work and our work is beautifully expressed in the words of Paul: "I press on to take hold of that for which Christ Jesus took hold of me." It was because he knew that the mighty and the faithful One had grasped him with the glorious purpose of making him one with Christ that he did his utmost to grasp the glorious prize.

Fix your eyes on Christ. Gaze on the love that shines in those eyes and that asks whether you can trust Him, who sought, found, and brought you near, now to keep you. It is because Jesus has taken hold of me and because He keeps me that I dare to say, "Savior, I abide in you."

Abiding in Christ

THE UNITY OF THE SPIRIT

I . . . beseech you to walk worthy of the calling with which you were called, with all lowliness and gentleness, with longsuffering, bearing with one another in love, endeavoring to keep the unity of the Spirit in the bond of peace.
EPHESIANS 4:1–3 (NKJV)

THE HOLY SPIRIT dwells not only in Christ in heaven and in the believer on earth, but particularly with Christ's body and all its members. The unbridled work of the Spirit can only be found where a right relationship exists between an individual and the whole body. His primary concern in his daily walk is to endeavor to maintain the unity of the Spirit. The principal virtues of the Christian life are holiness and meekness, in which each denies self for the sake of the others.

The need of such teaching is illustrated in the first epistle to the Corinthians. In the church at Corinth there were abundant operations of the work of the Spirit. The gifts were strikingly manifested, but the fruit of the Spirit was remarkably absent. The congregants did not understand that there is a diversity of gifts but the same Spirit. All have been baptized into one Spirit, into one body, and all drink of one Spirit. They had not learned the more excellent way—the way of love. Love seeks not its own and finds its life and happiness in serving others.

Keep the unity of the Spirit. It is God's command to every believer. It is the new commandment: to love one another—in a new form, tracing love back to the Spirit from which it draws its life. If you would obey the command, note carefully that it is unity of the *Spirit*. There is unity of creed or custom, of denomination or worship style, in which the bond is more of the flesh than of the Spirit. There is much in you that is of self and of the flesh that can excel in a unity that is of this earth, but it may greatly hinder the unity of the Spirit.

The Spirit of Christ

WASHED IN HIS BLOOD

WE KNOW WHAT the word *washing* means. We wash our bodies every day to cleanse them from the least defilement. Our clothes are washed to remove every stain or spot. Sin has an effect upon our souls as a kind of pollution. The blood of Jesus procures for us more than pardon for our guilt. When we are convicted by the Holy Spirit and go to God for forgiveness and cleansing, the blood has the power of a full deliverance from the sense of defilement and washes us whiter than snow.

To him who loves us and has freed us from our sins by his blood, and has made us to be a kingdom and priests to serve his God and Father—to him be glory and power for ever and ever! Amen.
REVELATION 1:6

John speaks of this twofold work of grace in his first epistle: "If we confess our sins, He is faithful and just to forgive us our sins and to cleanse us from all unrighteousness" (1:9 NKJV). To the same effect, he said previously, "But if we walk in the light, as he is in the light"—that is, in the pardoning and sanctifying love of God—"we have fellowship with one another, and the blood of Jesus, his Son, purifies us from all sin" (1 John 1:7). This refers to the abiding and uninterrupted cleansing of sin in the case of him who walks in the light in fellowship with God.

Where does this washing take place? In the heart. It is in the deep, hidden, inner life of man that this washing of the blood is experienced. Jesus said, "The kingdom of God is within you" (Luke 17:21). Sin has penetrated into the heart, and the whole nature has become saturated with it. So, too, must the blood penetrate the whole inner being. As deeply as the power of sin has gone, so deeply must we be cleansed by the blood.

The blood of Jesus carries with it His victory over sin and death; it inspires us with the consciousness of His victorious power and bestows upon us victory over sin and the enemy of our souls.

The Blood of Christ

CHRIST THE INTERCESSOR

Therefore he is able to save completely those who come to God through him, because he always lives to intercede for them.
HEBREWS 7:25

ALL GROWTH IN the spiritual life is dependent upon a clearer insight into what Jesus is to us. The more we realize that Christ is everything to us and that all of Christ is for us, the more we learn to live the true life of faith—dying to self, and living completely in Christ. The Christian life is no longer a struggle to live rightly but rather a resting in Christ and finding Him our life. This is especially true in the life of prayer.

Prayer also comes under the law of faith, and when seen in the light of the fullness and completeness that is in Jesus, the believer understands that prayer need not be a matter of strain or anxious care but an experience of what Christ does through us. It is a participation in the life of Christ, which ascends to the Father as prayer. We can begin to pray not only trusting in the merits of Jesus and in the intercession by which our unworthy prayers are made acceptable, but in that union by which He prays in us and we in Him.

This is illustrated clearly on the last night of Christ's earthly life. In His high-priestly prayer (John 17) He shows us how and what He prays to the Father and what He will pray after His ascension into heaven. His entrance into the work of His eternal intercession *would be the beginning and the power of their new prayer life in His name*. A vision of Jesus interceding for us gives us courage to pray in His name.

There is no need of His people that He conveys in intercession that the Godhead can deny: His mediation on the throne is as real and indispensable as the cross. Nothing takes place without Christ's intercession. It engages all His being and power; it is His unceasing occupation at the right hand of the Father.

Believing Prayer

ALL THINGS ARE POSSIBLE WITH GOD

IF THE GREAT HINDRANCE to the power of God's Spirit working in our lives is the idea that the standard is an impossible one, we must listen to the voice of Christ when He tells us that what is impossible with men is possible with God. God can do for us what

And those who heard it said, "Who then can be saved?" But He said, "The things which are impossible with men are possible with God."
LUKE 18:26–27 (NKJV)

appears to be beyond our reach. God by His Spirit desires to work in us all that He worked in the apostle Paul. We have this confidence in the words of our text. Now let us think about what is implied in the gift of the Holy Spirit.

Few words are used with such a variety of meanings as the word *spirit*. Its meanings range from anything in which the mind of man exerts and proves its power to the very highest revelation of God's holiness and love. Within the sphere of Bible truth we often have a very partial and defective view of what is meant by the Spirit of God and of Christ. We need to realize what God means when He promises us the Spirit of Christ.

When Jesus Christ came into the world as a human being, He purposed by His life to obey His Father in perfect holiness and love; it is this life that God intends to impart to those who believe in Christ. When Christ died, it was that He might lay down His life and then—just as the grain of wheat dies and reappears in the full head of wheat with its hundredfold reproduction of the seed—live again in our lives here on earth. The Father gave Him for this purpose. When He ascended to the throne, the Spirit was poured out into the hearts of His people: "God sent the Spirit of his Son . . . crying, 'Abba, Father'" (Galatians 4:6). The Spirit communicates the holiness and disposition of Christ with divine power to all who believe.

The Believer's Call to Commitment

THE WILL OF GOD

"Your kingdom come, your will be done on earth as it is in heaven."
MATTHEW 6:10

You ought to say, "If it is the Lord's will, we will live and do this or that."
JAMES 4:15

IN DAYS OF ILLNESS, when doctors and medicines fail, people turn to such Scriptures as "Your will be done" and "If it is the Lord's will . . ." But these may easily become a stumbling block to divine healing. How can we know whether or not it is God's will that we remain ill? I would answer that as long as this is an open question how can we believe for healing? How can we pray with faith?

We must be guided by the Word of God in order to know His divine will. The promise of James 5:14–15 is so absolute that it is impossible to deny it. This promise only confirms other passages, equally strong, that tell us that Jesus Christ has obtained for us the healing of our diseases because He has borne our sicknesses. We have a right to healing because it is a part of the salvation that we have in Christ; therefore, we may expect it with certainty. Scripture tells us that sickness, in God's hands, is the means of chastening His children for their sins, but that this discipline ceases to be exercised as soon as the suffering child acknowledges and turns from his sin.

So if you truly want to know what the will of God is in this, don't let yourself be influenced by the opinions of others or by your own former prejudices, but rather listen to and study what the Word of God says. Examine it to see if it does not tell you that divine healing is a part of the redemption of Jesus and that God wills that every believer should have the right to claim it. See whether it does not promise that the prayer of every child of God for healing will be heard and health restored by the power of the Holy Spirit.

Divine Healing

WHAT IS TO BE TAUGHT

IT WAS NEARLY twenty years after the initial outpouring of the Holy Spirit that this incident took place. These disciples were recognized as those who believed in Jesus Christ as the Messiah. This belief, however, was not enough. The disciples who walked with the Lord Jesus on earth were also true believers, yet He commanded them not to rest until they had received the Holy Spirit.

There are two ways in which the Holy Spirit works in us. The first is preparatory, in which He acts on us but is not yet dwelling in us. The second is the higher phase of His working, when we receive Him as an abiding gift, an indwelling Person; we know that He has assumed responsibility for our whole inner being, working in us both to will and to do of His good pleasure. This is the ideal of the full Christian life.

While Apollos was at Corinth, Paul took the road through the interior and arrived at Ephesus. There he found some disciples and asked them, "Did you receive the Holy Spirit when you believed?" They answered, "No, we have not even heard that there is a Holy Spirit."
ACTS 19:1–2

Yes, the supreme need of a believer's life is to receive the Holy Spirit, and when we have Him, to be conscious of the fact and live in harmony with Him.

Just as only those who are thirsty will drink water with eagerness and only those who are sick will ask for a physician, so it is that only when believers acknowledge the sinful nature of their spiritual condition will the message of the full blessing of Pentecost find entrance into their hearts. The first disciples received the baptism on their knees. It will be on our knees that the full blessing will come to us today.

The Fullness of the Spirit

HUMILITY: THE SECRET OF REDEMPTION

Your attitude should be the same as that of Christ Jesus: Who, being in very nature God, did not consider equality with God something to be grasped, but made himself nothing, taking the very nature of a servant. . . . And being found in appearance as a man, he humbled himself and became obedient to death—even death on a cross! Therefore God exalted him to the highest place and gave him the name that is above every name.
PHILIPPIANS 2:5–9

WHEN THE OLD SERPENT, who had been cast out of heaven for his pride, spoke temptation into Eve's ear, those words carried with them the very poison of hell. And when she listened, and yielded her desire and her will to the prospect of being like God, knowing good and evil, the poison entered into her soul, destroying forever that blessed humility and dependence upon God that would have been our everlasting inheritance and happiness. It is pride that made redemption necessary; it is from our pride that we need, above everything else, to be redeemed.

Even as we need to look to the first Adam and his failure to know the power of sin within us, we need to know the Second Adam and His power to give us the life of humility as real and abiding and enabling as was the life of pride. We have our life from and in Christ even more certainly than from and in Adam.

The life of God that entered human nature through the Incarnation, is the root in which we are to stand and grow; it is the same almighty power that worked there, at the cross, and onward to the Resurrection, which works daily in us. It is of utmost importance that we study to know and trust the life that has been revealed in Christ as the life that is now ours, and waits for our consent to gain possession and mastery of our whole being.

Humility

— 224 —

WHOLEHEARTEDNESS

"You will seek me and find me when you seek me with all your heart."
JEREMIAH 29:13

EXPERIENCE TEACHES US that anyone who engages in a work less than wholeheartedly will seldom succeed. Imagine a student, or his teacher, a man of business, or a warrior, who does not give himself to the task at hand. That one cannot expect success.

Wholeheartedness is even more essential in spiritual work, and above all, of the high and holy task of prayer and of being always well pleasing to a holy God.

How is it with you? What does your heart tell you? Even though you have given yourself to fulfill your obligations faithfully and zealously, perhaps you need to acknowledge: "I am convinced that the reason for my unsatisfactory prayer life is that I have not lived with a wholehearted surrender of all that would hinder my fellowship with God."

Prayerlessness is not something that can be overcome as an isolated thing. It is related to the state of the heart. And it is a way of life. True prayer depends on an undivided heart. And I cannot give myself an undivided heart—one that enables me to say, "I seek God with my whole heart." It is impossible for us in our own strength; but God will do it. He said He would give us a heart to fear Him. He also said He would write His law on our heart. Such promises serve to awaken a desire to pray. However weak our desire may be, if there is a sincere determination to strive after what God has for us, He will work in our heart both to will and to do of His good pleasure. It is the great work of the Holy Spirit in us to make us willing. He enables us to seek God with our whole heart.

May we acknowledge that we have been double-minded, because while we have given ourselves to many earthly things with all our heart and strength, we cannot always say that we have given ourselves to fellowship with God with our whole heart.

Living a Prayerful Life

THE SECRET OF
TRUE OBEDIENCE

*"Obey me, and I will be
your God and you will be
my people. Walk in all the
ways I command you,
that it may go well
with you."*
JEREMIAH 7:23

THE SECRET OF TRUE obedience, I believe, is a clear and close personal relationship to God. All our attempts to achieve full obedience will fail until we have access to His abiding fellowship. *It is God's holy presence, consciously abiding with us, that keeps us from dis-*obeying Him.

On earth Christ was a learner in the school of obedience; from heaven He teaches it to His disciples on earth. The urgent need to receive our orders and instructions continually from God himself is implied in the words "Obey me, and I will be your God." The expression "obey the commandments" is seldom used in Scripture; it is rather "obey Me," or "obey, listen to *My voice.*"

In learning obedience, Christ used the same textbook as we have. And He appealed to the Word not only when He had to teach or to convince others; He needed it and He used it for His own spiritual life and guidance. To appropriate the Word in His own life and conduct, to know when each particular portion was applicable, Christ needed and received divine teaching. Even so does He teach us by giving us the Holy Spirit in our hearts as the Divine Interpreter of the Word.

The true scholar of a great master finds it easy to render him unwavering obedience because he trusts his teacher so implicitly. The student sacrifices his own wisdom to be guided by a higher wisdom. We need this confidence in our Lord Jesus. Just as we have trusted Him as our Savior to atone for our disobedience, let us trust Him as our teacher to lead us out of it and into a life of practical obedience.

A Life of Obedience

WILL YOU BE MADE WHOLE?

WHEN A PHYSICIAN works to heal a patient, it is to render the patient independent of his help. He restores the patient to health and then leaves him on his own. The work of our Lord Jesus is the very opposite. Jesus works not from without but from *within*. He enters by the power of His Spirit into our life. Christ's purpose in healing is also the exact opposite of physical healing, which aims, if at all possible, toward independence from the doctors. Christ's condition of success is to bring us into such dependence upon himself that we will not be able to live a moment without Him.

When Jesus saw him lying there and learned that he had been in this condition for a long time, he asked him, "Do you want to get well?" "Sir," the invalid replied, "I have no one to help me into the pool when the water is stirred." . . . Then Jesus said to him, "Get up! Pick up your mat and walk." At once the man was cured.
JOHN 5:6–9

Christ Jesus himself is our life in a sense that many Christians cannot conceive. The weak and frail Christian life owes itself to a lack of appropriation of divine truth. As long as we expect Christ to continually do something for us in single acts of grace, trusting Him from time to time to give us only that which will last a little while, we cannot be restored to perfect health. But when we grasp the fact that we need Him moment by moment in our lives in utter dependence upon His strength and provision, then the life of Christ becomes the health of our soul. Health is nothing but life in its normal, undisturbed activity. Christ gives us health by giving us himself; He becomes our strength for our walk.

The Ministry of Intercessory Prayer

THE UNCTION FROM THE HOLY ONE

But you have an anointing from the Holy One, and all of you know the truth. . . .As for you, the anointing you received from him remains in you, and you do not need anyone to teach you. But as his anointing teaches you about all things and as that anointing is real, not counterfeit—just as it has taught you, remain in him.
1 JOHN 2:20, 27

THEY SHALL ALL BE taught of God. This includes every believer. The teaching comes through the anointing. Not in the thoughts or feelings, but in that all-pervading fragrance that comes from the fresh oil having penetrated the whole inner man.

In the spiritual life it is of deep importance always to maintain harmony between the objective and the subjective: God in Christ above me, God by the Spirit within me. In us not as a location, but in us as one with us, entering into the most secret part of our being and pervading all, dwelling in our very body, the anointing remains in us, forming part of our essential being.

Above circumstances and feelings, the anointing remains. Not, indeed, as a fixed state or as something in our own possession, but according to the law of the new life, in the dependence of faith on the Holy One and in the fellowship of Jesus. The life of holiness comes through the Trinity: first, the Father, who makes holy; second, the Son, His Holy One in whom we are; and third, the Holy Spirit, who dwells in us and through whom we abide in Christ and Christ in us.

Let us study the divine anointing. It is God's way of making us partakers of holiness in Christ. The anointing, received of Him day by day, abiding in us, teaching us all things, especially teaches us to abide in Christ. Its subtle, all-pervading power must go through our whole life. The odor of the ointment must fill the house. The anointing that abides makes abiding in Christ a reality and a certainty.

The Path to Holiness

THE HERITAGE OF HOLINESS

LET US BLESS God for this precious statement. There is not a deeper or more distinctly divine word in Scripture than holy; in this statement the whole treasure of holiness, with all that revelation teaches us concerning it, is made the heritage of our children. God's holiness in our children is meant to be; as parents we are the God-ordained links for bringing them into perfect union. To do this,

For the unbelieving husband has been sanctified through his wife, and the unbelieving wife has been sanctified through her believing husband. Otherwise your children would be unclean, but as it is, they are holy.

1 CORINTHIANS 7:14

we must first *understand* and *apply* this precious truth.

The word *holy* expresses a relationship. Whatever was separated unto God and made His property was called holy. The first and simplest thought our faith must take in and fill with spiritual meaning is this: Our children belong to God. The very fact of their being born of believing parents makes them His in a very special sense. The Lord's redeemed, who love to call themselves His bondservants, have no desire to look upon their children in any other light than wholly and absolutely His.

The word *holy* also suggests a destiny. It is of great importance, as we study the word in Scripture, to notice how everything that is called holy had a use and purpose; every holy day and thing, place and person, had its service to fulfill. Let the Christian parent beware of looking upon holiness as a mere means to an end, simply as the way to get safely to heaven. It is infinitely more than that! Let him realize that his child is God's property, to be used in this world as God directs, to be trained with the sole purpose of doing God's will and showing forth His glory. The more clearly this is grasped and made the distinct goal of the work of prayer and education, the more quickly will we be able to comprehend its higher meaning and gain the path to the blessing that it offers.

Raising Your Child to Love God

CHRIST THE SACRIFICE

"Abba, Father," he said, "everything is possible for you. Take this cup from me. Yet not what I will, but what you will."
MARK 14:36

WHAT A CONTRAST within the space of a few hours! What a transition from the quietness of "Father, the time has come" (John 17:2) to falling on the ground and crying, "Abba, Father. . . . Take this cup from me. Yet not what I will." In order of time the high priestly "Father, the time has come" precedes the sacrificial "Abba, Father. . . . Not what I will"; but this was only to show beforehand what the intercession would be once the sacrifice was brought. In reality it was that prayer at the altar in which the prayer before the throne had its origin and its power. Because of the entire surrender of His will in Gethsemane, the High Priest on the throne had the power to ask what He would. He has the right to let His people share in that power also and ask what they will.

This Gethsemane lesson is one of the most sacred and precious of all. To a superficial learner it may appear to take away the courage to pray in faith. If the earnest supplication of the Son's "Take this cup from me" was not heard, if He had to say, "Yet not what I will," how much more do we need to say it? Now it appears impossible that the promises the Lord had given only a few hours previously—"Whatever you ask," "Whatever you wish"—could have been meant literally. But a deeper insight into the meaning of Gethsemane teaches us that it is precisely here that we have sure ground and an open way to assurance of an answer to our prayers. Let us draw near in reverent and adoring wonder, to gaze on this great sight of God's Son offering up prayer and supplications with strong crying and tears—and not obtaining what He asks! He is our Teacher and will open up to us the mystery of His holy sacrifice as revealed in this awesome prayer.

Teach Me to Pray

A LIFE OF PRAYER

OUR LORD GAVE the parable of the widow and the unjust judge to teach us that we should always pray and not give up (Luke 18:1–5). As the widow perse-

Be joyful always; pray continually; give thanks in all circumstances.
1 THESSALONIANS 5:16–18

vered in seeking one particular thing, the parable seems to refer to persevering prayer when God seems to delay or appears to refuse an answer. The words in the Epistles, which speak of continuing in prayer, of praying always in the Spirit, appear to refer more to the whole life being one of prayer. As the soul fills with longing for the manifestation of God's glory to us and in us, through us and around us, and with the confidence that He hears the prayers of His children, the inner life of the soul is continually rising upward in dependence and faith, in longing desire and trustful expectation.

What is needed to live such a life of prayer? The first thing is undoubtedly the entire sacrifice of one's life to God's kingdom and glory. He who seeks to pray without ceasing simply because he wants to be very pious, will never attain to it. It is by forgetting oneself and yielding one's life to live for God and His honor that the heart is enlarged to know the light of God and His will. Because everything is weighed and tested by the one thing that fills the heart—the glory of God—and because the soul has learned that only what is of God can honor Him, the whole life becomes one of looking up, of crying from the inmost heart for God to prove His power and love and reveal His glory.

The believer awakens to the consciousness that he is one of the watchmen on Zion's walls, one of the Lord's remembrancers, whose call really does touch and move the King in heaven to do what would otherwise not be done. To forget oneself, to live for God and His kingdom among men, is the way to learn to pray without ceasing.

Teach Me to Pray

WAITING PATIENTLY ON GOD

Rest in the LORD, and wait patiently for Him; do not fret because of him who prospers in his way, because of the man who brings wicked schemes to pass. . . . For evildoers shall be cut off; but those who wait on the LORD, they shall inherit the earth.

PSALM 37:7, 9 (NKJV)

"BY YOUR PATIENCE possess your souls" (Luke 21:19 NKJV). "For you have need of endurance" (Hebrews 10:36 NKJV). "But let patience have its perfect work, that you may be perfect and complete, lacking nothing" (James 1:4 NKJV). Through these words, the Holy Spirit shows us how important patience and endurance are in the Christian life. And nowhere is there a better place for cultivating or displaying it than in waiting on God. There we discover how impatient we are and how our impatience affects our life. We confess at times that we are impatient with others and with circumstances that hinder us or with our slow progress in the Christian life. And if we truly set ourselves to wait on God, we will find that we are impatient with Him because He does not immediately, or as soon as we would like, give us what we ask. It is in waiting on God that our eyes are opened to believe in His wise and sovereign will and to see that the sooner and more completely we yield to it, the more surely His blessing will come to us.

Patience honors Him; it allows Him to do His work, yielding self wholly into His hands. It lets God *be God*. If your waiting is for some particular request, wait patiently. If your waiting is the exercise of the spiritual life seeking to know and have more of God, wait patiently. Whether it is in the designated periods of waiting or the continuous habit of the soul, rest in the Lord, be still before Him, and wait patiently. You will inherit the land—and all else that God has planned for you.

Waiting on God

A Home Built on Faith

DON'T BE AFRAID; just believe! To thousands that word has been the messenger of comfort and hope. As they struggled under the burden of sin, or sought for help in trial or difficulty, it told them that there was deliverance from fear by believing in Jesus. Faith can banish fear. And yet how many who have found a blessing in this word have forgotten that it is a word that especially belongs to parents. In every other use it is but a loan; it is as parents that we have

While Jesus was still speaking, someone came from the house of Jairus, the synagogue ruler. "Your daughter is dead," he said. "Don't bother the teacher any more."
Hearing this, Jesus said to Jairus, "Don't be afraid; just believe, and she will be healed."
LUKE 8:49–50

full right to it. It is Jesus, the Lord of the home, of parents and children, who speaks: Don't be afraid; just believe. The word is a double lesson: In our children there is every reason for fear; in Jesus, every reason for faith.

When we think of the tendency toward evil our children inherit from us, and the mighty power Satan has in this world, we have good reason to fear. When we see both in Scripture and in the world around us how often the bright promise of childhood is cut short and the children of a Christian home stray into the ways of the world and of the flesh, we cannot remind each other too often of the importance of parental faith, duty, and obedience. *Only believe* must be written on the doorposts of our homes. It must be the motivation for all we are and do for our children.

Faith is first the spiritual understanding that receives the revelation of God and His purpose. *It hears His voice*; it listens to His call; it believes His promises. Then it is a divine energy, a living principle of action that carries out God's will and inherits all His blessings. It is in the knowledge of what He is—it is in His presence—that such a faith is possible.

Raising Your Child to Love God

CHRIST ALONE

Jesus, knowing that they intended to come and make him king by force, withdrew again to a mountain by himself.
JOHN 6:15

THE GOSPELS FREQUENTLY tell us of Christ's going into solitude for prayer. Luke mentions His praying eleven times. Mark tells us, in his very first chapter, that after an evening when all the city had come to see Him and He had healed many, "Very early in the morning, while it was still dark, Jesus got up, left the house and went off to a solitary place, where he prayed" (1:35). Before He chose His twelve apostles, "One of those days Jesus went out to a mountainside to pray, and spent the night praying to God" (Luke 6:12). This idea of complete privacy in prayer appears to have deeply impressed the disciples, giving rise to Mark's remark, "He went up on a mountainside to pray" (6:46); and Matthew's, "He went up on a mountainside by himself to pray. When evening came, he was there alone" (14:23). As a man, Jesus felt the need for absolute solitude.

In the life of a Christian, one of the deepest lessons to learn is that the Word without the living God avails little; that the blessing of the Word comes when it brings us to the living God; that the Word from the mouth of God brings with it the power to understand and to obey it. Let us learn the lesson that personal fellowship with God in secret can make the Word life and power for us.

Prayer allows us to lay our whole life before God and to ask for His teaching and His strength. Attempt for a moment to think what prayer meant to Jesus: It was adoring worship, basking in love, childlike petition for all that He needed. Do we realize what blessedness awaits the one who knows how to follow in Christ's steps? He will prove what great things God can do for the one who makes this his greatest joy—to be alone with Him.

The Believer's Daily Renewal

WAITING ON GOD FOR ALL THE SAINTS

THINK FOR A MOMENT of the multitudes of people who need that prayer; how many there are who are sick and weary and alone, and who feel that their prayers are not being answered, who sometimes fear that their hope is in vain. Remember, too, the many servants of God, ministers or missionaries, teachers or workers, whose hope in their work has been disappointed and whose long-

O my God, I trust in You; let me not be ashamed; let not my enemies triumph over me. Indeed, let no one who waits on You be ashamed; let those be ashamed who deal treacherously without cause.
PSALM 25:2–3 (NKJV)

ing for a manifestation of God's power and blessing remains unsatisfied. Think of those who have heard of this life of rest and perfect peace, of abiding light and fellowship, of strength and victory, but who cannot find the path to it. In each of these cases there is no explanation but that they have not yet learned the secret of waiting on God. They simply need what we all need: the full assurance that waiting on God is never an exercise in vain.

If this intercession for others becomes a part of our waiting on Him, we will help to bear each other's burdens and so fulfill the law of Christ. There will be introduced into our waiting on God that element of unselfishness and love that is the path to the highest blessing and the fullest communion with God. Christ did not seek to enjoy the Father's love for himself alone; He passed it on to us. So let us also love our neighbor.

Twice in this psalm David speaks of waiting on God for himself; here he thinks of all those who wait on Him. Let this be a reminder to God's children who are weary, or who are going through trials, that there are more people praying for them than they know. Let it move them and us, so that in our waiting we can at times forget our own needs and say to the Father, "These also wait on you. Answer them."

Waiting on God

YOU ARE THE BRANCHES

"I am the vine, you are the branches."

JOHN 15:5

IT IS REALLY A SIMPLE thing to be a branch of a tree or a vine. The branch grows out of the vine or the tree, and in due time bears fruit. It has no responsibility except to receive its nourishment from the root and stem through the sap. Similarly, if by the Holy Spirit we understood our relationship to Jesus Christ, our work would be transformed into an effectual influence. Instead of being an exhausting experience, our work would be new and fresh, linking us to Jesus as never before.

Of course the vine does the vital work. It sends its roots down into the soil underground—the roots often far-reaching—and finds the necessary nourishment and moisture. If fertilizer is added to the soil, the vine naturally sends its roots toward it; then the roots turn the moisture and fertilizer into a sap that energizes the growth of the rich fruit to be borne. I have heard of a particular vine that has borne more than two thousand clusters of grapes in one season. People were understandably astonished at such extraordinary production. It was discovered that the vine stretched its roots hundreds of yards underground to the River Thames. There in the rich soil of the riverbed it found abundant nourishment and moisture, and the roots drew the sap that incredible distance into the vine, resulting in an abundant harvest.

Whether I preach a sermon, teach a Bible class, or visit the sick of my congregation, all the responsibility of the work is on God, who supplies the strength.

The flow of power to the branches is not intermittent. It is a vital relationship that is ongoing and healthy. The branch abiding in the Vine is our position as a servant. Every day I must be conscious of my part to abide in Him, to rest and trust and know that without the Vine I am nothing.

Absolute Surrender

THE BLESSING OF A VICTORIOUS PRAYER LIFE

Now to him who is able to do immeasurably more than all we ask or imagine, according to his power that is at work within us, to him be glory in the church and in Christ Jesus throughout all generations.
EPHESIANS 3:20–21

IF WE ARE DELIVERED from the sin of prayerlessness and understand how this deliverance may continue to be experienced, what will be the fruit of our liberty? He who grasps this truth will seek after this freedom with renewed enthusiasm and perseverance. His life and experience will show that he has obtained something of unspeakable worth. He will be a living witness of the blessing found in victory.

Think of the confidence in the Father that will replace the reproach and self-condemnation that characterized our lives before. Think how the hour of prayer may become the happiest time in our whole day, and how God may use us there to share in carrying out His plans, making us a fountain of blessing to the world around us. We can hardly conceive of the power God will bestow when we are freed from the sin of prayerlessness and pray with the boldness that reaches heaven in the almighty name of Christ to bring down blessing.

Prayer is not merely coming to God to ask something of Him. It is, above all, fellowship with God and being brought under the power of His holiness and love.

This does not come to us all at once. God has great patience with His children. He bears with us in fatherly patience at our slow progress. Let each child of God rejoice in all that God's Word promises. The stronger our faith, the more earnestly will we persevere to the end.

May God strengthen us to believe that there is certain victory prepared for us and that the blessing will be more than the heart of man has conceived! God will do this for those who love Him.

Living a Prayerful Life

PRAYER FOR THE HOLY SPIRIT

*May the grace of the Lord
Jesus Christ, and the love
of God, and the fellowship
of the Holy Spirit
be with you all.*
2 CORINTHIANS 13:14

LORD GOD, I THANK YOU that you have led me throughout this week of preparation and that I can now hope to eat with you and your Son on the Lord's Day at the table of your covenant. I thank you for every opportunity for meditation and prayer so that I may not appear carelessly in the sanctuary. In this quiet evening hour, I come once more to ask you for the filling of your Holy Spirit.

You have taught us that without Him there can be no true prayer, no real fellowship. You have given to every one of your children the Holy Spirit, by whom we may have access in Christ to the Father. I ask you that the Spirit might now work in me so as to impart to me the disposition I need to draw near to you together with all your chosen ones. I know that I have sometimes been unfaithful to you. Father, forgive me, and do not take your Holy Spirit from me.

Work in me true penitence so that I may remember my sin with a contrite heart. I desire to remember, confess, and cast away every sin that would cling to me. (Let us all here think of our own particular sins and confess them before God in preparation for the Lord's Table.)

I would renounce all confidence in myself and my own good deeds. I want a humble, tender spirit toward you and confidence in your work of grace alone. Then shall my observance of the Supper be truly a fellowship with the Father, Son, and Holy Spirit. Grant this for the sake of your Son. Amen.

The Lord's Table

THE MINISTRY OF THE SPIRIT AND PRAYER

CHRIST HAD JUST SAID (11:9), "Ask and it will be given to you"; God's giving is inseparably connected with our asking. He applies this principle especially to the gift of the Holy Spirit. As surely as a father on earth gives bread to his child, so God gives the Holy Spirit to them that ask Him. One great law rules

"If you then, though you are evil, know how to give good gifts to your children, how much more will your Father in heaven give the Holy Spirit to those who ask him!"
LUKE 11:13

the whole ministry of the Spirit: *We must ask; God must give.* When the Holy Spirit was poured out at Pentecost with a flow that never ceases, it was in answer to prayer.

Of all the gifts of the early church to which we should aspire, there is none more needed than the gift of prayer—prayer that brings the Holy Spirit into the midst of believers. This power is given to those who say, "We will give ourselves to prayer."

Prayer links the King on the throne with the church at His feet. The church, the human link, receives its divine strength from the power of the Holy Spirit, who comes in answer to their prayers. *Where there is much prayer, there will be much of the Spirit; where there is much of the Spirit, there will be ever-increasing prayer.* If prayer was the power by which the early church flourished and triumphed, shouldn't it be the need of the church of our day?

We have the privilege of offering ourselves to God to labor in prayer for the blessings He has in store for the church. Shouldn't we beseech God to make this truth live in us? And implore Him that we will not rest until we count the practice of intercession our highest privilege? It is the only certain means of obtaining blessing for the church, the world, and our own lives.

The Ministry of Intercessory Prayer

It Is Not in Ourselves

In me (that is, in my flesh) nothing good dwells; for to will is present with me, but how to perform what is good I do not find.
ROMANS 7:18 (NKJV)

TO HAVE LIFE IN himself is the prerogative of God alone, and of the Son, to whom the Father has also given it. To seek life, not in itself, but in God, is the highest honor of the creature. To live in and to himself is the folly and guilt of sinful man; to live to God in Christ is the blessing of the believer. To deny, to hate, to forsake, and to lose his own life: such is the secret of the life of faith. There is no path to true life, to abiding in Christ, other than the way taken by our Lord before us—through death.

At the beginning of the Christian life, very few see this truth. They are still ignorant of the terrible struggle of the flesh against God and its absolute refusal in the believer to be subject to the law of God. But bitter experiences of failure soon teach them the insufficiency of what they know about Christ's power to save; deep heart-longings are awakened to know Him better. He lovingly points them to His Cross.

You, a living person born of God, are already in Me; you are already dead to sin and alive to God, He explains. But are you ready now, in the power of this death, to give up self entirely to death on the cross, to be kept there until your self-will is conquered? It is in the slaying of self that the wonderful powers with which God has fitted you to serve Him can be set free and offered to Him to be accepted, sanctified, and used.

Remember, self that seeks to serve God is more dangerous than self that refuses to obey God. Look upon it with holy fear, and hide yourself in Christ. Jesus Christ will indeed take possession of you and dwell in you; and in the restfulness, peace, and grace of the new life, you will have unceasing joy at the wondrous exchange that has been made—the coming out of self to abide in Him alone.

Abiding in Christ

HOLINESS AND RESURRECTION

AS A BELIEVER you have a part in this new life. You have been given a "new birth into a living hope through the resurrection of Jesus Christ from the dead" (1 Peter 1:3). But this life can work in power only as you seek to know it, to yield to it, and to let it have full possession of you. If you do this, one of the most important things to see is that just as it was by virtue of the Spirit of holiness that Christ was raised, so also the Spirit of that same holiness must be in you the mark and the power of your life.

Regarding his Son, who as to his human nature was a descendant of David, and who through the Spirit of holiness was declared with power to be the Son of God by his resurrection from the dead: Jesus Christ our Lord.
ROMANS 1:3–4

Realize that Christ came to reveal what true holiness could be under the conditions of human life and weakness. He came to work it out for you so that He might communicate it to you by His Spirit. With your whole heart try to grasp this truth: The will of God accepted without condition is the power of holiness. As long as the believer is living the mixed life, part in the flesh and part in the spirit, with some of self and some of Christ, he seeks in vain for holiness. It is the new life that is the holy life: the full apprehension of it in faith and the full surrender to it in conduct will be the highway of holiness.

Jesus lived and died and rose again to prepare for us a new nature, to be received day by day in the obedience of faith. We "have put on the new self, which is being renewed in knowledge in the image of its Creator" (Colossians 3:10). Let the inner life, hidden with Christ in God, and also hidden deep within the recesses of our inmost being, be acknowledged, waited on, yielded to. It will work itself out in all the beauty of holiness.

The Path to Holiness

WAITING CONTINUALLY

So you, by the help of your God, return; observe mercy and justice, and wait on your God continually.
HOSEA 12:6 (NKJV)

IF WAITING ON GOD is the essence of true Christianity, the maintenance of an attitude of entire dependence on Him must be continual. There may be times of waiting for a particular answer, but the attitude and habit of the soul must remain unchangeable and uninterrupted.

Waiting continually *is* a possibility, though many think that our crowded lives make it impossible. They feel they cannot always be thinking of it. This is because they do not understand that it is a matter of the heart and that what the heart is full of, occupies it, even when our thoughts are on other things. A father's heart may be filled continually with intense love and longing for a sick wife or child at home, even though pressing business requires all his thoughts. When the heart has learned how entirely powerless it is to keep itself or to produce any good; when it has learned how surely and absolutely God will keep it; when it has, in despair of itself, accepted God's promise to do for it the impossible; it learns to rest in God and, in the midst of occupations and temptations, waits continually.

Do not limit God by your thoughts of what may be expected. Fix your eyes on this one truth: God in His very nature as the giver of life cannot do otherwise than every moment work in His child. Do not say, "If I wait continually, God will work continually." Rather, turn it around and say, "God works continually; I may wait on Him continually." Take time to catch the vision of God working continually—without a moment's intermission. Then your waiting continually will come naturally. Full of trust and joy, the habit of the soul will be: "On You I wait all the day" (Psalm 25:5 NKJV).

Waiting on God

IN STILLNESS OF SOUL

THERE IS A VIEW of the Christian life that regards it as a sort of partnership, in which God and man each have to do their part. It admits that there is little that man can do, and even that little is defiled with sin; still, the view holds, man must do his utmost; only then can he expect God to do His part. To those who think this way, it is extremely difficult to understand what Scripture means when it speaks of our being still and doing nothing, of our resting and waiting to see the salvation of God. It appears to them a perfect contradiction when we speak of this quietness and ceasing from all effort as the secret of the most productive activity of man. And yet this is just what Scripture does teach.

"In repentance and rest is your salvation, in quietness and trust is your strength."
ISAIAH 30:15

Rest in the LORD, and wait patiently for Him.
PSALM 37:7 (NKJV)

As Jesus was entirely dependent on the Father for all His words and all His works, so the believer can do nothing of himself. What he can do of himself is altogether sinful. He must therefore cease entirely from his own doing and wait for the working of God in him. As he ceases from self-effort, faith assures him that God is working in him to complete the work; what God does is to renew, sanctify, and awaken all his energies to their highest power.

So as the believer yields himself as a truly passive instrument in the hand of God, and works with renewed confidence in God's almighty power rather than his own, in that proportion will he experience the deepest possible expression of the Christian life. Passivity does not mean inactivity; it means that as we live out our Christian responsibilities, we do not trust in our own strength but in God's at work within us.

Abiding in Christ

Remain in His Love
at All Times

The fruit of the Spirit is love.
GALATIANS 5:22

ONE OF THE REASONS why God cannot bless us is *the lack of love* in the church. When the body is divided, strength is diminished. Only when believers stand as one body—one before God in the fellowship of love one toward another, one before the world in a love that the world can see—will they secure the blessing they seek from God.

One of the fathers of the church said that the best way to understand the Trinity was through the revelation of divine love—the Father, the loving one, the Fountain of Love; the Son, the beloved one, the Reservoir of Love in whom love was poured out; and the Spirit, the living love that united both and then overflowed into this world. The Spirit of Pentecost—the Spirit of the Father and the Spirit of the Son—is love. When the Holy Spirit comes to us and to others, will He be less a Spirit of love than He is in God? Of course not. He cannot change His nature. The Spirit of God is love, and the fruit of the Spirit is love.

Before Christ promised the Holy Spirit, He gave a new commandment: "Even as I have loved you, so you must love one another" (John 13:34). To them His dying love was to be the law of their conduct and interaction with one another. His message to those fishermen, so full of pride and selfishness was "Learn to love each other as I have loved you." And by the grace of God they did. On the Day of Pentecost they were of one heart and one soul.

And then He said, "By this all men will know that you are my disciples, if you have love for one another"(John 13:35). Christ said in effect: "I give you a badge, and that badge is *love*; that is to be your mark. If we were to ask the world if it has seen our "badge of love," what would its answer be?

Absolute Surrender

LEARNING OF CHRIST

"LEARN FROM ME. . . ." Here our Lord reveals the inmost secret of His own inner life. He brought it down to us from heaven, and it equips Him to be our teacher as well as our Savior. "I am gentle and humble in heart": It is the virtue

"Take my yoke upon you and learn from me, for I am gentle and humble in heart, and you will find rest for your souls."
MATTHEW 11:29

that makes Him the Lamb of God, our suffering Redeemer, our heavenly teacher and leader. It is the attitude He asks us to have when we come to learn from Him; from this beginning, everything else will fall into place. For Bible study as well as for daily living, it is the condition for learning of Christ. He wants to make us gentle and humble in heart. As learners, we must not only believe in Him but study to be gentle, humble, teachable.

It is an all-important issue because it lies at the root of a true relationship between us and God. Christ became the Son of Man to show us the blessed unceasing dependence upon God we are to have. In this spirit angels veil their faces and prostrate themselves before God. God is everything to them. This is the essence of the true Christian life: to be nothing before God and men, to wait on God alone, to delight in Christ, to learn of the One who is gentle and humble.

The key to the school of Christ, to true knowledge of Scripture, is this attitude of mind and heart. I am convinced that its lack has caused a large part of the weakness and unfruitfulness we all have experienced. Only as we are gentle and humble in heart can Christ teach us by His Spirit what God has for us. Let us begin with ourselves and count this the first condition of discipleship.

In our communion with God, attitude and character are everything.

The Believer's Daily Renewal

GRIEVING THE SPIRIT

Do not grieve the Holy Spirit of God, with whom you were sealed for the day of redemption.
EPHESIANS 4:30

WITH THE SPIRIT of God's Son living in us and having His reign over us, grieving our Father should no longer be a part of our lives. The believer who desires to live continually in the consciousness that he has been sealed with the Holy Spirit will find in his faith the assurance that the power and presence of that Spirit within him makes it possible to live without grieving Him. And yet the danger is so near and so strong. Unless we live entirely under the power of the Spirit, we may not hear the warning. It is essential to make a study of all the possible hindrances to His work in us. The context (v. 25) speaks of falsehood, anger, stealing, corrupt speech, and transgressions of the law of love. These were to be put far away; everything that is against God's law must grieve the Holy Spirit.

Think of all the commands of the Lord Jesus as expressed through the Beatitudes concerning being poor in spirit, meek, merciful, and pure in heart; through all His teaching concerning bearing our cross, denying self, forsaking the world and following Him; down to His last commands to His disciples to love one another as He loved them and to serve each other. These are some of the distinctive marks of the heavenly life Christ came to bring. Everything that is not in harmony with these must grieve the Spirit and prevent the enjoyment of His presence.

When Paul tells us "Everything that does not come from faith is sin" (Romans 14:23), he reminds us that while God's Word announces the great principles of our action, it leaves the individual believer under the teaching of the Spirit for the application of those principles in his daily life. In the gray areas, in things regarding differences among Christians, the believer grieves the Spirit when he does not wait for His guidance or does not follow through on what appears to be the mind of the Spirit.

The Believer's Call to Commitment

LET HIM THAT IS HEALED GLORIFY GOD

"HE JUMPED TO HIS FEET and began to walk. Then he went with them into the temple courts, walking and jumping, and praising God" (Acts 3:8).

It is a prevalent idea that holiness is easier in sickness than in health; that

Immediately he received his sight and followed Jesus, praising God. When all the people saw it, they also praised God.
LUKE 18:43

silence and suffering incline the soul to seek the Lord and enter into communion with Him better than in the distractions of active life. For these reasons, sick people hesitate to ask for healing from the Lord; for they say to themselves, *How can we know whether sickness may not be better for us than health?* To think this way is to ignore that healing and its fruits are divine. Sickness can glorify God only in the measure in which it gives occasion to manifest His power (John 9:3; 11:4).

Why should those who have been healed in answer to the prayer of faith glorify the Lord more than those who have been healed through earthly remedies? Here is the reason: Healing by means of medicine shows us the power of God in nature, but it does not bring us into living and direct contact with Him, while divine healing is an act proceeding from God, without anything but the Holy Spirit.

In the latter case, contact with God is the thing that is essential, and it is for this reason that examination of the conscience and the confession of sin should be the preparation for it. When the Lord heals the body it is that He may take possession of it and make it a temple that He may dwell in. The joy that then fills the soul is indescribable; it is not only the joy of being healed, but it is also joy mingled with humility and a holy enthusiasm that realizes the touch of the Lord and that receives new life from Him. In the exuberance of his joy, the healed one exalts the Lord, glorifies Him by word and deed, and his life is consecrated to God.

Divine Healing

THE CAUSE OF PRAYERLESSNESS

Those who belong to Christ Jesus have crucified the sinful nature with its passions and desires. Since we live by the Spirit, let us keep in step with the Spirit.
GALATIANS 5:24–25

SCRIPTURE TEACHES US that there are only two conditions possible for the Christian: one is to walk according to the Spirit and the other is to walk according the flesh. These two powers are in irreconcilable conflict with each other. So most Christians—even though they may be born again through the Spirit and have received the life of God—still continue to live their life not according to the Spirit but according to the flesh.

In Galatians 5 Paul mentions as the work of the flesh not only grave sins such as adultery, murder, and drunkenness but also the more ordinary sins of daily life: anger, strife, and arguing. The majority of Christians have no real knowledge of the deep sinfulness and godlessness of the carnal nature to which they unconsciously yield. The flesh can say prayers well enough, calling itself religious for so doing and thus satisfy the conscience. But the flesh has no desire or strength for the prayer that strives after an intimate knowledge of God, that rejoices in fellowship with Him, and that continues to lay hold of His strength.

The Christian who is still carnal (fleshly) has neither the disposition nor the strength to follow after God. He remains satisfied with his prayer of habit or custom. But the glory and the blessedness of secret prayer is a hidden thing to him, until one day his eyes are opened, and he begins to see that the flesh in its disposition to turn away from God is the archenemy that makes powerful prayer impossible.

Do not seek to find in circumstances the explanation for this prayerlessness over which we mourn. Seek it where God's Word declares it to be—in the hidden aversion of the heart to a holy God.

Living a Prayerful Life

PRAYER IN HARMONY WITH THE PERSON OF GOD

IN THE NEW TESTAMENT we find a distinction made between faith and knowledge: "For to one is given the word of wisdom through the Spirit, to another the word of knowledge through the same Spirit, to another faith by the same Spirit, to another gifts of healings by the same Spirit" (1 Corinthians 12:8–9 NKJV). In a child or a childlike

"Father, I thank You that You have heard Me. And I know that You always hear Me, but because of the people who are standing by I said this, that they may believe that You sent Me."
JOHN 11:41–42 (NKJV)

Christian there may be faith but little knowledge. Childlike simplicity accepts the truth without difficulty and rarely cares to give itself or others any reason for its faith except that God said it. But God would have us love and serve Him not only with all our heart but also with all our mind; that we might grow up into the divine wisdom and beauty of all His ways and words and works.

This truth has its full application in our prayer life. While prayer and faith are so simple that a newborn convert can pray with power, the doctrine of prayer often presents problems. Is the power of prayer a reality? How can God grant to prayer such power? How can the action of prayer be harmonized with the will of God? How can God's sovereignty and our will, God's liberty and ours, be reconciled? These and other similar questions are valid subjects for Christian meditation and inquiry. The more earnestly and reverently we approach such mysteries, the more we will fall down in adoring awe to praise Him who has in prayer given such power to men and women.

Teach Me to Pray

WAITING FOR THE COMING OF HIS SON

WAITING ON GOD and waiting for His Son were both initiated in view of the other and cannot be separated. Waiting on God for His presence and power in our daily life is the only true preparation for waiting for Christ in humility and true holiness. Waiting for Christ's coming to take us to heaven gives waiting on God its tone of hopefulness and joy. The Father, who in His own time will reveal His Son from heaven, is the God who, as we wait on Him, prepares us for the revelation of His Son. This present life and the coming glory are inseparably connected in God and in us.

"Looking for the blessed hope and glorious appearing of our great God and Savior Jesus Christ" (Titus 2:12–13 NKJV) is one of the great bonds uniting God's church throughout the ages. "He comes, in that Day, to be glorified in His saints and to be admired among all those who believe" (2 Thessalonians 1:10 NKJV). Then we will all meet, and the unity of the body of Christ will be seen in its divine glory. It will be the meeting place and the satisfaction of God's love: Jesus receiving His people and presenting them to the Father; His people meeting Him and worshiping Him as never before; His people meeting each other in the bond of God's love. Let us wait, long for, and love the appearing of our Lord and heavenly Bridegroom.

Tender love to Him and to each other is the true and only bridal spirit. Jesus refuses to accept our love unless it is expressed also to His disciples. Waiting for His coming means waiting for the glorious unity of the body while we attempt to maintain that unity in humility and love here on earth. Those who love most are the most ready for His coming.

Waiting on God

OBEYING HIS COMMANDMENTS

WHEN THE SINNER, in coming to Christ, seeks to prepare himself by works, the voice of the Gospel sounds, "Not of works." Once in Christ, however, lest the flesh should abuse the word "Not of works," the Gospel lifts its voice as loudly to say, "Created in Christ Jesus

"If you keep My commandments, you will abide in My love, just as I have kept My Father's commandments and abide in His love."
JOHN 15:10 (NKJV)

for good works" (Ephesians 2:10 NKJV). To the sinner out of Christ, works may be his greatest hindrance, keeping him from union with the Savior. To the believer in Christ, works are his strength and blessing, for by them faith is made perfect (James 2:22 NKJV), the union with Christ is cemented, and the soul is established and more deeply rooted in the love of God.

Our union with Jesus Christ is not something of the intellect or sentiment, but a real, vital union in heart and life. The Holy Spirit breathes the holy life of Jesus, with His feelings and disposition, into us. The believer's calling is to think, feel, and will what Jesus thought, felt, and willed. To live the life of Christ means to him to be delivered from the life of self; the will of Christ is to him the only path of liberty from the slavery of his own self-will.

Love will assimilate the commands into your inmost being as food from heaven. They will no longer come to you as a law standing outside and against you, but as the living power that has transformed your will into perfect harmony with all your Lord requires.

And if even for a moment the commandments appear grievous, just remember whose they are. They are the commandments of Him who loves you. Each new surrender to keep the commandments, each new sacrifice in keeping them, leads to deeper union with the will, the spirit, and the love of the Savior.

Abiding in Christ

WHO WILL DELIVER ME?

O wretched man that I am! Who will deliver me from this body of death? I thank God—through Jesus Christ our Lord! So then, with the mind I myself serve the law of God, but with the flesh the law of sin.

ROMANS 7:24–25 (NKJV)

DO YOU REALIZE the wonderful place this text has in the epistle to the Romans? It stands at the end of chapter 7 as the gateway to the eighth. In the first sixteen verses of chapter 8, the Holy Spirit is mentioned sixteen times; there we have the description and promise of the life that a child of God can live in the power of the Holy Spirit.

In our text we have the words of a man who has come to the end of himself. In the previous verses he describes how he has struggled in his own power to obey the law of God and failed. But in answer to his own question of who will deliver him from this body of death, he cries, "through Jesus Christ our Lord!"

In the first two sections of the epistle, Paul deals with justification and sanctification. In dealing with justification, he lays the foundation of the doctrine in the teaching about sin—not in the singular but in the plural: "sins." These represent actual transgressions. In the second part of the fifth chapter, he begins to deal with sin not as actual transgression, but as a power. Imagine the loss if we did not have the second half of chapter 7! We would have missed the question we all want answered! And what is the answer? The one who is truly regenerated is the one whose will has been renewed and who can say, "I delight in God's law."

You will find in our text, in contrast to chapter 8, that the Holy Spirit is not mentioned. The man is struggling on his own to fulfill God's law. (The law is mentioned nearly twenty times.) It describes a believer doing his best to obey the law of God *without* being filled with the Spirit.

Absolute Surrender

TEACHABLENESS

THE FIRST QUALITY of a student is the willingness to be taught. This implies a consciousness of our own ignorance, a readiness to give up our own way of thinking or doing, and to examine things from the teacher's standpoint, a quiet confidence that the master "knows" and will teach us to "know" also. Anyone who would know Christ and His Word

The man without the Spirit does not accept the things that come from the Spirit of God, for they are foolishness to him, and he cannot understand them, because they are spiritually discerned.
1 CORINTHIANS 2:14

will study carefully to understand what the Word says but also seek the Spirit's interpretation.

Ironically, "unlearning" is an important part of learning; wrong impressions, prejudices, and presumptions are insurmountable obstacles to learning. Until these have been removed, the teacher labors in vain. The knowledge he communicates only touches the surface; deep beneath the surface, the student is guided by that which has become second nature to him. The first task of the teacher is to expose and then make the student see and remove those hindrances.

We cannot truly and fruitfully learn of Christ if we are not ready to unlearn as well. Through heredity, education, and tradition we have ideas about faith and God's Word that are often hindrances because we are convinced they are the truth. Learning of Christ requires a willingness to subject every truth we hold to His inspection for criticism and correction.

Teachableness is a form of humility. In our morning devotional time we place ourselves as students of Christ; let teachableness be the distinguishing mark of the learner. If you sense this is lacking, listen to His voice: "Take my yoke upon you" and all that this implies—learning from the One who is gentle and humble of heart; the One who submitted himself to His Father and learned obedience.

The Believer's Daily Renewal

FILLED WITH THE SPIRIT

And do not be drunk with wine, in which is dissipation; but be filled with the Spirit, speaking to one another in psalms and hymns and spiritual songs, singing and making melody in your heart to the Lord.

EPHESIANS 5:18–19 (NKJV)

"DO NOT GRIEVE the Spirit!" and "Be filled with the Spirit!" are commands that encompass our responsibility to the Spirit. The first warns against anything of the flesh or self that would lead to unbelief or disobedience; the second calls us to commit our whole personality to the Father, who reveals and maintains the life of Christ within us.

To understand the command "Be filled with the Spirit" we need only turn to the Day of Pentecost. For three years the disciples lived day and night in close fellowship with the Lord. His presence was everything to them. When He spoke about His departure, He promised that the Spirit would come not to take His place but to reveal himself as their Lord. Through the Spirit He would be as present with them as when He was on earth, only in a more intimate and glorious way. He would no longer be near them without the power to enable them to do what He taught them. He would live and work in them as the Father lived and worked in Him. Their former fellowship with Him during His earthly ministry would be but a shadow of the constant union with Him that the Spirit would reveal in power.

The command "Be filled with the Spirit" shows that what the disciples received and enjoyed at Pentecost is for us too. The church has existed at a level far inferior to the life of Pentecost. Few believe in the possibility of unbroken fellowship with Christ, conquering sin by His holy presence, inspiring us to commitment and self-sacrifice, and guiding us each day into all His will by His Spirit. His redemptive ministry includes not only salvation to those who repent but full salvation to all whom He has sanctified by the offering of himself.

The Believer's Call to Commitment

NOT BY OUR OWN POWER

AS SOON AS THE crippled man had been healed at the gate of the temple, the people ran toward Peter and John. Peter, seeing this miracle was being attributed to their power and holiness, lost no time setting them straight by telling them that all the glory of this miracle belonged to Jesus.

When Peter saw this, he said to them: "Men of Israel, why does this surprise you? Why do you stare at us as if by our own power or godliness we had made this man walk?"
ACTS 3:12

Peter and John were undoubtedly full of faith and holiness; otherwise, God might not have chosen them as instruments in this healing. They knew their holiness was not of themselves but of God through the Holy Spirit. They hastened to declare that in this incident they counted for nothing and that it was the work of the Lord alone. This is the object of divine healing: to be a proof of the power of Jesus, a witness in the eyes of men of what He is, proclaiming His divine intervention, and attracting hearts to Him.

It is necessary to insist on this because of the tendency of believers to think the opposite. Those who have recovered their health in answer to "the prayer of a righteous man" (James 5:16) are in danger of being too occupied with the human instrument that God is pleased to employ and to think that the power lies in man's piety.

No, it is not by our own power or holiness that we obtain these graces, but by a simple, childlike faith, one that knows it has no power or holiness of its own, and which commits itself completely to Him who is faithful and whose power can fulfill His promise. It is only as we feel our own powerlessness, and expect all from God and His Word, that we realize the glorious way in which the Lord heals sickness through faith in His name.

Divine Healing

THE CROSS IN CONTRAST TO THE FLESH AND THE WORLD

I know that nothing good lives in me, that is, in my sinful nature. . . . The sinful mind is hostile to God. It does not submit to God's law, nor can it do so.
ROMANS 7:18; 8:7

THE CROSS AND THE flesh are deadly enemies. The cross would condemn and put to death the flesh. The flesh desires to cast aside and conquer the cross. Many, as they hear of the cross as the indispensable preparation for the fullness of the Holy Spirit, will find out what there is in them that must yet be crucified. We are to understand that our entire nature is sentenced to death, and we must die, by the cross, so that the new life in Christ may rule in us.

The very essence of the flesh is to hate God and His holy law. The wonder of redemption is that Christ has borne on the cross the judgment and curse of God on the flesh and has forever nailed it to the cursed tree. If a man only believes God's Word about this mind of the flesh, and then longs to be delivered from it, he learns to love the cross as his deliverer from the power of the Enemy. Our old man—our former nature—is crucified with Christ, and our one hope is to receive this by faith and to hold it fast.

What the flesh is in the small circle of my own person, so the world is in the larger circle of humankind. The flesh and the world are two manifestations of the same "god of this world," who is served by both. When the cross deals with the flesh as cursed, we at once discover what the nature and the power of the world are: "They hated both me and my Father." The proof of this was that they crucified Christ. But Christ obtained the victory on the cross and freed us from the power of the world.

Against the two great powers of the god of this world, God has given us two great powers from heaven: the cross and the Holy Spirit.

Living a Prayerful Life

THE OBEDIENCE OF CHRIST

TO THE OBEDIENCE of Christ we owe everything. The one thing God asked of Adam in the Garden was obedience. The one thing by which a creature can glorify God or enjoy His favor and blessing is obedience.

For as by one man's disobedience many were made sinners, so also by one Man's obedience many will be made righteous.
ROMANS 5:19 (NKJV)

From Adam we have inherited a tendency to willfulness, to selfishness, to disobedience. By our own choice we become "the children of disobedience." Christ came to show us how noble, how blessed, how pleasing to God a life of obedience is. He overcame disobedience and gives us the power to replace ours with His obedience.

The truer our grasp of the righteousness of Christ in the power of the Spirit, the more intense will be our desire to share in the obedience out of which it sprang.

The obedience of Jesus was not an act of obedience now and then, or even a series of acts, but the spirit of His whole life. He said in Hebrews 10:9 (NKJV), "Behold, I have come to do Your will, O God." When He said, "I do not seek My own will but the will of the Father who sent Me" (John 5:30 NKJV), He was ready to go to any length in denying His own will and doing the Father's. He meant it. This is the obedience to which He calls us and for which He empowers us.

In the obedience of One the obedience of many has its root, life, and security. Turn and look upon, study, and believe in Christ as the obedient One. As His righteousness is our hope, let His obedience be our model for all of life.

A Life of Obedience

THE SECRET OF EFFECTIVE PRAYER

> *"Therefore I tell you, whatever you ask for in prayer, believe that you have received it, and it will be yours."*
> MARK 11:24

RECEIVING SOMETHING FROM God by faith—believing in the answer with perfect assurance that it has already been given—is not necessarily the experience itself or the actual possession of what we have asked for. At times there may be a considerable wait involved. In other cases the believer may enjoy immediately what he has asked. Of course, in the case of having to wait for the answer, we have a greater need for faith and patience.

We need this faith to be effective intercessors, for grace to pray earnestly and persistently for the lost or needy around us. We must hold fast the divine assurance that as surely as we believe, we will receive. The more we praise God for the answer, the sooner it will be ours.

If you do not immediately see an increase in your desire to pray, do not allow circumstances to hinder or discourage you. Even without any change in feelings, you have accepted the spiritual gift by faith. The Holy Spirit may seem hidden, but you may count on Him to pray through you, even if it is only sighing. In due time you will become conscious again of His full presence and power.

Ask God. Believe that you have received what you ask. If you still find it difficult to do this, say that you believe on the strength of His Word.

"Believe that you have received." Begin with the faith you have, even though weak. Step by step, be faithful in prayer and intercession. The more simply you hold to this truth and expect the Holy Spirit to work, the more surely will the Word be made true for you.

The Ministry of Intercessory Prayer

HOLINESS AND REVELATION

WHY WAS IT HOLY GROUND?

Because God had come there and occupied it. It is the presence of God that makes holy. In the burning bush God makes himself known as dwelling in the midst of the fire.

The nature of fire may be either beneficial or destructive. The sun may give life and fruitfulness or it may scorch to death. All depends upon occupying the right position, upon where we stand in relation to it. And so wherever God the Holy One reveals himself, we shall find the two sides together: God's holiness as judgment against sin, destroying the sinner who remains in it, and as mercy freeing His people from it. Of the elements of nature, there is none of such spiritual and mighty energy as fire. What it consumes it changes into its own spiritual nature, rejecting as smoke and ashes what cannot be assimilated. And so the holiness of God is that infinite perfection by which He keeps himself free from all that is not divine, and yet has fellowship with the creature, destroying and casting out all that will not yield to Him.

It is with our face in the dust; it is in the putting off not only of our shoes but also of all that has been in contact with the world and self and sin that the soul draws nigh to the fire in which God dwells, the fire that burns but does not consume. Oh that every believer might learn and understand how the burning bush was a type of the crucified Christ, and how, as we die with Him, we receive that baptism of fire. Only then can we learn what it is to be holy as He is holy.

When the Lord saw that he had gone over to look, God called to him from within the bush, "Moses! Moses!" And Moses said, "Here I am." "Do not come any closer," God said. "Take off your sandals, for the place where you are standing is holy ground." . . . At this, Moses hid his face, because he was afraid to look at God.
EXODUS 3:4–6

The Path to Holiness

THE NEWNESS OF THE SPIRIT

But now we have been delivered from the law, having died to what we were held by, so that we should serve in the newness of the Spirit and not in the oldness of the letter.

ROMANS 7:6 (NKJV)

THE WORK OF THE indwelling Spirit is to glorify Christ and reveal Him within us. Corresponding to Christ's threefold office of Prophet, Priest, and King, we find that His work in the believer is set forth in three aspects: enlightening, strengthening, and sanctifying. Of the enlightening, Christ particularly speaks in His farewell discourse, when He promises the Spirit as the Spirit of truth, who will bear witness of Him, will guide into all truth, and will take the things of Christ and declare them unto us. In His epistles to the Corinthians, where wisdom was so sought and prized, the two aspects are combined; they are taught that the Spirit can only enlighten as He sanctifies. In Acts, His strengthening for the work is in the foreground. As the promised Spirit of power, He equips for a bold testimony in the midst of persecution and difficulty.

We all know how an impression is intensified by the force of contrast. Just as the apostle contrasted the service of sin and of righteousness, so here he brings out what the power and work of the Spirit is in contrast to bondage to the law. Paul very boldly says that not only are we dead to sin and made free that we might become servants of righteousness, but we are made dead to the law, so that having died to that wherein we were held, we serve in newness of Spirit and not in the oldness of the letter.

A carnal Christian is one who, though regenerate, has not yet yielded himself entirely to the Spirit so as to become spiritual. They have a portion of the Spirit, but allow the flesh to prevail. So there is a difference between a carnal and a spiritual Christian, depending on which element is strongest in them.

The Spirit of Christ

PRAYER AND THE DESTINY OF MAN

Then God said, "Let Us make man in Our image, according to Our likeness. . . ." So God created man in His own image; in the image of God He created him; male and female He created them.
GENESIS 1:26–27 (NKJV)

THE MORE WE MEDITATE on what prayer is and its power with God, the more we ask, "What is man that You are mindful of him, and the son of man that You visit him?" (Psalm 8:4 NKJV). Sin has so degraded man that from what he is now we can form no concept of what he was meant to be. We must turn back to God's own record of man's creation to discover what God's purpose was and what capacities man was endowed with for that purpose. Man's destiny is clear from God's language at Creation. It was to *fill*, to *subdue*, and to *have dominion* over the earth and all that is in it.

When an earthly sovereign sends an ambassador to another country, it is understood that he will advise as to the policy to be adopted, and that advice is acted upon. He is at liberty to apply for troops and any other means needed for carrying out the policy. If his policy is not approved, he is recalled, making way for someone who better understands his sovereign's desires. As God's representative, man was to have ruled. On his advice and at his request, heaven was to have bestowed its blessing on earth. His prayer was to have been the channel by which the close relationship between the King in heaven and man was to have been maintained. The destinies of the world were given into the power of the wishes, the will, and the prayer of man.

Of course, with the entrance of sin into the picture, this plan underwent a catastrophic change: Man's fall brought all creation under the curse. Only redemption could effect a glorious restoration.

Teach Me to Pray

WAITING FOR THE PROMISE OF THE FATHER

He commanded them not to depart from Jerusalem, but wait for the Promise of the Father, "which," He said, "you have heard from Me."
ACTS 1:4 (NKJV)

IN ONE SENSE, the fulfillment can never come again as it came at Pentecost. In another sense, we need to wait for the Father to fulfill His promise in us with as deep a reality as it was with the first disciples.

The Holy Spirit is not a person distinct from the Father in the way two persons on earth are distinct. The Father and the Spirit are never without or separate from each other. The Father is always in the Spirit; the Spirit works nothing except what the Father works in Him. Each moment the same Spirit that is in us is in God, too. He who is full of the Spirit will be the most apt to wait on God more earnestly.

The Spirit given at Pentecost was not a project that God failed with in heaven and so sent to earth. God does not give away anything in that sense. When He gives grace or strength or life, He gives it by giving himself. His gifts are inseparable from himself. It is all the more true with the Holy Spirit. He is God—present and working in us. The only way to see more of His work is to wait on the Father.

This gives new meaning and promise to our life of waiting. It teaches us to maintain the place where the disciples waited at the footstool of the throne. It reminds us of how helpless they were to meet their enemies or to preach to Christ's enemies until they were given power. So we also can only be strong in the life of faith or the work of love when we are in direct communication with God and Christ and they maintain the life of the Spirit in us. There is nothing the church cannot do if her members will learn to wait on God.

Waiting on God

SHOWING LOVE TO FELLOW BELIEVERS

WE KNOW THAT GOD is love and that Christ came to reveal this not as a doctrine but as a life. His life, in its wonderful self-abasement and self-sacrifice, was above everything the embodiment of

"This is My commandment, that you love one another as I have loved you."
JOHN 15:12 (NKJV)

divine love, which showed humankind in a way they could understand, how God loves. In His love to the unworthy and the ungrateful, in humbling himself to walk among men as a servant, in giving himself up to death, He lived and acted out the life of divine love that was in the heart of God. He lived and died to show us the love of the Father.

And now, just as Christ was to show forth God's love, believers are to show forth to the world the love of Christ. They are to prove to others that Christ loves them, and in loving, fill them with a love that is not of this Earth. By living and by loving just as He did, they are to be perpetual witnesses to the love that gave itself over to death. Christians are to live so that men are compelled to say, "See how Christians love one another."

In their daily interactions with one another, Christians are "made a spectacle to the world, both to angels and to men" (1 Corinthians 4:9 NKJV); and in the Christlikeness of their love to one another they are to prove what manner of spirit they are. In all the diversity of character, creed, language, or station in life, Christians are to prove that love has made them members of one body and of one another and has taught them each to forget and to sacrifice self for the sake of the other. Their life of love is the primary evidence of Christianity, the proof to the world that God sent Christ and that He has shed abroad in them (His followers) the same love with which He loved Him. Of all the evidences of Christianity, this is the most powerful and the most convincing.

Abiding in Christ

THE LIFE AND THE LIGHT

"I am the light of the world. Whoever follows me will never walk in darkness, but will have the light of life."
JOHN 8:12

BECAUSE CHRIST IS GOD, He is the Word of God. Because He has the life of God in himself, He is the revealer of that Life. And so as the living Word He is the life-giving Word. The written Word can be made void and ineffective when we trust human wisdom for its understanding. When it is accepted as the seed in which the life of the living Word is hidden—made alive by the Holy Spirit—it becomes the Word of life to us.

It is only as the written Word ministers the life of the Eternal Word, and as the Holy Spirit, who knows the things of God, makes them life and truth to us, that our study of Scripture can be edifying to us.

Hunger for the will of God as your daily food. Thirst for the living spring of the Spirit within you. Receive the Word into your life, your conscious will; and make it your joy. The life it brings will shed light on all.

The reason I so frequently repeat this truth is very simple. My own experience has taught me how long it takes before we understand that the Word of God must be received into the life—not only into the mind—and how long it takes for us to fully believe it and act on it! Meditate on this truth until it becomes part of you. The Word comes from the life of God, carries that life in itself, and seeks to enter your life and mine and fill us with the life of God. This life is the light of men, the light of the knowledge of the glory of God. Only the Spirit that lives in God knows the things of God, and only the Spirit living in me can teach me the things of God by imparting them to my life.

The Believer's Daily Renewal

PARDON AND HEALING

IN HUMANKIND TWO natures are combined. We are at the same time spirit and matter, heaven and earth, soul and body. For this reason, on the one side we are sons of God and on the other we are doomed to destruction because of the Fall. Sin in our soul and sickness in our body bear witness to the right that death

"But so that you may know that the Son of Man has authority on earth to forgive sins. . . ." Then he said to the paralytic, "Get up, take your mat and go home."
MATTHEW 9:6

has over us. It is the twofold nature that has been redeemed by divine grace. When Isaiah foretells the deliverance of his people, he adds, "No one living in Zion will say, 'I am ill'; and the sins of those who dwell there will be forgiven" (Isaiah 33:24).

This prediction was accomplished beyond all expectation when Jesus the Redeemer came to earth. By His own acts and afterward by the commands He left for His disciples, He showed us clearly that the preaching of the gospel and the healing of the sick were both part of the salvation He came to offer.

This truth is nowhere better demonstrated than in the story of the paralytic. Jesus begins by saying to him, "Which is easier: to say, 'Your sins are forgiven,' or to say, 'Get up and walk'? But so that you may know that the Son of Man has authority on earth to forgive sins . . . he said to the paralytic, 'Get up, take your mat and go home.'" Sin in the soul and sickness in the body both bear witness to the power of Satan, and "the reason the Son of God appeared was to destroy the devil's work" (1 John 3:8).

Jesus came to deliver men from sin and sickness that He might make known the love of the Father. In His actions, in His teaching of the disciples, in the work of the apostles, pardon and healing are always found together.

Divine Healing

THE FIGHT AGAINST PRAYERLESSNESS

Let us fix our eyes on Jesus, the author and perfecter of our faith. . . . Consider him who endured such opposition from sinful men, so that you will not grow weary and lose heart.
HEBREWS 12:2–3

WE MUST NOT COMFORT ourselves with thoughts of standing in a right relationship to the Lord Jesus while the sin of prayerlessness has any power over us. But if we first recognize that a right relationship to the Lord Jesus above all else includes prayer, with both the desire and power to pray according to God's will, then we have something that gives us the right to rejoice and rest in Him.

Discouragement is the result of self-effort, and so blocks out all hope of improvement or victory. Indeed, this is the condition of many Christians when called on to persevere in prayer as intercessors. They feel it is something entirely beyond their reach: they do not have the power for the self-sacrifice and consecration necessary for such prayer. They have tried in the power of the flesh to conquer the flesh—a wholly impossible thing. They have endeavored by Beelzebub to cast out Beelzebub—and this will never happen. It is Jesus alone who can subdue the flesh and the devil.

We have spoken of a struggle that will certainly result in disappointment and discouragement. This is the effort made in our own strength. But there is another struggle that will certainly lead to victory. The Scripture speaks of "the good fight of faith," a fight that springs from and is carried on by faith. Jesus Christ is the author and finisher of faith. When we come into right relationship with Him, we can be sure of His help and power.

Living a Prayerful Life

THE DIVINE INVITATION

THE KING OF HEAVEN and earth says to you: In honor of His Son, He has prepared a great supper. He has invited all the children of men, dear and precious to the Father, to the great festival of His divine love. He is prepared to receive and honor them there as guests and friends. He will feed them with

"Tell those who have been invited that I have prepared my dinner: My oxen and fattened cattle have been butchered, and everything is ready. Come to the wedding banquet."
MATTHEW 22:4

heavenly food. He will bestow upon them the gifts and power of everlasting life.

We have been given a priceless invitation. What an incredible honor to be asked to dine with the King of Glory! Let us prepare ourselves for this feast! Let us clothe ourselves with the humble spirit and disposition of one who is invited to the court of the King of Kings.

Think of what it cost God to prepare this feast. Nothing less than the suffering and death of His Son was required to remove our sin and make way for us to enjoy the blessings of heaven. This is what we celebrate. Ponder the wonders of this royal banquet. It is as free and as generous as it can be. The poorest and the most unworthy are called to enjoy it.

Some excuse themselves, saying they are too busy—one with his many possessions, another with his work, and still another with his family obligations. Let us lay aside everything that would distract us from accepting the invitation to dine with the King.

The Lord's Table

HOLINESS AND SEPARATION

I am the LORD your God,
who has set you apart
from the nations. . . .
"You are to be holy to me
because I, the LORD, am
holy, and I have set you
apart from the nations
to be my own."
LEVITICUS 20:24, 26

THOUGH THERE CAN BE no holiness without separation, there can be separation without holiness. Although the idea of holy always includes that of separation, it is itself something infinitely higher. It is not what I am or do or give that makes me holy but what God is and gives and does in me. God's taking possession of me makes me holy; it is the presence and the glory of God that makes holy.

Separation is only the setting apart and taking possession of the vessel to be cleansed and used; it is the filling of the vessel with the precious contents we entrust to it that gives it its real value. But separation is essential to holiness. "I am the LORD your God, who has set you apart from the nations." Until I have chosen and separated a vessel from those around it, and cleansed it, if need be, I cannot fill or use it. I must have it in my hand with full and exclusive command of it, or I will not pour into it the precious milk or wine. In that way God separated His people unto himself when He brought them up out of Egypt, when He gave them His covenant and His law so that He might work out His purpose of making them holy.

Divine love does its separating work step by step along a glorious path. As we accept this separation, the holiness of God will enter and take possession. Then we will realize that to be the Lord's property signifies infinitely more than to be acknowledged as His—it means that God by the power and indwelling of the Holy Spirit, fills our being, our affections, and our will with His own life and holiness. He separates us for himself and sanctifies us to be His dwelling place.

The Path to Holiness

POWER FOR PRAYER AND WORK

> *"I tell you the truth,*
> *anyone who has faith in*
> *me will do what I have*
> *been doing. He will do*
> *even greater things than*
> *these, because I am going*
> *to the Father. And I will*
> *do whatever you ask*
> *in my name."*
> JOHN 14:12–13

THE SAVIOR OPENED His public ministry to His disciples with the Sermon on the Mount. He closed it by the parting address preserved for us by John. In both messages He spoke more than once of prayer—but with a difference. The Sermon on the Mount was to disciples who had just entered His school, who scarcely knew that God was their Father, and whose prayers' chief reference was to their personal needs. In His closing address, He spoke to disciples whose training time had come to an end, and who were ready as His messengers to take His place and do His work.

In the former, the primary lesson is to be childlike, to pray in faith, and to trust the Father to give good gifts. Now He points to something higher. Now they are His friends to whom He has made known all He has heard from His Father. They are His messengers who have entered into His plans and into whose hands the care of His work and kingdom on earth is to be entrusted. They are to go out and do His work, and in the power of His approaching exaltation, even greater works. Prayer is to be the channel through which that power is received for their work. With Christ's ascension to the Father, a new epoch begins, both for their work and for their life of prayer.

He who would work *must pray.* In prayer, power for your work is obtained. As long as Jesus was here on earth, He did the greatest works. The same demons that the disciples could not cast out fled at His word. When Jesus went to the Father, He was no longer here in body to do the work. The disciples became His body. All His work from the throne must and could be done through them. And now it is done through us.

Teach Me to Pray

Waiting in Holy Expectancy

Therefore I will look to the Lord; I will wait for the God of my salvation; my God will hear me.
MICAH 7:7 (NKJV)

A LITTLE BOOK I read some time ago contained one of the best sermons I have seen on the text of this chapter. It told of a king who prepared a city for some of his poor subjects. Not far from their homes were large storehouses where everything they could possibly need was supplied if they would only send in their requests. There was just one condition: They must be on the lookout to receive the answer to their request so that when the king's messengers came with supplies, they would always be found waiting and ready to receive them. The sad story goes on to tell of one despondent subject who never expected to get what he asked for because he felt too unworthy. One day he was taken to the king's storehouses, and there to his amazement he saw all the packages addressed to him. Deliveries had been attempted, but the packages always came back. There was the garment of praise, and the oil of joy, and the eye salve he had asked for, and so much more. The messengers had been to his door, but always found it closed and no one around to receive the packages.

When we have made special requests to God, our waiting must involve the confidence that God hears us. Holy, joyful expectancy is the very essence of true waiting. It is important to remember that it is *God* who works in us. For this to happen, our efforts must cease. Our hope must be in the work of God, who raised Jesus from the dead. Our waiting must become more than ever a lingering before God in stillness of soul, depending on Him who raises the dead and calls the things that are not as though they were.

Every moment of a life in the will of God must be of His working. I have only to look to Him, to wait for Him, and to know that He hears me.

Waiting on God

So Will You Have Power in Prayer

PRAYER IS BOTH ONE of the means and one of the fruits of union with Christ. As a means it is of great importance. All the things of faith, all the pleadings of desire, all the yearnings after a fuller surrender, all the confessions of shortcoming and of sin, all the exercises in which the soul gives up self and clings to Christ, find their utterance in prayer.

> *"If you abide in Me, and My words abide in you, you will ask what you desire, and it shall be done for you."*
> JOHN 15:7 (NKJV)

But it is not so much as a means but as a fruit of abiding that the Savior mentions it in the parable of the Vine. He does not think of prayer as we too often do—exclusively as a means of getting blessing for ourselves. Rather, He sees prayer as one of the primary channels of influence by which, through us as workers together with God, the blessings of Christ's redemption are dispensed to the world. Ours will be the effectual, fervent prayer of a righteous man, availing much, like Elijah's prayer for ungodly Israel (James 5:16–18). Such prayer will be the fruit of our abiding in Him and the means of bearing much fruit.

In promising to answer prayer, Christ's one thought (see John 14:13 NKJV) is this: "that the Father may be glorified in the Son." In His intercession on earth (John 17), this was His sole desire and plea; in His intercession in heaven, it is still His chief object. As the believer abides in Christ, the Savior breathes this desire into him. The thought *only the glory of God* becomes more and more the keynote of the life hidden in Christ. At first this subdues, quiets, and makes the soul almost afraid to entertain a wish, lest it should not be to the Father's glory. But when His glory has finally been accepted, and everything yielded to it, it comes with mighty power to enlarge the heart and open it to the vast possibilities in the area of God's glory.

Abiding in Christ

THE BIBLE STUDENT

Blessed is the man who does not walk in the counsel of the wicked or stand in the way of sinners or sit in the seat of mockers. But his delight is in the law of the LORD, and on his law he meditates day and night.

PSALM 1:1–2

MANY STUDENTS HAVE come away from seminary confessing that they have been taught everything but how to study the Word of God and how to motivate others to study it.

God's Word is our only authentic revelation of God's will. All human statements of divine truth, however correct they may be, are defective and carry a measure of human authority. In the Word, the voice of God speaks to us directly. Every child of God is called to direct communion with the Father through the Word. As God reveals all His heart and grace in it, His child can, if he receives it from God, assimilate the life and power of the Word into his own heart and life. Few secondhand reports of messages or events can be fully trusted. Every believer, therefore, has the right and the calling to live in direct communication with God. In the Word, God has revealed—and still reveals—himself to each individual.

This Word of God is a living Word. It carries a divine quickening power in it. The human expression of the truth is often a mere concept or image of the truth appealing to the mind alone. Faith that the Word is God's own, with His presence and power in it, makes it effective. The words in which God has chosen to clothe His own divine thoughts are God-breathed, and the life of God dwells in them. The Word was not only inspired when first given, the Spirit of God still breathes in it. God is still in and with His Word. As Christians, especially teachers and students, we need to embrace this truth. It will enable us to give the simple divine Word a credence that no human teaching can have.

The Believer's Daily Renewal

PERSEVERING PRAYER

THE NECESSITY OF praying with perseverance is the secret of all spiritual life. What a blessing to be able to ask the Lord for grace until He gives it, knowing with certainty that it is His will to answer prayer! But what a mystery for us is the call to persevere in prayer, to remind Him of His promises, and to do so without growing weary, until He arises and grants us our petition!

More than once the Bible explains to us the need for persevering prayer. There are many grounds, the chief of which is the justice of God. God has declared that sin must bear its consequences; sin has rights over a world that welcomes and remains enslaved by it. When the child of God seeks to quit this order of things, it is necessary that the justice of God should consent to this. Time, therefore, is needed for the privileges that Christ has procured for believers to be weighed before God's tribunal. Another reason is the opposition of Satan, who always seeks to prevent the answer to prayer. The only means by which this unseen enemy can be conquered is through faith.

Finally, perseverance in prayer is necessary for ourselves. Delay in the answer is intended to prove and strengthen our faith; it ought to develop in us the steadfast will that no longer lets go of the promises of God but that renounces its own side of things to trust in God alone. It is then that God, seeing our faith, finds us ready to receive His favor and grants it to us. And even though there may be delays, He will not make us wait a moment too long. If we cry unto Him day and night, He will answer us in due time.

> *Then Jesus told his disciples a parable to show them that they should always pray and not give up. . . . "Will not God bring about justice for his chosen ones, who cry out to him day and night? Will he keep putting them off? I tell you, he will see that they get justice, and quickly."*
> LUKE 18:1, 7–8

Divine Healing

THE HOLINESS OF GOD

But just as he who called you is holy, so be holy in all you do; for it is written: "Be holy, because I am holy."
1 PETER 1:15–16

IT HAS OFTEN BEEN said that the church has lost the concept of sin and the holiness of God. In the secret place of prayer we may learn anew how to give God's holiness the place it should have in our faith and our life. Nowhere can we get to know the holiness of God and come under its influence and power except in private prayer. It has been well said: "No man can expect to make progress in holiness who is not often and long alone with God."

If we remain prayerless, let our hearts be deeply ashamed. By so doing we make it impossible for God to impart His holiness to us. Let us ask God to forgive us this sin and to draw us to himself by His heavenly grace and to strengthen us to have fellowship with Him, the One who is holy.

The meaning of the words *the holiness of God* is not easily expressed. But we may begin by saying that they imply the unspeakable aversion and hatred with which God regards sin. If you want to understand what that means, remember that He preferred to see His Son die than that sin should reign in us. Think of the Son of God, who gave up His life rather than act in the smallest matter against the will of the Father. He had such a hatred of sin that He preferred to die rather than let men be held in its power. That is something of the holiness of God; it is a pledge that He will do anything for us in order to deliver us from sin.

I ask that you not think lightly of that grace: you have a holy God who longs to make you holy. Obey the voice of God that calls you to give time to Him in the stillness of your prayer room so that He may cause His holiness to rest on you.

Living a Prayerful Life

HOLINESS AND SERVICE

THROUGH ALL OF SCRIPTURE we have seen that whatever God sanctifies is to be used in the service of His holiness. Holiness and selfishness, holiness and inactivity, holiness and helplessness, are utterly incompatible. Our Lord speaks of himself as "the one whom the Father set apart as his very own and sent into the world" (John 10:36). And when He says, "I sanctify myself" (John 17:19), He adds the purpose: the service of the Father and His redeemed ones "that they too may be truly sanctified" (John 17:19).

If a man cleanses himself from the latter, he will be an instrument for noble purposes, made holy, useful to the Master and prepared to do any good work.
2 TIMOTHY 2:21

Holiness is essential to effectual service. In the church of Christ there is a vast amount of work done that yields very little fruit. Many throw themselves into service without true holiness and with little of the Holy Spirit. They often work diligently, and as far as human influence is concerned, successfully. And yet true spiritual results are few. The Lord cannot work through these people because He does not rule in their inner life.

There is no holiness in God except that which is actively engaged in loving and saving and blessing. It must be so in us, too. Every thought of holiness, every act of faith or prayer, every effort in pursuit of it must be motivated by the desire and the surrender of its object. Let your whole life be one distinctly and definitely surrendered to God for His use and service. You will find that in the union and interchange of worship and work God's holiness will rest upon you.

The Path to Holiness

THE CHIEF END OF PRAYER

"I am going to the Father. And I will do whatever you ask in my name, so that the Son may bring glory to the Father."
JOHN 14:12–13

"THAT THE SON MAY bring glory to the Father": for this reason Jesus on His throne in glory will do all we ask in His name. Every answer to prayer He gives will have this as its object; when there is no prospect of the Father being glorified, He will not answer. As with Jesus, the essential element in our petitions must be the glory of the Father—the aim, the end, the very soul and life of our prayers.

Jesus said that nothing glorifies the Father more than His doing what we ask. He will not, therefore, let any opportunity pass by for answering these prayers. Let us make His aim ours. Let the glory of the Father be the link between our asking and His doing. Prayer like that cannot fail to be heard and answered.

It is not that we do not at times want to pray with that motive, but we grieve that we seldom do. We know the reason for our failure: the gulf between the spirit of daily life and the spirit of prayer is too great. We begin to see that the desire for the glory of the Father is not something that we can stir up and present to our Lord only when we prepare ourselves to pray. It is when our whole life—in every part—is surrendered to God's glory that we can truly pray to His glory.

When our prayers cannot be answered, the Father is not glorified. It is our duty to live and pray so that our prayers can be answered and so glorify God. For the sake of God's glory, let us learn how to pray.

Teach Me to Pray

That You May Bear Much Fruit

WE ALL KNOW WHAT fruit is—the produce of the branch that refreshes and nourishes humankind. The fruit is not for the branch, but for those who come to harvest it. As soon as the fruit is ripe the branch gives it up, to begin

> "He who abides in Me, and I in him, bears much fruit. . . . By this My Father is glorified, that you bear much fruit."
> JOHN 15:5, 8 (NKJV)

again its work of benevolence in preparing fruit for another season. A fruit-bearing tree does not live for itself, but entirely for those to whom its fruit brings refreshment and life. And so the branch's whole existence is for the sake of the fruit, while its object and glory is to make the heart of the vinedresser glad.

What a beautiful image of the believer who is abiding in Christ! He not only grows in strength as his union with the Vine becomes progressively surer and firmer but he also bears fruit, much fruit to God's glory. He has the power to offer to others something to eat and by which they may live. Among all who surround him he becomes like a tree of life, of which they can taste and be refreshed. He is in his circle a center of life and blessing simply because he abides in Christ; he receives from Him the Spirit and the life that he can then impart to others. If you would bless others, learn to abide in Christ; and if you do abide, you will indeed be a blessing.

If Christ, the Heavenly Vine, has taken the believer as a branch, then He has pledged himself, in the very nature of things, to supply the sap, spirit, and nourishment to make it bear fruit. The soul needs to concern itself with only one thing—to abide closely, fully, and entirely in Him. Christ will give the fruit. He works in us all that is needed to make us a blessing.

Abiding in Christ

WHO ARE YOU?

Set your minds on things above, not on earthly things. For you died, and your life is now hidden with Christ in God.
COLOSSIANS 3:2–3

UPON ENTERING GOD'S presence in the morning hour, a great deal depends upon our realizing not only who *God* is but who we are and what our relationship to God is. The question *Who are you?* is asked (not in words but in spirit) of each one who claims right of access and an audience with the Most High. We must have an answer in our inmost consciousness; and that consciousness must be a living sense of the place we have in Christ before God. The mode of expressing it may differ at various times, but in substance it will always be the same.

Who am I? Let me think about who I am and not be afraid to tell God who it is that shall meet with Him and spend the day. I know, by the Word and Spirit of God, that I am in Christ and that my life is hid with Christ in God. In Christ I died to sin and the world. I am taken out of them, separated from them, and delivered from their power. I have been raised together with Christ and in Him I live unto God. Because my life is hid with Christ in God, I come to God to claim and obtain the divine life that is hidden in Him for my needs this day.

"Yes, this is who I am," I say to God in humble, holy reverence. Seek and expect nothing less than grace to live out here on earth the hidden life of heaven. I can say with confidence, "Christ is my life." The longing of my soul is for Christ to be revealed by the Father within my heart. Nothing less can satisfy me. My life is hidden with Christ in God. He can be my life in no other way than as He is in my heart. I can be content with nothing less than Christ in my heart—Christ as my Savior from sin, Christ as the gift and bringer of God's love, Christ as my indwelling Friend and Lord.

The Believer's Daily Renewal

SICKNESS AND DEATH

SCRIPTURE STATES seventy or eighty years as the ordinary measure of a human life. The believer who receives Jesus as the healer of the sick will feel at liberty to expect a life of seventy years, but not necessarily longer. The man of faith places himself under the direction of the Spirit, which will enable him to discern the will of God regarding him if something should prevent his attaining the age of seventy.

Of this we are sure according to the Word of God that our heavenly Father wills, as a rule, to see His children in good health that they may labor in His service. For the same reason, He wills to set them free from sickness as soon as they have made confession of sin and prayed with faith for their healing.

Surely he will save you from the fowler's snare and from the deadly pestilence. . . . You will not fear the terror of night, nor the arrow that flies by day, nor the pestilence that stalks in the darkness, nor the plague that destroys at midday. . . . "With long life will I satisfy him and show him my salvation." . . . They will still bear fruit in old age, they will stay fresh and green.
PSALMS 91:3, 5–6, 16; 92:14

For the believer who has walked with his Savior, and whose body is under the influence of the Holy Spirit, it is not necessary that he should die of sickness. To fall asleep in Jesus Christ seems to be the ideal when the time comes for the believer to leave this life.

Faith is not a logical reasoning that ought in some way to oblige God to act according to His promises. It is rather the confident attitude of the child who honors his Father and who counts on His love to fulfill His promises, and who knows that He is faithful to communicate to the body as well as to the soul the new strength that flows from the moment of redemption until the moment of departure.

Divine Healing

THE HOLY SPIRIT
AND PRAYER

Because you are sons, God sent the Spirit of his Son into our hearts, the Spirit who calls out, "Abba, Father."
GALATIANS 4:6

IS IT NOT UNFORTUNATE that our thoughts about the Holy Spirit are so often coupled with grief and self-reproach? Yet He bears the name of Comforter, or Counselor, and is given to lead us to find in Christ our highest delight and joy. God grant that our meditation on the work of the Holy Spirit may cause rejoicing and the strengthening of our faith!

The Holy Spirit is the Spirit of prayer. He is called in Zechariah 12:10 "a spirit of grace and supplication." Twice in Paul's epistles there is a remarkable reference to Him in the matter of prayer: "For you did not receive a spirit that makes you a slave again to fear, but you received the Spirit of sonship. And by him we cry, 'Abba, Father'" (Romans 8:15).

Have you ever meditated on the words *Abba, Father*? By that address our Savior offered His greatest prayer to the Father, accompanied by the total surrender and sacrifice of His life and love. The Holy Spirit is given for the express purpose of teaching us right from the very beginning of our Christian life to utter those words in childlike trust and surrender.

The Christian left to himself does not know how to pray or what he ought to pray for. But God has stooped to meet us in this helplessness of ours by giving us the Holy Spirit to pray for us. That operation of His Spirit is deeper than our thoughts or feelings, but is acknowledged and answered by God.

Think of it! In every prayer the triune God takes a part—the Father who hears, the Son in whose name we pray, and the Spirit who prays for us and in us. How important it is that we are in right relationship to the Holy Spirit and that we understand His work!

Living a Prayerful Life

THE GREATER THE TASK we undertake the more important the preparation. Four days before Passover the Israelites made preparations. The Lord Jesus also desired that care be taken to obtain an upper room, furnished and ready, where the Passover might be prepared for Him and His disciples to take a Last Supper. When we are called upon to meet God and to sit down at His table, we should see to it that we do not approach it unprepared. Otherwise, we will lose the blessing He has prepared for us.

On the first day of the Feast of Unleavened Bread, when it was customary to sacrifice the Passover lamb, Jesus' disciples asked him, "Where do you want us to go and make preparations for you to eat the Passover?" . . . "He will show you a large upper room, furnished and ready. Make preparations for us there."
MARK 14:12, 15

For the right preparation two things are necessary. First, our hearts should be occupied and filled with Him who has invited us. Thoughts of Jesus and expectations of what His love will do for us lighten the heart and are the best preparation for meeting Him. The second part is to consider our worthiness as guests; are we acceptable and welcome to the Lord of the feast? To set aside thoughts of ourselves and to think on Jesus alone—this is the attitude that leads to a blessed observance of the Supper.

We obtain nothing without taking sufficient time for it. Even where free grace works apart from our striving, we must give it time. It is only when in quietness we resolve to look to Jesus alone that we shall be prepared for the banquet. It is only when we confide in Him in the ordinary tasks of daily life that we can expect blessing from communion with Him at His table. It is in the conflicts of life that hunger and thirst for Him are quickened and the table becomes a feast.

The Lord's Table

HOLINESS AND THE BODY

Offer your bodies as living sacrifices, holy and pleasing to God.
ROMANS 12:1

"WHEN CHRIST CAME into the world, he said, 'A body you prepared for me. . . . Here I am. . . . I have come to do your will, O God' "(Hebrews 10:5, 7). Leaving this world again, it was in His own body that He bore our sins upon the tree. So it was in the body, no less than in soul and spirit, that He did the will of God. When praying for the Thessalonians' sanctification, Paul says, "May God himself, the God of peace, sanctify you through and through. May your whole spirit, soul and body be kept blameless at the coming of our Lord Jesus Christ" (1 Thessalonians 5:23).

A good comparison is that the body is around the soul and spirit like the walls of a city. Through them the enemy may enter. In time of war, the defense of the walls is of prime importance. Let us remember it was through the body that sin entered. "The woman saw that the fruit of the tree was good for food"; this was a temptation to the flesh. Through this the soul was reached: "pleasing to the eye." Through the soul it then passed into the spirit: "and also desirable for gaining wisdom" (Genesis 3:6). Many Christians are unknowingly tripped up by Satan on the question of what is lawful and good. To have every appetite of the body under the rule and regulation of the Holy Spirit appears to some unnecessary, to others too difficult. And yet it must be so if the body is to be holy, as God's temple, and we are to glorify Him in our body and our spirit.

With the body, as it is with the spirit, it is God who works; God in Christ is our keeper and our sanctifier. The guarding of the walls of the city must be entrusted to Him who rules within. Abiding in Him in a life of trust and joy, we shall receive the power to prove, even in the body, how fully and wholly we are in Him who is made unto us sanctification.

The Path to Holiness

THE SPIRIT OF PRAYER

OF THE OFFICES of the Holy Spirit, the one that leads us most deeply into the understanding of His place in the divine economy of grace is the work He does as the Spirit of prayer. We have the Father *to* whom we pray and who hears our prayer. We have the Son *through* whom we pray and through whom we receive and appropriate the answer because of our union with Him. And we have the Holy Spirit, *in* whom we pray, and who prays in us according to the will of God with such deep unutterable sighings that God has to search the hearts to know what is the mind of the Spirit.

Likewise the Spirit also helps in our weaknesses. For we do not know what we should pray for as we ought, but the Spirit Himself makes intercession for us with groanings which cannot be uttered. Now He who searches the hearts knows what the mind of the Spirit is, because He makes intercession for the saints according to the will of God.
ROMANS 8:26–27 (NKJV)

Just as wonderful and real as the work of God on His throne is the work of the Holy Spirit in us in the prayer that waits and obtains an answer. The intercession within is as divine as the intercession above.

What the Father has purposed and the Son has procured can be appropriated and take effect in the body of Christ only through the continual intervention and active operation of the Holy Spirit. This is especially true of intercessory prayer. The coming of the kingdom, the increase of grace, knowledge, and holiness in believers, their growing devotion to God's work, the effectual working of God's power on the unconverted through the means of grace, all await us from God through Christ. The Holy Spirit has been assigned the task of preparing the body of Christ to reach out, receive, and hold on to what has been provided.

The Spirit of Christ

THE ALL-INCLUSIVE CONDITION

"If you abide in Me, and My words abide in you, you will ask what you desire, and it shall be done for you."
JOHN 15:7 (NKJV)

IN ALL GOD'S DEALINGS with us, His promises and their conditions are inseparable. If we fulfill the conditions, He fulfills the promises. What He is to be to us depends upon what we are willing to be to Him. "Come near to God and he will come near to you" (James 4:8). And so in prayer, the unlimited promise "Ask what you desire" has one simple and natural condition: "if you abide in Me." The Father always hears His Son. God is *in Christ*, and can be reached only because He is in Him. To be *in Him* is our guarantee that our prayers are heard. Fully and wholly *abiding in Him*, we have the right to ask whatsoever we will, and the promise that it will be done is ours as well.

When we compare this promise with the experience of most believers, we are startled by an awesome discrepancy. Who can count the prayers that rise to God without an answer? Why is this? Either we do not fulfill the condition, or God does not fulfill the promise.

Believers are not willing to admit either, and therefore have devised a way of escape from the dilemma. They add to the promise the qualifying clause our Savior did not put there: if it is God's will. That way, they maintain both God's integrity and their own. How sad that they do not accept and hold the Word as it stands, trusting Christ to vindicate His truth. Then God's Spirit would lead them to see the divine propriety of such a promise to those who truly abide in Christ—in the sense in which He means it—and to confess that failure to fulfill the condition is the sole explanation for unanswered prayer.

To those who abide in this way, the promise comes as their rightful heritage: Ask what you desire.

Teach Me to Pray

WAITING ON GOD FOR HIS COUNSEL

OUR TEXT REFERS to the sin of God's people in the wilderness. God had wonderfully redeemed them and was prepared to supply all their needs. But

They soon forgot His works; they did not wait for His counsel.
PSALM 106:13 (NKJV)

when needs arose "they did not wait for His counsel." They did not remember that the almighty God was their leader and provider; they did not ask what His plans were. They simply acted on their own thoughts and feelings and tempted and provoked God by their unbelief. Let us take the warning and see what Israel teaches us.

Our whole relationship to God is based on doing His will and being open to His leading. He has promised to make known His will to us by His Spirit, our guide into all truth. And our position is to be that of waiting for His counsel as the only guide for our thoughts and actions. God always works according to the counsel of His will. The more that counsel of His will is looked for, found, and honored, the more surely and mightily will God do His work for us and through us.

There may be elements of God's will, application of His Word, experience of His close presence and leading, and a manifestation of the power of His Spirit about which we know nothing. God is willing to open these up to those who are set on allowing Him to have His way and who are willing to wait for Him to make it known.

When we come together, praising God for all He has done and taught and given, we may at the same time be limiting Him by not expecting greater things. It was when God had given Jericho into his hands that Joshua thought the victory over the city of Ai was sure and did not wait for counsel from God. And so while we think we know and trust the power of God for what we might expect, we may be hindering Him by not practicing the habit of waiting for His counsel.

Waiting on God

THAT YOU MIGHT NOT SIN

In Him there is no sin.
Whoever abides in
Him does not sin.
1 JOHN 3:5–6 (NKJV)

AS LONG AS THE believer abides, and as far as he abides, he does not sin. Our holiness of life has its roots in the personal holiness of Jesus. "If the root is holy, so [also] are the branches" (Romans 11:16 NKJV). The believer who claims the promise in full faith has the power to obey the command, and sin is kept from overpowering him. Ignorance of the promise, unbelief, or carelessness, however, opens the door for sin to reign. And so the life of many believers is a course of continual stumbling and sinning.

But when a believer seeks full admission into a life of continual, permanent abiding in Jesus, the Sinless One, then the life of Christ can keep him from actual transgression. "In Him there is no sin. Whoever abides in Him does not sin." Jesus saves such a believer from his sin—not by the removal of his sinful nature, but by keeping him from yielding to it.

Dear reader, I am not surprised if you find the promise of our text almost too high. Do not, however, let your attention be diverted by the question as to whether it were possible to be kept for your whole life without sinning. Faith only has to deal with the present moment. Let failure and sin, instead of discouraging you, urge you to seek even more your safety by abiding in the Sinless One.

Look upon *His holy human nature as something He prepared for you to partake of with himself*, and you will see that there is something even higher and better than being kept from sin—that is, being restrained from evil. There is the positive and larger blessing of being a vessel purified and cleansed, filled with His fullness, and made a channel for showing forth His power, His blessing, and His glory.

Abiding in Christ

THE WILL OF GOD

THE WILL OF GOD is the living power to which the world owes its existence. Through that will and according to that will the world is what it is. It is

"Your kingdom come, your will be done on earth as it is in heaven."
MATTHEW 6:10

the expression or embodiment of the divine Will in its wisdom, power, and goodness. What it has in beauty and glory it owes to God's having willed it. As that Will formed it, so it upholds it every day. Creation does what it was destined for; it shows forth the glory of God: "Whenever the living creatures give glory, honor and thanks to him who sits on the throne and who lives for ever and ever, the twenty-four elders fall down before him who sits on the throne, and worship him who lives for ever and ever. They lay their crowns before the throne and say: 'You are worthy, our Lord and God, to receive glory and honor and power, for you created all things, and by your will they were created and have their being'" (Revelation 4:9–11).

This is true of inanimate nature. It is even truer of intelligent creatures. The divine Will created a creature-will in its own image and likeness with the living power to know, accept, and cooperate with that Will to which it owes its being. The angels count it their highest honor and happiness to be able to will and to do what God wills and does. The glory of heaven is that God's will is done there.

Redemption is the restoration of God's will to its place in the world. To this end Christ came and showed in a human life that man has but one thing to live for—doing the will of God. He showed us the way to conquer self-will: by obeying God's will even unto death. So He atoned for our self-will, conquering it for us, opening a path through death and resurrection into a life entirely united with and devoted to the will of God.

The Believer's Daily Renewal

THE BLOOD OF THE CROSS

*For it pleased the Father
that in Him all fullness
should dwell, and by Him
to reconcile all things to
Himself . . . having made
peace through the
blood of His cross.*
COLOSSIANS 1:19–20
(NKJV)

WE ARE SO ACCUSTOMED when speaking about the cross of Christ to think only of the work that was done for us. We generally take little notice of the disposition of our Lord that gave the Cross its value.

The Lord Jesus, who came to deliver us from sin and all its devastation, had to deal with the power of sin as well as with its guilt. We need to understand that our Lord by His atonement on the cross removed the guilt of sin, but that this was only possible by the victory He had first won over the *power* of sin. The Lord Jesus had to abolish the power of sin. He could do this only in His own person. Therefore, He came in the closest possible likeness of sinful flesh, in the weakness of flesh, with the fullest capacity to be tempted as we are. From His baptism with the Holy Spirit and the temptation of Satan that followed, up to His soul's awful agony in Gethsemane and the offering of himself on the cross, His life was an unceasing battle against self-will and self-honor, against the temptations of the flesh and of this world, in order to reach His goal—the setting up of His kingdom.

It is because Jesus surrendered and conquered the power of sin in His personal life that He can deliver us from both its power and its guilt. The Cross is the divine sign that proclaims to us that the only way to life in God is through the sacrifice of our self-life.

Beloved Christian, whose hope is in the blood of the cross, give yourself over to the experience of its full blessing. Each drop of that blood points to the surrender and death of self-will as the way to God and life in Him. It assures you of the power of a life that maintains the disposition of Jesus.

The Blood of Christ

Sin and Sickness

HERE, AS IN OTHER Scriptures, the forgiveness of sins and the healing of sickness are closely related. James declares that forgiveness of sins will be granted with our healing; and for this reason he admonishes that confession of sin accompany the prayer that claims healing. Sickness is primarily a consequence of sin. It is because of sin that God permits sickness at all. It is in order to show us our faults, to chasten us, and to purify us from them. Sickness is a visible sign of God's judgment on sin. This is not to say that the one who is sick is necessarily a greater sinner than someone who has good health. On the contrary, it is often the most holy among the children of God whom He chastens, as we see from the example of Job. Neither is it always to point out some fault that we could easily determine ourselves. Rather, it is to draw the attention of the one who is sick to that which remains in him of the "old man," his old life, and all that hinders his being entirely consecrated to God. To confess our sins is to lay them down before God and to subject them to His judgment with the decided intent not to fall into them again. A sincere confession will be followed by new assurance of forgiveness.

When we have consented to make a sincere confession and have obtained pardon, we are ready to lay hold of the promise of God; it is no longer difficult to believe that the Lord will raise us up. His presence is revealed, and His divine life comes to quicken our body.

And the prayer offered in faith will make the sick person well; the Lord will raise him up. If he has sinned, he will be forgiven. Therefore confess your sins to each other and pray for each other so that you may be healed. The prayer of a righteous man is powerful and effective.
JAMES 5:15–16

Divine Healing

The Holy Spirit and the Cross

God sent his Son, born of a woman, born under law, to redeem those under law, that we might receive the full rights of sons.
GALATIANS 4:4–5

THE HOLY SPIRIT always leads us to the cross. It was so with Christ. The Spirit taught Him and enabled Him to offer himself without spot to God.

It was so with the disciples. The Spirit led them to preach Christ as the Crucified One. Later on He led them to glory in the fellowship of the Cross, by which they were deemed worthy to suffer for Christ's sake.

When Christ had borne the cross, He received the Spirit from the Father that He might be poured out. When the three thousand newly converted, mentioned in the book of Acts, bowed before the Crucified One, they received the promise of the Holy Spirit. The union between the Spirit and the Cross is indissoluble; they belong inseparably to one another.

When Moses smote the rock, the water streamed out, and Israel drank of it. When the Rock, Christ, was smitten, and He had taken His place as the slain Lamb on the throne of God, there flowed out from under the throne the fullness of the Holy Spirit for the whole world.

Christ yielded himself unreservedly to the cross. It was the only way to redeem the lost. Integral to the act of self-sacrifice and death was a disposition borne in Him by the Spirit—a disposition that would be imparted to His disciples and to all who put their trust in Him. The cross demands our entire life. To comply with this demand requires nothing less than an act of the will, and for this we are unfit in the natural sense. But if we submit our will to Him who stands waiting to receive us, we will be enabled to do what we could not otherwise do.

Living a Prayerful Life

HOLINESS AND THE WILL OF GOD

It is God's will that you should be sanctified.
1 THESSALONIANS 4:3

IN THE WILL OF GOD we have the union of His wisdom and power. Wisdom decides and declares what is to be and power secures the performance. The declarative will is only one side; its complement, the executive will, is the living energy in which everything good has its origin and existence. So long as we only look at the will of God in the former light, as law, we feel it is a burden, because we do not have the power to perform it—it is too high for us. But when faith looks to the power that works in God's will and carries it out, then faith has the courage to accept and fulfill God's will because it knows God himself is working it out. Seek your sanctification not only as part of the will of God, as a declaration of what He wants you to be, but also as a revelation of what He surely will work out in you.

Will we attempt to accept Christ as Savior without accepting His will? Will we profess to be the Father's children and spend our life debating how much of His will we will do? Shall we be content to go on from day to day with the painful consciousness that our will is not in harmony with God's? Or will we at once and forever give up our will for His—to that which He has already written on our hearts? This surrender is possible. It *can* be made. In a simple, definite transaction with God, we can say that we accept His holy will as ours. Faith knows that God will not pass by such a surrender unnoticed but will accept it.

In the confidence that He takes us up into His heart and breathes His will into us—with the love and the power to perform it—let us enter into God's will and begin a new life, standing and abiding in the very center of His most holy will.

The Path to Holiness

THE WORD AND PRAYER

"If you abide in Me, and My words abide in you, you will ask what you desire, and it shall be done for you."
JOHN 15:7 (NKJV)

GOD'S WORD PREPARES us for prayer by revealing what the Father would have us ask. In prayer, it is God's Word that strengthens us by giving our faith its grounds for asking. And after prayer, it is God's Word that brings the answer, for through it the Spirit shows us that we have heard the Father's voice.

Prayer is not a monologue but a dialogue; God's voice in response to mine is its most essential part. Listening to God's voice is the secret of the assurance that He will listen to mine. What God's words are to me is the test of what He is to me and also of the sincerity of my desire after Him in prayer.

Jesus points to this connection between His Word and our prayer when He says the words of our text. The deep importance of this truth becomes clear as we notice the other expression from which this one is taken: "Abide in Me, and I in you. As the branch cannot bear fruit of itself, unless it abides in the vine, neither can you, unless you abide in Me" (John 15:4 NKJV).

In God's Word God gives us himself. His Word is nothing less than the eternal Son, Jesus Christ. All Christ's words are God's words, full of divine life and power. "It is the Spirit who gives life; the flesh profits nothing. The words that I speak to you are spirit, and they are life" (John 6:63 NKJV).

To pray, or give utterance to certain wishes and appeal to certain promises, is an easy thing, and can be learned by anyone through human wisdom. But to pray in the Spirit and speak words that reach and touch God, that affect and influence the powers of the unseen world—such praying and speaking depend entirely upon our hearing God's voice.

Teach Me to Pray

WAITING ON GOD FOR INCONCEIVABLE THINGS

OUR TEXT EMPHASIZES how God *acts* for those who wait on Him. The King James Version speaks of *what* God has prepared for us. Our responsibility is to wait on God. What will then be revealed is beyond what the human heart can conceive. Whether it is *what* He has prepared or what He will *do* for

For since the beginning of the world men have not heard nor perceived by the ear, nor has the eye seen any God besides You, who acts for the one who waits for Him.
ISAIAH 64:4 (NKJV)

us, either is more than we who are finite human beings should expect from an almighty God. But He wants us to expect it. He wants us to believe and trust Him for what to us is the impossible.

The previous verses to our text refer to the low state of God's people. The prayer has been poured out, "Look down from heaven" (63:15). "Why have you . . . hardened our heart from Your fear? Return for Your servants' sake" (v. 17 NKJV). And 64:1–2 (NKJV) is still more urgent, "Oh, that You would rend the heavens! That You would come down! That the mountains might shake at Your presence—as fire burns brushwood, as fire causes water to boil—to make Your name known to Your adversaries, that the nations may tremble at Your presence!"

The need of God's people, and the call for God's intervention, is as urgent in our day as it was then. Nothing but a special intervention of almighty power will accomplish what is needed. We must desire and believe, we must ask and expect, that God will do what is inconceivable. The miracle-working God, who surpasses all our expectations, must be the God of our confidence.

Yes, let us enlarge our hearts to wait on a God able to do much more than we can ask or think.

Waiting on God

THAT YOUR JOY
MAY BE FULL

"These things I have spoken to you, that My joy may remain in you, and that your joy may be full."
JOHN 15:11 (NKJV)

WE ALL KNOW the value of joy. It alone is the proof that what we have really satisfies the heart. As long as duty, or self-interest, or other motives influence me, no one can know what the object of my pursuit or possession is really worth to me. But when it gives me joy, and they see me delight in it, they know that to me at least it is a treasure. So there is nothing quite so attractive as joy, no preaching so persuasive as the sight of hearts made glad. This makes gladness such a strong element in Christian character. There is no proof of the reality of God's love and the blessing He bestows, which people so quickly feel the strength of, as when the joy of God overcomes all the trials of life. And for the Christian's own welfare, joy is just as indispensable; the joy of the Lord is his strength (see Nehemiah 8:10), and confidence, courage, and patience find their inspiration in joy. With a heart full of joy no work can make us weary and no burden can depress us; God himself is our strength and song.

Whether we look backward and see the work He has done, or upward and see the reward He has in the Father's love that passes knowledge, or forward in anticipation of continual joy experienced as sinners are brought home, His joy is ours. With our feet on Calvary, our eyes on the Father's face, and our hands helping sinners home, we have His joy as our own.

"As sorrowful, yet always rejoicing" (2 Corinthians 6:10 NKJV): These precious words teach us how the joy of Christ can overrule the sorrow of the world, can make us sing even while we weep, and can maintain in the heart, even when cast down by disappointment or difficulties, a deep consciousness of a joy that is unspeakable and full of glory (1 Peter 1:8).

Abiding in Christ

WHAT IS IMPOSSIBLE WITH MEN IS POSSIBLE WITH GOD

CHRIST TOLD THE RICH young ruler, "Sell everything you have and give to the poor, and you will have treasure in heaven. Then come, follow me"

Jesus replied, "What is impossible with men is possible with God."
LUKE 18:27

(v. 22). The young man became sad when he heard this. Christ turned to the disciples and said, "How hard it is for the rich to enter the kingdom of God!" The disciples were greatly astonished and answered, "If it is so difficult to enter the kingdom, who then can be saved?" Christ gave this answer: "What is impossible with men is possible with God."

Your daily spiritual life is proof that God works impossibilities; your spiritual life is a series of impossibilities made possible and actual by God's almighty power. Let us desire and ask for God's power—with all reverence—to keep us and enable us to live like Christ.

Every tree grows on the root from which it springs. An oak tree three hundred years old grows on the same root from which it had its beginning. Christianity had its beginning in the omnipotence of God, and in every soul it must have its continuance by that same power. All the possibilities for spiritual growth have their origin in the apprehension of Christ's power to work all God's will in us.

When God called Abraham to be the father of that people from which Christ was to be born, God said to him, "I am God Almighty; walk before me and be blameless" (Genesis 17:1). God trained Abraham to trust Him as the Omnipotent One. We see it in his departure to a land that he knew not and in his faith as a pilgrim among the Canaanites. We see it in his faith that waited twenty-five years for a son in his old age. Abraham even believed God would raise Isaac from the dead on Mount Moriah when he was told to sacrifice him. He was strong in faith, giving glory to God, because he counted Him who had promised able to perform.

Absolute Surrender

Feeding on the Word

*Your words were found,
and I ate them, and Your
word was to me the joy
and rejoicing of my heart.*
JEREMIAH 15:16 (NKJV)

FIRST, WE *find* God's Word. This only happens to those who diligently seek for it. Next, we *consume* the Word. This is personal appropriation for our own sustenance, the taking into our being the words of God. "'Man shall not live by bread alone, but by every word that proceeds from the mouth of God'" (Matthew 4:4 NKJV). Finally, we *rejoice* in the Word: "'The kingdom of heaven is like treasure hidden in a field, which a man found and hid; and for joy over it he goes and sells all that he has and buys that field'" (Matthew 13:44 NKJV).

Consuming, or eating, is the central thought. It is preceded by the finding and is accompanied and followed by rejoicing. Eating is the aim of searching; it is the cause for rejoicing.

To understand the difference between finding and eating God's words, compare the grain a farmer has stored in his granary with the bread he has on his table. All the diligent labor he has expended in sowing, harvesting, and storing his grain, all the satisfaction he has gained from his work, cannot profit him unless he eats a daily portion of the bread his body requires. The harvesting and storing the high yield are only things we can look at. In the eating, the opposite takes place; here the small quantity, the slow, steady perseverance, characterizes the appropriation. Do you see the application of this to Bible study? You need to find God's words and then, by careful thought, master them so as to have them stored in your mind and memory for your own use and that of others. In this work there may often be great joy, the joy of harvest or of victory, the joy of treasure secured or difficulties overcome. Yet we must remember that finding and possessing the words of God are not the same as *eating* them, which alone brings divine life and strength to the soul.

The Believer's Daily Renewal

THE BLOOD OF THE LAMB

WHEN WE HEAR OUR Lord Jesus referred to as the Lamb of God, two thoughts come to mind. One is that He is the Lamb of God because He was slain as a sacrifice for sin. The other is that He is lamblike: gentle and patient. The first emphasizes the work that He as a lamb had to accomplish; the second emphasizes the gentleness that characterized Him.

"These are they who have come out of the great tribulation; they have washed their robes and made them white in the blood of the Lamb."
REVELATION 7:15

When Jesus was on earth, He said, "Come to me . . . learn from me, for I am gentle and humble in heart, and you will find rest for your souls" (Matthew 11:28–29). This meekness is what places such virtue on His blood. He inflicted a deadly wound on sin, gaining the victory in His own person. He subjected himself to the will of God, and through His whole life, under the severest temptations, He sacrificed himself for the glory of God with a lowliness, patience, and meekness that were the delight of the Father and all the holy angels.

In Him we see humility crowned by God and all-conquering gentleness exalted to the throne. He is able to reveal this very same disposition in our hearts. Just as a garment that is to be colored must be plunged into the dye and become saturated by it, so the soul that constantly bathes and cleanses itself in the blood of the Lamb becomes filled with that disposition that the blood represents. The gentleness and the humility of the Lamb will become the adornment of the soul.

This is why praise is offered in heaven for the blood of the Lamb of God. This is why the Father has placed Him in the midst of the throne as the Lamb that was slain. And this is why believers, in awe and love, glory in the blood of the Lamb and praise His meekness and lowliness as their greatest joy and their one desire.

The Blood of Christ

THE SWORD OF THE SPIRIT

And take the helmet of salvation, and the sword of the Spirit, which is the word of God.
EPHESIANS 6:17 (NKJV)

THE HOLY SPIRIT IS the power of God. The Spirit-filled Christian is strengthened and equipped for God's service and the spiritual warfare related to God's kingdom. He warns them that "we do not wrestle against flesh and blood, but against principalities, against powers, against the rulers of the darkness of this age, against spiritual hosts of wickedness in the heavenly places" (6:12 NKJV). It is crucial for them to live every day clothed in the whole armor of God, standing strong in Christ and in the strength of His might. The believer not only has to meet evil spirits that tempt him but he also has to regard himself as a soldier in the army that Christ leads against the kingdom of darkness in all its forms. In the warfare of the church, the victory of the Cross over the power of Satan is carried out in the same power that raised Christ from the grave.

When Paul says, "Put on the whole armor of God" (v. 11), he begins by defining the various parts of the defense. The Christian needs to realize that his entire personality is defended in the protection of his Lord. Properly defended, he is always ready to take action on the offensive. Paul mentions only one offensive weapon—the sword. That sword is the sword of the Spirit, the Word of God.

To know its power and how to use it effectively, we need only look to our leader, the captain of the Lord's host. When Jesus Christ met Satan in the wilderness, He conquered him by the Word of God alone. He had studied that Word, loved it, obeyed it, and lived it. The Holy Spirit found in Him the familiar words with which He could meet and conquer every satanic suggestion. To take the sword of the Spirit in the hour of battle indicates that I have lived in that Word and it abides in me; I have lived it out and it is the master of my personality.

The Believer's Call to Commitment

THE BODY IS FOR THE LORD

ONE OF THE MOST LEARNED of theologians has said that the redemption and glorification of the body is the chief end of the ways of God. So little is this truth understood by believers that they do not seek for the power of the Holy Spirit in their bodies. Many of them, believing that their body belongs to them, use it as they please. Not understanding how much the sanctification of the soul and spirit depend upon the body, they do not grasp all the meaning of the words "The body is for the Lord."

"Food for the stomach and the stomach for food"—but God will destroy them both. The body is *not meant for sexual immorality, but* for the Lord.
1 CORINTHIANS 6:13
(emphasis added)

Many believers fail to watch over their bodies, to observe a holy sobriety so as to render them fit for the service of God. In the same way, all of what goes to maintain the body—to clothe it, strengthen it, rest it, or afford it enjoyment—should be placed under the control of the Holy Spirit.

One of the chief benefits, then, of divine healing will be to teach us that our body ought to be set free from the yoke of our own will to become the Lord's property. God does not grant healing until He has attained the end for which He permitted the sickness. He desires that this discipline should bring us into a more intimate communion with Him; He would make us understand that we have regarded our body as our own property, while it belonged to the Lord; and that the Holy Spirit seeks to sanctify all its actions. He leads us to understand that if we yield our body unreservedly to the influence of the Holy Spirit, we will experience His power in us, and He will heal us by bringing into our body the very life of Jesus.

Divine Healing

IT MAY BE EXPERIENCED BY ALL

"I will sprinkle clean water on you, and you will be clean; I will cleanse you from all your impurities and from all your idols. . . . And I will put my Spirit in you and move you to follow my decrees and be careful to keep my laws."

EZEKIEL 36:25, 27

A VESSEL INTO WHICH anything precious is to be poured must first be cleansed. So if the Lord is to give you a new and full blessing, cleansing must also take place. Spend time in silent meditation and ask God to expose what your life really is made up of. How much pride, self-seeking, worldliness, self-will, and impurity is there?

This discovery must be followed by the actual putting away of what is impure. You must resolve to undergo a complete transformation. The sins that still cleave to you are to be cast off and done away with. You can give over to God those sins against which you feel utterly ineffective. You can give them up to Him to be dealt with as He desires and He will fulfill His promise. In this way you come to a new discovery, reception, and experience of what Christ is and is prepared to do for you.

What then is required on our part? Only this: When you see that Jesus will carry out this work, you open the door and receive Him into your heart as Lord and King. A house that has remained closed for twenty years can be penetrated by the light in a moment if the doors and windows are thrown open. In like manner, a heart that has remained enveloped in darkness and uselessness because it did not know that Jesus was willing to take the victory over sin into His own hands, can have its whole experience changed in a moment.

Through Jesus Christ, God will so cleanse you from all unrighteousness that day by day you may walk before God with a pure heart. What you really need is the discovery that He is prepared to work this change in you and that you may receive it by faith here and now.

The Fullness of the Spirit

THE HOLY TRINITY

GOD IS AN EVER-FLOWING fountain of pure love and blessedness. Christ is the reservoir wherein the fullness of God was made visible as grace, and has been opened for us. The Holy Spirit is the stream of living water that flows from under the throne of God and of the Lamb.

May the grace of the Lord Jesus Christ, and the love of God [the Father], and the fellowship of the Holy Spirit be with you all.
2 CORINTHIANS 13:14

The Redeemed, God's believing children, are the channels through which the love of the Father, the grace of Christ, and the powerful operation of the Spirit are brought to earth to be imparted to others.

What a clear picture we get here of the wonderful partnership in which God includes us as dispensers of the grace of God! The time we spend in prayer covering our own needs is only the beginning of the life of prayer. The glory of prayer is that we have power as intercessors to bring the grace of Christ and the energizing power of the Spirit upon those souls that are still in darkness. The more we yield ourselves to fellowship with the triune God, the sooner we will gain the courage and ability to intercede for others in our families, in our neighborhoods, and in our churches.

The more closely the channel is connected with the reservoir, the more certainly will the water flow unhindered through it. The more we are occupied in prayer with the fullness of Christ and the Spirit who proceeds from Him, the more firmly will we abide in fellowship with Him and the more surely will our lives be full of joy and strength. Are we truly channels that remain open, so that water may flow through to the thirsty, lost souls in a dry and barren land?

Meditate on this: God is an ever-flowing fountain of love and blessing, and I, as His child, am a living channel through which the Spirit and His life can be brought to earth every day!

Living a Prayerful Life

HOLY AND BLAMELESS

For he chose us in him before the creation of the world to be holy and blameless in his sight.
EPHESIANS 1:4

THERE ARE SAINTS WHO are holy but hard, holy but distant, or holy but sharp in their judgments of others— holy in man's eyes, but also unloving and selfish. The half-heathen Samaritan, for instance, was more kind and self-sacrificing than the holy Levite and priest. Even though this may be true, it is not the teaching of Scripture that is at fault. In linking "holy" and "blameless" so closely, the Holy Spirit leads us to seek for the embodiment of holiness as a spiritual power in the blamelessness of practice and of daily life.

We can see how this blamelessness is particularly related to our relationship with others when we see how it is linked with love: "May the Lord make your love increase and overflow for each other and for everyone else. . . . May he strengthen your hearts so that you will be blameless and holy" (1 Thessalonians 3:12–13). The holiness (the positive, hidden divine life principle) and the blamelessness (the external human life practice) both find their strength, by which we are to be established in them, in our abounding and ever-flowing love.

If holiness is a divine fire, love is its flame. In God's children, true holiness is the same: The divine fire burns to bring into its own blessedness all that comes within its reach. If we would be holy, we must begin by being very gentle and patient, forgiving and kind—generous in our relationships with all God's children. Pray unceasingly that the Lord might cause us to abound in love toward one another. The holiest will be the humblest and most self-forgetting, the gentlest and most self-denying, the kindest and most thoughtful of others for Jesus' sake.

If we abound in this kind of love, we shall be blameless in holiness.

The Path to Holiness

OBEDIENCE: THE PATH TO POWER IN PRAYER

THE FATHER'S PROMISE to give whatever we ask is shown again in the words of John 15:16: "I chose you," the Master says, "and appointed you to go

The prayer of a righteous man is powerful and effective.
JAMES 5:16

and bear fruit—fruit that will last." Then He adds, "Then the Father will give you [the fruit-bearing ones] whatever you ask in my name" (John 15:16). So it appears that the "qualification" for obtaining what we ask for in prayer is to bear fruit as a result of our abiding in Christ.

Some question whether such a statement is at variance with the doctrine of free grace. Look at the words in 1 John 3:18, 21–22: "Let us not love with words or tongue but with actions and in truth. . . . If our hearts do not condemn us, we have confidence before God and receive from him anything we ask, because we obey his commands and do what pleases him." Also note our James text: "The prayer of a righteous man is powerful and effective"; that is, a man of whom it can be said, "He who does what is right is righteous, just as he is righteous" (1 John 3:7).

The spirit of so many of the psalms is a confident appeal to the integrity and righteousness of the supplicant. In Psalm 18, David says, "The LORD has dealt with me according to my righteousness; according to the cleanness of my hands he has rewarded me. . . . I have been blameless before him and have kept myself from sin. The LORD has rewarded me according to my righteousness" (vv. 20, 23–24). If we carefully consider such utterances in the light of the New Testament, we will find them to be in perfect harmony with the explicit teaching of the Savior's parting words: "If you obey my commands, you will remain in my love" (John 15:10); "You are my friends if you do what I command" (John 15:14). The word is indeed meant literally: "I chose you and appointed you to go and bear fruit. . . . *Then* the Father will give you whatever you ask in my name" (John 15:16).

Teach Me to Pray

WAITING ON GOD FOR INSTRUCTION

Show me Your ways, O LORD; teach me Your paths. Lead me in Your truth and teach me, for You are the God of my salvation; on You I wait all the day.

PSALM 25:4–5 (NKJV)

THIS PSALM IS DISTINCTIVE because of the author's repeated expression of his need for divine teaching and his childlike confidence that it will be given. Study the psalm until your heart is filled with two thoughts: the absolute need for divine guidance and the absolute certainty of receiving it. It is with these thoughts in mind that the psalmist declares, "On You I wait all the day." Waiting for guidance or instruction throughout the day is a very blessed part of waiting on God.

The Father in heaven is so interested in His children and so longs to have them in step with His will and His love that He is willing to hold their guidance in His own hands. He knows so well that we do not naturally do what is holy except when He works it in us, that He makes His demands the same as promises of what He will do to watch over us and lead us through the day. We may count on Him to teach us His way and to show us His path not only in special trials and hard times but also in everyday life.

Are we convinced that the way to receive this guidance is by daily waiting on Him for instruction? We must acknowledge our need and declare our faith in His help. We will have a deep, restful assurance that He hears and answers. "The humble He teaches His way" (Psalm 25:9 NKJV).

"On You I wait all the day." As simple as it is to walk all day in the light of the sun, it can become simple and delightful for a soul who has practiced waiting on God to walk all day in the enjoyment of God's light and leading. The one thing needed for such a life is the knowledge and faith that God is our only source of wisdom and goodness.

Waiting on God

THE CRUCIFIED ONE

"I HAVE BEEN CRUCIFIED with Christ": Here the apostle expresses his assurance of his fellowship with Christ in His sufferings and death, and his full participation in all the power and the

"I have been crucified with Christ; it is no longer I who live, but Christ lives in me."
GALATIANS 2:20 (NKJV)

blessing of that death. The apostle Paul is so convinced of this and the fact that he is now indeed dead that he adds: "It is *no longer I who live*, but Christ lives in me" (emphasis added).

I must learn to look upon the Cross as not only atonement to God but also a victory over the devil; it is not only deliverance from the guilt but also from the power of sin. I must gaze on Him on the cross, seeing Him as the One who offered himself in order to receive me into the closest possible union and fellowship. Through Him I can partake of the full power of His death to sin and the new life of victory to which it is but the gateway. My part is simply to yield myself to Him in undivided surrender, with much prayer and strong desire, asking to be admitted into the ever-closer fellowship and conformity of His death by the power of the Spirit in which He died that death.

It is a deep mystery, this cross of Christ. I am afraid there are many Christians who look upon the cross, Christ dying on it for their sins, who have little heart for fellowship with the Crucified One.

We know how Peter knew and confessed Christ as the Son of the living God while the cross was still an offense to him (Matthew 16:16–17, 21, 23). The faith that believes in the blood that pardons and the life that renews can only reach its perfect growth as it abides beneath the Cross and in living fellowship with Him seeks for perfect conformity with Jesus the Crucified.

Abiding in Christ

THE INWARD AND
THE OUTWARD

You foolish people! Did not the one who made the outside make the inside also?
LUKE 11:40

EVERY SPIRIT SEEKS to create for itself a form or shape in which to embody its life, the outward being the visible expression of the hidden inward life. Of course, the outward is generally known before the inward; and through it the inward is developed and reaches its full perfection. The apostle says in 1 Corinthians 15:46, "The spiritual did not come first, but the natural, and after that the spiritual." To understand and maintain the right relationship between the inward and the outward is one of the greatest secrets of the Christian life.

If Adam had not listened to the Tempter, his trial would have resulted in the perfection of his inward life. His sin, his ruin, and all his misery came because he gave himself over to the power of the visible outward world. Instead of seeking his happiness in the hidden inward life of obedience, love, and dependence on God, he focused his desire on the tangible world around him, on the pleasure and the knowledge of good and evil that it could give him.

All false religion—from the most degrading idolatry to the corruption of Judaism and Christianity—has its root in what is outward. What can please the eye, interest the mind, or gratify earthly pleasure displaces truth in the inward part, that hidden wisdom in the heart and life that God alone can give.

The great characteristic of the New Testament is that it is a dispensation of the inner life. The promise of the new covenant is "I will put my law in their minds and write it on their hearts" (Jeremiah 31:33); "I will give you a new heart and put a new spirit in you" (Ezekiel 36:26). It is in a heart into which God has placed the Spirit of His Son, a heart in which the love of God is shed abroad, that true salvation is found.

The Believer's Daily Renewal

WHAT'S IN A NAME?

WHAT IS A PERSON'S NAME? It is that word or expression by which the person is called or known. When I mention or hear a name, it brings to mind the whole man—what I know of him and the impression he has made on me. The name of a king includes his honor, his power,

> *"And whatever you ask in My name, that I will do, that the Father may be glorified in the Son. If you ask anything in My name, I will do it."*
> JOHN 14:13–14 (NKJV)

and his kingdom. His name is the symbol of his power. And so each name of God embodies and represents some part of the glory of the unseen One. The name of Christ is the expression of all He has done and all He is and lives to do as our Mediator.

What does it mean to do something in someone's name? It is to come with the power and authority of that one, as his representative and substitute. We know how such use of another's name always presumes a common interest. No one would give another the free use of his name without first being assured that his honor and interest were as safe with that person as with himself.

And what does it mean when Jesus gives us power in His name, the free use of it, with the assurance that whatever we ask in it will be given to us? The ordinary comparison of one person giving another person the liberty to ask something in his name comes altogether short here. Jesus solemnly gives to *all* His disciples a general and unlimited power of the free use of His name at *all* times for *all* they desire. He could not do this if He did not know that He could trust us with His interests, that His honor would be safe in our hands. The free use of the name of another is always the token of great confidence and of close union. He who gives his name to another stands aside to let that person act for him.

Teach Me to Pray

THE HOLY SPIRIT

From the beginning God chose you to be saved through the sanctifying work of the Spirit and through belief in the truth.

2 THESSALONIANS 2:13

THE NAME *Holy Spirit* teaches us that it is particularly the work of the Spirit to impart holiness to us and make it our own.

Try to realize the meaning of this: The expression that through the whole Old Testament has belonged to the Holy God is now appropriated to that Spirit that is within you. The holiness of God in Christ becomes holiness in you because His Spirit is in you. The words *Holy* and *Spirit* and the divine realities they express are now inseparably and eternally united. *You can only have as much of the Spirit as you are willing to have of holiness.* And you can only have as much holiness as you have of the indwelling Spirit.

Some pray for the Spirit because they long to have His light and joy and strength, but their prayers bring little increase of blessing or power. It is because they do not truly know or desire Him as the *Holy* Spirit. They do not know His burning purity, His searching and convicting light, His putting to death the deeds of the body, of self with its will and its power, and His leading into the fellowship of Jesus as He gave up His will and His life to the Father.

How is it that this Holy Spirit makes us holy? He reveals and imparts the holiness of Christ. How do we obtain the working of the Holy Spirit? The answer is clear. He is the Spirit of the Holy Father and of Christ, the Holy One of God: He must be received from them.

Bow to the Father in the name of Christ, His Son; believe very simply in the Son as Him in whom the Father's love and blessing reach us. Then we may be assured that the Spirit, who is already within us as the Holy Spirit, will do His work in ever-increasing power.

The Path to Holiness

THE HOLY SPIRIT, THE
SPIRIT OF HEALING

WHAT IS IT THAT distinguishes the children of God from the children of the world? What is their glory? It is that God dwells in the midst of them and reveals himself to them in power. God sends the Holy Spirit to His church, which is the body of Christ, to act in her with power, and her life and her prosperity depend on Him. In every age the church may look for manifestations of the Spirit, for they form our indissoluble

There are different kinds of gifts, but the same Spirit. . . . to another faith by the same Spirit, to another gifts of healing by that one Spirit. . . . All these are the work of one and the same Spirit, and he gives them to each one, just as he determines.
1 CORINTHIANS 12:4, 9, 11

unity: "one body and one Spirit" (Ephesians 4:4).

The gift of healing is one of the most beautiful manifestations of the Spirit. It is recorded of Jesus, "how God anointed Jesus of Nazareth with the Holy Spirit and power, and how he went around doing good and healing all who were under the power of the devil, because God was with him" (Acts 10:38). The Holy Spirit in Him was a healing Spirit, and He was the same in the disciples after Pentecost. Thus the words of our text express what was the continuous experience of the early churches.

Divine healing is the work of the Holy Spirit. Christ's redemption extends its powerful working to the body, and the Holy Spirit is in charge of transmitting it to us and maintaining it in us. It is God's will that His Son should be glorified, and the Holy Spirit does this when He comes to show us what the redemption of Christ does for us. The redemption of the mortal body appears almost more marvelous than that of the immortal soul. In these two ways God wills to dwell in us through Christ and thus to triumph over the flesh. As soon as our body becomes the temple of God through the Spirit, Jesus is glorified.

Divine Healing

The Importance of Obedience

IT WAS BECAUSE CHRIST humbled himself and became obedient unto death, even death on the cross, that God so highly exalted Him. In this connection Paul exhorts us: "Your attitude should be the same as that of Christ Jesus" (Philippians 2:5). We see, above everything else, that the obedience of Christ, so pleasing to God, must become the basic characteristic of our disposition and of our entire walk.

The Scripture says that we are to be led by the Spirit and that we must walk by the Spirit. My right relationship to the Holy Spirit is that I allow myself to be guided and ruled by Him. Notice how the Lord Jesus, giving His great promise about the Holy Spirit on His last night, emphasized this point: "If you love me, you will obey what I command. And I will ask the Father, and he will give you another Counselor to be with you forever" (John 14:15–16). Obedience was essential as preparation for the reception of the Spirit.

How little we believe that Christ asks for, expects this, from us—because He has undertaken to make it possible for us. How much is it manifested in our prayer, our walk, or in the depths of our spiritual life that we seek to please the Lord in all things? *Christ holds himself responsible to work this out in me every moment, if I only trust Him for it.*

I begin to understand the important phrase with which Paul begins the book of Romans: "obedience that comes from faith" (Romans 1:5). Faith brings me to the Lord Jesus not only for forgiveness of sin but also every moment to enjoy the power that enables me as a child of God to abide in Him and to be numbered among His obedient children.

Living a Prayerful Life

THE SPIRIT OF PRAYER

THESE WORDS ARE connected with the preceding context: "Be strong in the Lord. . . . Put on the whole armor of God" (Ephesians 6:10–11 NKJV). Our battle is against the spiritual hosts of wickedness in heavenly places. We are to put on the whole armor of God, both defensive and offensive, with prayer and supplication, praying at all times in the Spirit. Even putting on the armor and wielding the sword of the Spirit are to be done in total dependence upon God.

Praying always with all prayer and supplication in the Spirit, being watchful to this end with all perseverance and supplication for all the saints; and for me, that utterance may be given to me, that I may open my mouth boldly to make known the mystery of the gospel.
EPHESIANS 6:18–19 (NKJV)

A life of prayer is the secret of a life of victory. Praying always in the Spirit is the mark of a normal Christian life. As unceasingly as my lungs take in air and my heart continues to beat by the divine power that upholds my physical life, the Holy Spirit continually breathes in me that prayer life through which the powers of the divine life are maintained. Salvation is not won by works, by my own effort, or by struggling. It is a gift. But I am God's workmanship, created in Christ Jesus *for* good works that God declares are already prepared for me to walk in. Unceasing prayer is possible, even commanded, because the eternal Spirit maintains it as the spiritual breathing of the soul.

Praying at all times is never to be selfish in nature, remembering only our own needs. Paul speaks here of the unity of the saints as forming one great army as the host of the Lord, living by one Spirit and striving together for the establishment of His kingdom in the world. Continual prayer for all believers is not only the responsibility of each member but the essential factor upon which the welfare and the victory of the whole body depends.

The Believer's Call to Commitment

WAITING ON GOD FOR MORE THAN WE KNOW

And now, Lord, what do I wait for? My hope is in You. Deliver me from all my transgressions.
PSALM 39:7–8 (NKJV)

THERE MAY BE TIMES when we do not know what we are waiting for, but we know we need to be in His presence. Other times we *think* we know, and it would be better to just wait on Him without an agenda. He is able to do for us immeasurably more than all we ask or think, and we are in danger of limiting Him when we always confine our desires and prayers to our own thoughts. It is a good thing at times to say with the psalmist, "And now, Lord, what do I wait for?" That is, I hardly know; I can only say, "My hope is in You."

We clearly see a limiting of God in the case of Israel. When Moses promised them meat in the wilderness, they doubted, saying, "Can God prepare a table in the wilderness? . . . He struck the rock, so that the waters gushed out. . . . Can He give bread also? Can He provide meat for His people?" (Psalm 78:19–20 NKJV). If they had been asked whether God could provide streams in the desert, they would have answered yes. God had done it; He could do it again. But when the thought came that God might do something new, they limited Him. Their expectation could not rise beyond past experience or their own thoughts of what was possible. In the same way, we may limit God by our concept of what He has promised or what He is able to do. Let us be careful not to limit the Holy One of Israel by the way we pray. Let us believe that the very promises of God we claim have divine merit beyond our thought or imagination.

In waiting on God, you may grow weary because you don't know what to expect. But be encouraged. Ignorance is often a good sign. He is teaching you to leave everything in His hands and to wait on Him alone.

Waiting on God

IT IS IN THE LEISURE hours, when we are free from constraint and observation, that we are more apt to reveal what is truly important to us. In the spiritual life this is true as well. While in college or school, for instance, the mind of a stu-

If the owner of the house had known at what hour the thief was coming, he would not have let his house be broken into.
LUKE 12:39

dent is inclined toward systematic work so that his time for devotions or Bible study is often kept as regularly as classes or lesson study. When extended periods of relaxation occur, and we are free to do exactly as we wish, we may find that Bible study and fellowship with God in prayer do not come so naturally. And so the time of leisure becomes a test of character, the proof as to whether one could say with Job, "I have treasured the words of his mouth more than my daily bread" (23:12). The abrupt relaxation of regular habits and the subtle thought that we are at liberty to do as we please, sets many a person back in his Christian life.

The progress of months may be lost by the neglect of one week. We do not know at what hour the thief will come. The spirit of the morning watch means constant vigilance all day and every day. Just as we need during leisure hours to eat regular meals and breathe fresh air, so we need to daily eat the bread of life and breathe the air of heaven. The morning devotional hour is not only a duty but an unspeakable privilege and pleasure. Fellowship with God, abiding in Christ, loving His Word and meditating on it throughout the day is life and strength to the Christian, health and gladness to the new nature.

God has created and redeemed us so that through us He may—as the sun illuminates the world—shine His light and life and love upon the people around us. In order to do this, we need to be in daily communication with the fountain of light.

The Believer's Daily Renewal

THE LORD IS FOR THE BODY

The body is not meant for sexual immorality, but for the Lord, and the Lord for the body.
1 CORINTHIANS 6:13
(emphasis added)

THERE IS RECIPROCITY IN God's relationship with man. That which God has been for me, I ought in turn to be for Him. And that which I am for Him, He desires to be for me. In saying, "The body is for the Lord," we express the desire to regard our body as wholly consecrated, offered in sacrifice to the Lord and sanctified by Him. In saying, "The Lord is for the body," we express the precious certainty that our offering has been accepted and that by His Spirit the Lord will impart to our body His strength and holiness and that He will keep us.

This truth has various applications. Our temper is often a result of our physical constitution. A nervous, irritable state produces words that are sharp, harsh, and lacking in love. But let the body with this physical tendency be taken to the Lord, and it will soon experience the power of the Holy Spirit to overcome the rising of impatience, sanctify the body, and render it blameless.

These words, "The Lord is for the body," are applicable also to the physical strength that the Lord's service demands. Many believers have experienced that the promise "Those who hope in the LORD will renew their strength" (Isaiah 40:31) touches the body, and that the Holy Spirit increases their physical strength.

But it is especially in divine healing that we see the truth of these words, "The Lord is for the body." Yes, Jesus, the sovereign and merciful healer, is always ready to save and to heal. Therefore, give Him your body. Give it to Him with your sickness and your sin. Believe that the Lord has taken charge of your body, and He will manifest with power that He truly is the Lord who is for the body.

Divine Healing

THE MORE ABUNDANT LIFE

A MAN MAY HAVE LIFE, and still through lack of nourishment or through illness there may be no abundance of life or power. This was the distinction between the Old Testament and the New. In the former there was life under the

> *"The thief comes only to steal and kill and destroy; I have come that they may have life, and have it to the full."*
> JOHN 10:10

law but not the abundance of grace of the New Testament. Christ had given life to His disciples, but they could receive the abundant life only through His resurrection and the gift of the Holy Spirit.

All true Christians have received life from Christ. The majority, however, know nothing about the more abundant life that He is willing to bestow. Paul speaks constantly of this. He says of himself that the grace of God was exceedingly abundant, that he could do all things through Christ. He thanked God, who always caused him to triumph in Christ. He was more than a conqueror through Him who loves us. We must not be satisfied with a weakened life but must seek an abundant life.

What is it that particularly constitutes this abundant life? We cannot too often repeat it or in different ways too often explain it: The abundant life is nothing less than Jesus having full mastery over our entire being through the power of the Holy Spirit.

Not long ago I read an interesting thought: "Live in what must be." Do not live limited by your human imagination of what is possible. Live in the Word—in the love and infinite faithfulness of the Lord Jesus. Even though it goes slowly, with many a faltering step, the faith that always thanks Him—not for experiences but for the promises on which it can rely—goes on from strength to strength, ever increasing in the blessed assurance that God himself will perfect His work in us.

Living a Prayerful Life

IN CHRIST OUR SANCTIFICATION

That is what some of you were. But you were washed, you were sanctified, you were justified in the name of the Lord Jesus Christ and by the Spirit of our God.

1 CORINTHIANS 6:11

IN CHRIST'S LIFE the holiness that before had only been revealed in symbol and as a promise of good things to come took possession of a human will and was made one with human nature. In His death every obstacle was removed that could prevent the transmission of that holy nature to us: Christ truly became our sanctification. In the Holy Spirit the actual communication of that holiness took place.

This life is meant for the sinful and the weary, for the unworthy and the impotent. It is a life that is the gift of the Father's love and a life that He will reveal in each one who comes in childlike trust to Him. It is a life that is meant for our everyday life. In every varying circumstance and situation this life will make and keep us holy.

Before our Lord left the world, He said, "And surely I am with you always, to the very end of the age" (Matthew 28:20). In the Holy Spirit the Lord Jesus is with His people here on earth. Though unseen and not in the flesh, His personal presence is as real on earth as when He walked with His disciples. In regeneration the believer is taken out of his old place "in the flesh." He is no longer in the flesh, but in the Spirit (Romans 8:9). He is actually in Christ. The living Christ is around him by His holy presence. Wherever and whatever he is, however ignorant of his position or however unfaithful to it, he is in Christ.

Be content to leave all your weakness, foolishness, and faithlessness to Him in the quiet confidence that He will do for you more than you could ever ask or think. And so from now on let it be as it is written: He that glories, let him glory in the Lord.

The Path to Holiness

THE HOLY SPIRIT AND PRAYER

TO UNDERSTAND HOW the coming of the Holy Spirit was indeed to begin a new epoch in the prayer-world, we must remember who He is, what His work is, and the significance of His not being given until Jesus was glorified. It is in the Spirit that God exists, for He is Spirit. It is in the Spirit that the Son was begotten of the Father. It is in the fellowship of the Spirit that the Father and the Son are one. The eternal, never-ending giving to the Son that is the Father's prerogative, and the eternal asking and receiving that is the Son's right and blessedness—it is through the Spirit that this communion of life and love is maintained. It has been so from all eternity. It is especially so now, when the Son as Mediator ever lives to pray for us.

"In that day you will no longer ask me anything. I tell you the truth, my Father will give you whatever you ask in my name. Until now you have not asked for anything in my name. Ask and you will receive, and your joy will be complete."
JOHN 16:23–24

The great work of reconciling in His own body God and man, which Jesus began on earth, is now carried on in heaven. To accomplish this, He took up in His own person the conflict between God's righteousness and our sin. In His own body on the cross He once for all ended the struggle. Then He ascended to heaven so that from there He might in each member of His body carry out the deliverance and manifest the victory He had obtained. To do this, He ever lives to pray, and in His unceasing intercession, He places himself in living fellowship with the unceasing prayer of His redeemed ones. It is His intercession that shows itself in our prayers and gives them power that they never had before. All this is done through the Holy Spirit.

Teach Me to Pray

WAITING ON GOD FOR REDEMPTION

There was a man in Jerusalem called Simeon, who was righteous and devout. He was waiting for the consolation of Israel, and the Holy Spirit was upon him. . . . There was also a prophetess, Anna . . . [who] spoke about the child to all who were looking forward to the redemption of Jerusalem.
LUKE 2:25, 36, 38

HERE WE HAVE THE MARKS of a waiting believer. *Righteous* in all his conduct, *devout*, devoted to God and always walking in His presence; *waiting for the consolation of Israel*, looking for the fulfillment of God's promises: *and the Holy Spirit was upon him*. Through devoted waiting, Simeon was prepared for the blessing. Anna spoke of Him (the Christ child) to all who looked for redemption in Jerusalem. The mark of a godly group of men and women in Jerusalem, in the middle of surrounding formalism and worldliness, was that they were waiting on God for His promised redemption.

Now that the Consolation of Israel has come and our redemption has been accomplished, we wait on God in the full power of the redemption, but we still wait for its full revelation. Our waiting on God is now in the wonderful knowledge that we are accepted in the beloved and that we are living in that love in the actual presence of God. The old saints took their stand on the Word of God. Waiting and hoping on that Word, we, too, rest on it—but it is a far greater privilege to be joined to Christ Jesus!

We are just as dependent on God for the revelation of redemption in us as were the saints of old in their anticipation of it. The sense of complete and absolute powerlessness, and the confidence that God can and will do all, must be the signs of our waiting on God today. As gloriously as God proved himself in the past as the faithful and wonder-working God, He will prove himself to us today.

Waiting on God

THE POWER OF DAILY RENEWAL

EVERY DAY OUR NATURAL life is renewed. The sun rises with its light and warmth, the flowers open, the birds sing, and life is everywhere stirred and strengthened. As we rise from a night's

Though outwardly we are wasting away, yet inwardly we are being renewed day by day.
2 CORINTHIANS 4:16

sleep and refresh ourselves with food, we feel we have gathered new strength for the duties of the day. Awareness of our need for prayer and reading the Word each day is the confession that our inward life needs daily renewal, too. Only by fresh nourishment from God's Word and fresh communion with God himself in prayer can the vitality of the spiritual life be maintained and grow. Just as our bodies need rest and nourishment for daily life as well as for times of sickness, stress of work, and fatigue, so the inward man must be renewed daily.

Even our time of quiet and prayer and study of the Word is only effective when the Spirit of God works through them. Our study would be lacking if we did not emphasize the daily renewal of the inward person, which the Spirit himself performs. In Romans 12:2 we read of the progressive transformation of the Christian life that comes by "the renewing of [the] mind." In Ephesians 4:22–23, the word "to put off your old self" indicates an act done once for all, but the word "be made new in the attitude of your minds" is in the present tense and indicates a progressive work. It says in Colossians 3:10, "Put on the new self, which is being renewed in knowledge in the image of its Creator." We are to look to the blessed Spirit on whom we can count for daily renewal of the inner person in the place of prayer.

The Believer's Daily Renewal

A Manifestation of God's Power

IS IT PERMISSIBLE to pray in this way, to ask the Lord to enable His servants to speak His Word with great boldness and that He stretch out His hand to heal?

The Word of God encounters as many difficulties in our day as it did then, and the needs today are equally pressing. Imagine the apostles in the midst of Jerusalem: on the one hand there were the rulers of the people with their threatenings; on the other, the blind multitude refusing to believe in the crucified Christ. The world today may not be so openly hostile to the church because it has lost its fear of her, but its flattering words are more to be dreaded than its hatred. Dissimulation is sometimes worse than violence. The help of God is as necessary now as it was then. The apostles well knew that it was not the eloquence of their preaching that caused the truth to triumph but the manifest presence of the Holy Spirit through miracles. It was necessary that the living God stretch forth His hand in healings, miracles, and signs in the name of Jesus. It was then that His servants rejoiced and were strengthened by His presence. It was then that they could speak His Word with boldness and teach the world to fear His name.

The divine promises are also for us. It is nowhere to be found in the Bible that this promise was not for future times. In all ages God's people need to know that the Lord is with them and to possess the irrefutable proof of it. Therefore, this promise is for us; let us pray for its fulfillment.

Divine Healing

LET THE SPIRIT TEACH YOU

DO YOU EVER WONDER why there are not more men and women who can witness, with joyful hearts, that the Spirit of God has taken possession of them and given them new power to witness? What is it that hinders us? The Father in heaven is more willing than an earthly father to give bread to his child, and yet the cry arises: "Is the Spirit restricted or hampered? Is this His work?"

Who is it that overcomes the world? Only he who believes that Jesus is the Son of God. This is the one who came by water and blood—Jesus Christ. . . . And it is the Spirit who testifies, because the Spirit is the truth.
1 JOHN 5:5–6

Some will acknowledge that the hindrance undoubtedly lies in the fact that the church is under the sway of the flesh and the world. They understand too little of the heart-changing power of the cross of Christ. Because of this, the Spirit does not have vessels into which He can pour His fullness.

But I bring you a message of joy. The Spirit who is in you, in however limited a measure, is prepared to bring you under His teaching, to lead you to the cross, and by His heavenly instruction to make you aware of what the crucified Christ wants to do for you and in you.

He will show you how the neglect of private prayer has hindered your fellowship with Christ; He will reveal the cross to you and the powerful operation of the Spirit. He will teach you what is meant by self-denial, taking up your cross daily, and losing your life in order to follow Him.

In spite of your having acknowledged your ignorance, your lack of spiritual insight and fellowship with the cross, He is willing to teach you and to make known to you the secret of a spiritual life beyond all your expectations.

Living a Prayerful Life

The Holy One of God

"We believe and know that you are the Holy One of God."
JOHN 6:69

ONLY ONCE IS THE expression "holy one of the Lord" found in the Old Testament. It is applied to Aaron, in whom holiness, as far as it could then be revealed, had found its most complete embodiment. The title waited for its fulfillment in Him who alone, in His own person, could perfectly reveal the holiness of God on earth—Jesus the Son of the Father. In Him we see true holiness, as divine, as human, as our very own.

In the Son we see divine holiness tested. He is tried and tempted. He suffers, being tempted. He proves that holiness has indeed a moral worth: it is ready to make any sacrifice, even to give up life and cease to be rather than consent to sin.

But this is only one side of holiness. The fire that consumes also purifies: it makes partakers of its own beautiful light-nature capable of assimilation. In Him was seen the affinity holiness has for all that are lost and helpless and sinful. He proved that holiness is not only the energy that separates itself *from* all that are impure but also in holy love separates *to* itself even the most sinful, to save and to bless. In Him we see how the divine holiness is the harmony of infinite righteousness with infinite love.

He is the one Holy One whom God sees, of such an infinite compass and power of holiness that He can be holiness to each of His brethren. Just as He is to God the Holy One, in whom God delights and for whose sake He delights in all who are in Christ, even so now Christ may be to us the only Holy One in whom we delight.

Study and pray to believe and understand that it is in Christ as the Holy One of God, in whom the holiness of God is prepared for you, that you may continue to abide. Study holiness in the light of His countenance.

The Path to Holiness

WAITING ON GOD TO SUPPLY

IF AN ARMY HAS BEEN sent out to march into enemy territory and news is received that it is not advancing, the question is at once asked, "What is the cause of the delay?" The answer will very often be: "Waiting for supplies." If provisions of gear or ammunition have

The LORD upholds all who fall, and raises up all who are bowed down. The eyes of all look expectantly to You, and You give them their food in due season.
PSALM 145:14–15 (NKJV)

not arrived, they dare not proceed. It is no different in the Christian life: Day by day we need our supplies from above. And there is nothing so necessary as cultivating a spirit of dependence on God and of confidence in Him that refuses to go on without the needed supply of grace and strength.

It is especially at the time of prayer that we ought to cultivate this spirit of quiet waiting. Before you pray, bow quietly before God; remember and realize who He is, how near He is, how certainly He can and will help. Be still before Him and allow His Holy Spirit to awaken in your soul the childlike disposition of absolute dependence and confident expectation. Wait on God as you would a living person. He is the living God who is aware of you and is longing to fill all of your needs. Wait on God until you know you have met Him; your prayer time will never be the same.

Waiting on Him will become the most blessed part of prayer, and the answer to your prayer will be twice as precious because it is the fruit of fellowship with Him.

God provides in nature for the creatures He has made. How much more will He provide in grace for those He has redeemed! Learn to say about every want, failure, or lack of the grace you need: I have waited too little on God. He would have given me in due season all I needed.

Waiting on God

THE PATTERN FOR DAILY RENEWAL

Do not lie to each other, since you have taken off your old self with its practices and have put on the new self, which is being renewed in knowledge in the image of its Creator.
COLOSSIANS 3:9–10

IN EVERY PURSUIT it is important to have clearly defined goals. It is not enough that there is some progress; you will want to know whether you are moving in the right direction. If you are working in partnership with someone else, you will need to know that your aim and his are in perfect accord. If our daily renewal is to attain its objective, we will need to know clearly its purpose and then hold to it. The divine life, which is the work of the Holy Spirit within us, is not a blind force. We are to be workers *together* with God; our cooperation is to be intelligent and voluntary—the new man is being renewed day by day in righteousness.

There is no knowledge that our natural understanding can draw from the Word unless it is that which is void of life and power—unlike the real truth and substance that spiritual knowledge brings. The renewing of the Holy Spirit gives true knowledge—such that does not consist of thought and concept, but a living reception of the things of which words and thoughts are but images. However diligent our Bible study may be, there is no true knowledge gained beyond the spiritual renewal that is experienced; only renewal in the spirit of your mind brings true divine knowledge.

We have been predestined, redeemed, and called, and we are being taught and shaped by the Holy Spirit to be conformed to the image of the Son, to be imitators of God, and to walk as Christ walked. How can daily renewal be carried on; what can daily Bible study and prayer profit, unless we set our heart on what God has set His on: the new man being renewed day by day after the image of Him who created him.

The Believer's Daily Renewal

THE POWERFUL AND EFFECTIVE PRAYER

JAMES KNEW THAT a faith that obtains healing is not the fruit of human nature; therefore he adds that the prayer must be "powerful." Only such prayer can be effective. In this he stands on the example of Elijah, a man "just like us," drawing the inference that our prayer can be and ought to be of the same nature as his. How did Elijah pray?

Elijah had received from God the promise that rain was about to fall upon the earth and he had declared this to Ahab. Strong in the promise of his God, he mounted Carmel to pray (1 Kings 18:42). He knew that it was God's will to send rain, but he also knew he needed to pray or the rain would not come.

Therefore confess your sins to each other and pray for each other so that you may be healed. The prayer of a righteous man is powerful and effective. Elijah was a man just like us. He prayed earnestly that it would not rain, and it did not rain on the land for three and a half years. Again he prayed, and the heavens gave rain, and the earth produced its crops.
JAMES 5:16–18

This is how prayer is to be made for the sick. The promise of God must be relied on and His will to heal recognized. After the prayer of faith, comes the prayer of perseverance, which does not lose sight of what has been asked until God has fulfilled His promise. It might seem strange to us that after having prayed with the certainty of being heard and seeing in it the will of God, we should still need to pray. In Gethsemane Jesus prayed three times in succession. On Mount Carmel Elijah prayed seven times; and we, if we believe the promise of God without doubting, shall pray until we receive the answer. If we learn to persevere in prayer, we will obtain, as Jesus did when He was on earth, the healing of the sick, often a miraculous healing that glorifies God.

Divine Healing

WHAT HINDERS THE BLESSING?

Then Jesus said to his disciples, "If anyone would come after me, he must deny himself and take up his cross and follow me. For whoever wants to save his life will lose it, but whoever loses his life for me will find it."
MATTHEW 16:24–25

MANY SINCERELY SEEK the full blessing of Pentecost and yet do not find it. The question comes, What causes this failure? Sometimes the answer is the presence of some sin that is still permitted. Worldliness, lack of love or humility, ignorance of intimate walking in the way of faith—these and many more causes could be mentioned. There are, however, many who think they have come to the Lord with the source of their failure and have sincerely confessed it and put it away and yet the blessing does not come. For them it is particularly necessary to point out that there remains one great hindrance—the root from which all other hindrances come.

It is nothing other than self with its varied forms of self-seeking, self-pleasing, self-confidence, and self-satisfaction. Peter had uttered such a glorious confession of his Lord that Jesus said to him: "Blessed are you, Simon son of Jonah, for this was not revealed to you by man, but by my Father in heaven" (Matthew 16:17). But when the Lord began to speak of His death by crucifixion, Peter was motivated by Satan to say: "Never, Lord! This shall never happen to you!" (v. 22). The Lord then said that not only must He lay down His life, but this same sacrifice was to be made by every disciple.

Why should a Christian be called upon to part with his life? The answer is very simple. It is because that life is completely under the power of sin and death. The self-life must be wholly taken away to make room for the life of God. Your own life and the life of God cannot both fill your heart.

The Fullness of the Spirit

THE SPIRIT OF THE CROSS
IN OUR LORD

SOMETIMES WE SEEK for the operation of the Spirit with the purpose of obtaining more power for work, more love in our life, more holiness in the heart, more light on Scripture or on our path. But all these gifts are subordinate to the great purpose of God. The Father bestowed the Spirit on the Son, and the

I pray that out of his glorious riches he may strengthen you with power through his Spirit in your inner being, so that Christ may dwell in your hearts through faith.
EPHESIANS 3:16–17

Son gave Him to us for the purpose of revealing and glorifying Christ Jesus in us.

The heavenly Christ must become for us a real and living personality who is always with us and in us. Our life on earth can be lived every day in unbroken fellowship with our Lord Jesus. This is the first and greatest work of the Holy Spirit in the believer, that we should know and experience Christ as our life.

The thought has come to me that perhaps our concept of the Lord Jesus in heaven is too limited. We think of Him in the splendor and glory of God's throne. We also think of the incredible love that moved Him to give himself for us. But we forget that, above all, He was known here on earth as the Crucified One.

I feel deeply that the Cross is Christ's highest glory. The Holy Spirit neither has done nor can do anything greater or more glorious than He did when Christ "through the eternal Spirit offered himself unblemished to God" (Hebrews 9:14). It was the spirit of the cross that made Christ the object of His Father's good pleasure, of the worship of the angels, of the love and confidence of all the redeemed.

Because of this, it is evident that the Holy Spirit can do nothing greater or more glorious for us than to bring us into the fellowship of that Cross and work out in us the same spirit that was seen in our Lord Jesus.

Living a Prayerful Life

WAITING ON GOD FOR THOSE IN DARKNESS

I will wait for the LORD, who is hiding his face from the house of Jacob. I will put my trust in him.
ISAIAH 8:17

HERE WE HAVE A SERVANT of God waiting on Him not for himself but for his people, from whom God was hiding His face. It suggests to us how our waiting on God, though it begins with our personal needs or with the desire for a revelation of Him, does not need to stop there. We may be walking in the full light of God's approval, while God is hiding His face from His people around us. Far from being content to think that this is the punishment they deserve for their sin or the consequence of their indifference, we are called with tender hearts to think of their sad condition and to wait on God on their behalf. The privilege of waiting on God is one that brings with it great responsibility. Christ entered God's presence and at once used His position of privilege and honor as intercessor. With the same determination, if we know what it is to enter in and wait on God, we must use our access for those who still live in darkness.

Believe that God can and will help. Let the spirit of the prophet Isaiah come into you as you meditate on his words, and set yourself to wait for God on behalf of His people who have gone astray. Instead of feeling judgment, condemnation, or despair, realize your calling to wait on God. If others fail in doing it, give yourself to it all the more. The deeper the darkness, the greater the need to appeal to our one and only Deliverer. The more you see self-confidence in people around you, not knowing they are poor and miserable and blind, the more urgent the call is to you who profess to see the evil and have access to Him who alone can help, to be on your knees waiting on God.

Waiting on God

THE GUARANTEE OF THE
NEW COVENANT

SCRIPTURE SPEAKS OF the old covenant as not being faultless; God complains that Israel did not continue in it and so He disregarded them. The prob-

Jesus has become the guarantee of a better covenant.
HEBREWS 7:22

lem was that the old covenant did not secure its apparent object of uniting Israel and God. Therefore, God promises to make a new covenant, able to accomplish its purpose. "I will put My laws into their mind"; in this way God seeks to secure their unchanging faithfulness to Him. "Their sins and their lawless deeds I will remember no more" (see Hebrews 8:10–12 NKJV); this will be the means of assuring His unchanging faithfulness to them. A pardoning God and an obedient people: These are the two parties who are to meet and be eternally united in the new covenant.

The most beautiful provision of this new covenant is that of the guarantee in whom its fulfillment on both parts is assured. Jesus was made the guarantee of the better covenant. To man He became the guarantee that God would faithfully fulfill His part, so that man could confidently depend upon God to pardon, accept, and never again forsake them. And to God He likewise became the guarantee that man would faithfully fulfill his part so that God could bestow on him the blessing of the covenant. All that man must be and do is secured in Christ. The believer who abides in Him has divine assurance for the fulfillment of every promise of the covenant.

It is in the Resurrection that the glory of Christ as guarantee for the covenant consists: He ever lives. If His life unceasingly, moment by moment, rises to the Father for us and descends to us from the Father, then to abide moment by moment is easy, even simple. In each moment of conscious communion with Him let us say, "Jesus, our guarantor, keeper, ever-living Savior, in whose life I live, I abide in you."

Abiding in Christ

THE COST OF
DAILY RENEWAL

Therefore we do not lose heart. Though outwardly we are wasting away, yet inwardly we are being renewed day by day.
2 CORINTHIANS 4:16

IT IS NOT A SMALL or an easy thing to be a full-grown strong Christian. On God's side, it cost the Son of God His life; the mighty power of God is needed to re-create a person; and only the unceasing daily care of the Holy Spirit can maintain that life. From our side, it demands that when our new self is put on, the old is put off. All the dispositions, habits, pleasures of our own nature that make up the life we have lived are to be put away. All we have by our birth from Adam is to be sold if we are to possess the pearl of great price. We must cast away not only all sin but everything, however needful, legitimate, or precious, that may become an occasion for sin; we must "pluck out the eye" or "cut off the hand," as it were, to avoid sin. We must hate our own life—lose our own life—if we are to live in "the power of an endless life." To be a true Christian is a far more serious thing than most people realize.

This is especially true of the daily renewing of the inward person. Paul speaks of it as being accompanied and conditioned by the "destroying" of the "earthly tent" or outward man. The whole epistle (2 Corinthians) shows us how the fellowship of the sufferings of Christ, including conformity to His death, was the secret of his life of power and blessing to the church. "We always carry around in our body the death of Jesus, so that the life of Jesus may also be revealed in our body. For we who are alive are always being given over to death for Jesus' sake, so that his life may be revealed in our mortal body" (2 Corinthians 4:10–11). The full experience of the life in Christ in our person, our body, and our work for others, depends upon our fellowship in His suffering and death. There can be no renewal of the inward man without the sacrifice and death of the outward.

The Believer's Daily Renewal

WAITING ON GOD IN HUMBLE FEAR AND HOPE

FEAR AND HOPE ARE generally thought to be in conflict with each other. In the presence and worship of God, they are found side by side in perfect harmony. In God, all apparent contradictions are reconciled: righteousness and peace, judgment and mercy, holiness and love, infinite power and infinite gentleness. There is a fear of punishment that is cast out entirely by perfect love. But there is another fear that speaks of awe and respect. In the song of Moses and the Lamb they sang, "Who shall not fear You, O Lord, and glorify Your name?" (Revelation 15:4 NKJV).

The true fear of God does not keep us from hope. On the contrary, it stimulates and strengthens hope. The lower we bow before Him, the deeper we feel we have nothing to hope in but His mercy and the bolder we are to trust Him. Let every exercise of waiting on God be pervaded by abounding hope—a hope as bright and boundless as God's mercy.

Think about the God on whom we wait: His eye is on those who fear Him, on those who hope in His mercy to deliver them and to keep them alive. He doesn't say He will always prevent the *danger* of death and famine—this is sometimes needed to stir up men to wait on Him—but He does say He will deliver them and keep them alive. The dangers are often very real and dark; the situation, whether in the natural or spiritual life, may appear to be utterly hopeless. But there is always hope: God's eye is on us.

> *Behold, the eye of the LORD is on those who fear Him, on those who hope in His mercy, to deliver their soul from death, and to keep them alive in famine. Our soul waits for the LORD; He is our help and our shield. For our heart shall rejoice in Him, because we have trusted in His holy name. Let Your mercy, O LORD, be upon us, just as we hope in You.*
>
> PSALM 33:18–22 (NKJV)

Waiting on God

The Primary Aim of Bible Study Is Holiness

Sanctify them by the truth; your word is truth.
JOHN 17:17

IN HIS GREAT INTERCESSORY prayer, our Lord spoke of the words the Father had given Him, of His passing them on to His disciples, and of their receiving and believing them. This is what made them disciples. Their obedience to His words would enable them to live the life and do the work of a true disciple. Receiving the words of God and obeying them is the mark of true discipleship. Our Lord asked the Father to sanctify them through the Word and that He would keep them while they remained in the world after He left it.

No diligence in Bible study will benefit us unless it makes us humbler and holier people. In all our study of the Word, this must be our goal. The reason there is often so much Bible reading with so little resultant Christlike character is that salvation "through the sanctifying work of the Spirit and through belief in the truth" (2 Thessalonians 2:13) is not always sought. People imagine that if they study the Word and accept its truths, it will in some way, of itself, benefit them. But experience teaches that it does not. The fruit of holy character, a consecrated life, and power to bless others comes only when that is what we seek.

Only God can make us holy by His Word. The Word apart from God and His direct intervention avails nothing. The Word is an instrument; God himself must use it. God is the Holy One. He alone can make something holy. The unspeakable value of God's Word is that it is God's means of holiness. The terrible mistake of many is that they forget that God alone can use it or make it effective.

It is not enough that I have access to the dispensary of a physician. I need him to prescribe a medication for me. Without him, my use of medicine might even be fatal. The Word did not sanctify the scribes because they did not seek for this in the Word, and they did not allow God to do it for them.

The Believer's Daily Renewal

THE HOLY ONE OF ISRAEL

HERE IN ISAIAH we see how God the Sanctifier is to bring about the great redemption of the New Testament: The Holy One is the Redeemer. God redeems because He is holy and loves to make holy: Holiness will be redemption perfected. Redemption and holiness together

"I am the LORD, your God, the Holy One of Israel, your Savior. . . . I am the LORD, your Holy One, Israel's Creator, your King."
ISAIAH 43:3, 15

are to be found in the personal relationship to God. To come near, to know, to possess the Holy One and be possessed of Him is true holiness.

If the holiness of God is to become ours, to rest upon and enter into us, there must be a holy fear of sin, an aversion to all that would grieve our holy God. Side by side and in perfect harmony with that fear will be the deep longing to behold the beauty of the Lord, an admiration of His divine glory and a joyful surrender to be His alone.

Divine holiness is that infinite perfection of Divinity in which righteousness and love are in perfect harmony. It is that energy of the divine life by which God not only keeps himself free from all creature weakness or sin but also unceasingly seeks to lift the creature into union with himself and into full participation of His own purity and perfection. The glory of God as God, as the God of creation and redemption, is His holiness. It is in this that the separateness and exaltation of God, even above man's comprehension, truly consists.

Do you want to be holy? Come and claim Him as your God, as the One who can make you holy. Only remember that holiness is himself. Come to Him; worship Him; give Him glory. Let self be abased and be content that holiness belongs to Him; He alone can give it. As His presence fills your heart, as His holiness and glory are your delight—as the Holy One becomes all in all to you—you will be holy with the holiness He loves to impart.

The Path to Holiness

WAITING ON GOD
TO REVEAL HIMSELF

And it will be said in that day: "Behold, this is our God; we have waited for Him, and He will save us. This is the LORD; we have waited for Him; we will be glad and rejoice in His salvation."
ISAIAH 25:9 (NKJV)

IN THIS PASSAGE we have two important thoughts: First, God's people have been waiting on Him *together*. Second, the result of their waiting has been that God has revealed himself. They could joyfully respond, "Behold, this is our God. . . . This is the LORD." If we do not yet know the power and blessing of waiting together, we must learn it.

Note the phrase "We have waited for Him." It is stated twice. In times of trouble the hearts of the people had been drawn together, and they had with one heart set themselves to wait for their God. Is not this what we need in our churches, conventions, and prayer meetings? There are conditions in the church to which no human wisdom is equal: ritualism, rationalism, formalism, and worldliness, to name a few—all robbing the church of its power. Culture, money, and pleasure threaten its spiritual life. Whatever power the church has is inadequate to cope with the power of unfaithfulness, disobedience, and dissatisfaction both in so-called Christian countries and in those where the gospel is not known.

The purpose of more structured waiting on God in our gatherings would be much the same as in personal worship. It would bring about a deeper conviction that God must and will do all; a greater consciousness that the essential thing is to give God His place of honor and power. The purpose would also be to bring everyone in a praying congregation to a deeper sense of God's presence, so that when they go their separate ways, they have a consciousness of having met God, of having left their requests with Him, and of knowing that together they can do what individually is not possible.

Waiting on God

The Teaching of Psalm 119

ONE PORTION OF SCRIPTURE is wholly devoted to teaching us the place God's Word ought to have in our estimation. It is the longest chapter in the Bible, and almost without exception every one of its 176 verses mentions the Word under various names. Those who would like to know how to study the Bible according to God's will ought to make a careful study of Psalm 119. We cannot wonder why our Bible study does not benefit us more if we neglect the direction of this Psalm. Maybe you have never read it through as a whole. You would be wise to find the time to read it through, absorb its theme, or at least catch its spirit. If you find it difficult to do this by reading it once, read it more than once. This will help you to see the need of giving it more careful thought.

Oh, how I love your law! I meditate on it all day long. . . . See how I love your precepts; preserve my life, O LORD, according to your love. . . . I obey your statutes, for I love them greatly.
PSALM 119:97, 159, 167

The Word of God becomes a rich and inexhaustible basis for holding communion with God. As we gradually gain insight into these truths, we will find new meaning in the individual verses. And when we take up whole portions and meditate upon them, we will find how they lift us up into God's presence and into the life of obedience and joy that says "I have taken an oath and confirmed it, that I will follow your righteous laws" (v. 106). "Oh, how I love your law! I meditate on it all day long."

Begin to work into your morning prayers the devotional life found in this Psalm. Let God's Word lead you into communion with God every day and before everything else. Make its petitions your own and vow to allow God's Word to make you all the more eager to take that Word to others, whether for awakening souls toward God or strengthening them to follow more diligently in His ways.

The Believer's Daily Renewal

THE SPIRIT OF THE CROSS IN US

"Everything that I learned from my Father I have made known to you."
JOHN 15:15

ALL THAT CHRIST WAS and did was for us. And He desires to manifest in us that same spirit. The spirit of the cross was His blessedness and His glory. May it be for us also. He desires to duplicate His likeness in us and to give us a full share of all that is His.

Paul wrote, "Your attitude should be the same as that of Christ Jesus" (Philippians 2:5). The fellowship of the cross is not only a holy duty for us, but an unspeakably blessed privilege.

When the Lord told His disciples that they must take up the cross and follow Him, from their frame of reference, they could hardly have understood His meaning. But He wanted to stir up their thinking, and so prepare them for the time when they would see Him carrying His cross. From the Jordan forward, where He had presented himself to be baptized and counted among sinners, He carried the cross in His heart. That is to say, He was always conscious that the sentence of death, because of sin, rested on Him, and that He must bear it to completion. As the disciples thought about this, and wondered what He meant, only one thing helped them to grasp it: In their day, carrying a cross was the language of a man who had been sentenced to death and must carry his cross to the appointed place.

About the same time, Christ had said, "Whoever finds his life will lose it, and whoever loses his life for my sake will find it" (Matthew 10:39). He taught them that they must despise their present life when compared to their life in Christ. Their nature was so sinful that nothing less than death could deliver them.

So in a small sense they were prepared to see that the cross that Christ carried represented the power to deliver them from sin, and that they must first receive from Him the true spirit of the cross.

Living a Prayerful Life

ALL GROWTH IN the spiritual life is connected with a clearer insight into what Jesus is to us. The more I realize that Christ must be all to me and in me

"But I have prayed for you . . . that your faith may not fail."
LUKE 22:32

and that all in Christ is for me, the more I learn to live the true life of faith, which in dying to self lives wholly in Christ. The Christian life is no longer the vain struggle to live right, but resting in Christ and finding strength in Him as our life, to fight the fight and gain the victory of faith.

This is especially true of the life of prayer. As it, too, comes under the law of faith alone and is seen in the light of the fullness and completeness there is in Jesus, the believer understands that prayer need no longer be a matter of strain or anxious care but an experience of what Christ will do for us and in us. Further, prayer is participation in that life of Christ that on earth as in heaven ever ascends to the Father. We can begin to pray not only trusting in the merits of Jesus and in the intercession by which our unworthy prayers are made acceptable, but also in that close union by which He prays in us and we in Him. He lives in us. Because He prays, we pray. Just as the disciples, when they saw Jesus pray, asked Him to make them partakers of what He knew of prayer, so we, seeing Him as our Intercessor on the throne, know that we participate with Him in the life of prayer.

In the incarnation and resurrection of Jesus the wonderful reconciliation took place by which man became partaker of the divine life. But the real personal appropriation of this reconciliation in each of His members here below cannot take place without the unceasing exercise of His divine power. In all conversion and sanctification, in every victory over sin and the world, there is a flowing forth of the power of Him who is mighty to save.

Teach Me to Pray

WAITING ON GOD WITH THE WHOLE HEART

Trust in the LORD with all your heart, and lean not on your own understanding.
PROVERBS 3:5 (NKJV)

THE FRUIT OF OUR WAITING depends on the state of our heart. As a man's heart is, so is he before God. We can advance no further or deeper into the Holy Place of God's presence than our heart is prepared for it by the Holy Spirit.

It is with the heart that man believes and comes into contact with God. It is in the heart that God has given His Holy Spirit to reveal the presence and power of God working in us. In our efforts to follow God, it is the heart that must trust, love, worship, and obey. The mind is completely incapable of creating or maintaining the spiritual life. It is the heart that must wait on God.

It is the same in the physical life. My mind may dictate what to eat and drink and even understand how the food nourishes me. But reason cannot do the nourishing. The body's organs are for that purpose. And so reason may tell me what God's Word says, but it can do nothing about feeding my soul with the bread of life—the heart alone can do this by faith and trust in God.

Remember the difference between *knowing* with the mind and *believing* with the heart. Beware of the temptation to lean on your understanding. Present your heart to Him as that wonderful part of your spiritual nature in which God reveals himself and by which you can know Him. Develop confidence that though you cannot see into your heart, God is working there by His Holy Spirit. Allow the heart to wait at times in perfect silence and quiet; in its hidden depths God will work. Be confident of this. Give your whole heart, with its secret workings, into God's hands continually. He wants possession of your heart and He will take it.

"Be of good courage, and He shall strengthen your heart, all you who hope in the LORD" (Psalm 31:24 NKJV). *My soul, wait only on God!*

Waiting on God

THROUGH THE HOLY SPIRIT

HOW BEAUTIFUL IS the thought of a life always abiding in Christ! The longer we think of it, the more attractive it becomes. And yet how often the precious words "Abide in Me" are heard by a young disciple with a sigh! It is as if he

The anointing which you have received from Him abides in you . . . and just as it has taught you, you will abide in Him.
1 JOHN 2:27 (NKJV)

does not understand what they mean or how such full enjoyment can be reached. He longs for someone who can make it perfectly clear, and continually reassure him that such abiding is indeed within his reach. If only this one would listen carefully to the word we have from John this day; what hope and joy it would bring! It gives us divine assurance that we have the anointing of the Holy Spirit to teach us all things, including how to abide in Christ.

Thoughts like these come from an error that is very common among believers. They imagine that the Spirit, in teaching them, must reveal the mysteries of the spiritual life first to their intellect, and afterward in their experience. And God's way is just the opposite of this. What holds true of all spiritual truth is especially true of abiding in Christ: *We must live and experience truth in order to know it.* Life-fellowship with Jesus is the only school for the science of heavenly things. "You do not understand now, but you will know after this" (John 13:7 NKJV) is a law of the kingdom. By faith he knows that the blessed Spirit within is doing His work silently but surely, guiding him into a life of full abiding and unbroken communion.

On the strength of God's promise, trusting in His faithfulness, the believer yields himself to the leading of the Holy Spirit without insisting on having it made clear to the intellect first what He is to do, but consenting to let Him do His work in the soul, and afterward come to know what He has done.

Abiding in Christ

HAVING BEGUN IN THE SPIRIT . . .

Did you receive the Spirit by observing the law, or by believing what you heard? Are you so foolish? After beginning with the Spirit, are you now trying to attain your goal by human effort?
GALATIANS 3:2–3

AS WE LOOK AT the church as a whole we see so many indications of weakness, failure, sin, and shortcoming, that we are compelled to ask, How can this be? Is there any excuse for the church of Christ to be living in such a low state? Is it actually possible for God's people to always live in the joy and strength of their God?

We find in more than one of the epistles an answer to that question. In some of the epistles, such as 1 Thessalonians, Paul writes to the believers, in effect: "I want you to grow, to abound, to increase more and more." They were young, and although there were things lacking in their faith, their condition was satisfactory and gave Paul great joy. But there are other epistles where he takes a very different tone, especially the epistles to the Corinthians and the Galatians. He tells them in many different ways that the reason they were not living as believers are meant to live is that many of them were under the power of their flesh. Having begun in the Spirit, they tried to perfect the work that the Spirit had begun by their own fleshly effort.

God has called the church to live in the power of the Holy Spirit, yet it is living for the most part in the power of human flesh, of will and energy and effort apart from the Spirit of God.

If the Galatians who received the Holy Spirit in power were tempted to go astray by perfecting in the flesh what had been begun in the Spirit, how much more believers today who barely understand that they have received the Holy Spirit, or if they do, seldom think of it and seldom praise God for it!

Absolute Surrender

THE HOLY TRINITY

THIS PASSAGE HAS OFTEN been regarded as one of the highest expressions of what the life of a believer can be on earth. And yet this view may foster the idea that such an experience is to be regarded as exceptional, hiding the fact that in varying degrees it is to be the heritage of every child of God.

Each day we are to be content with nothing less than the indwelling of Christ by faith, a life rooted in love and strengthened to know more of the love of Christ. Each day God fills us afresh with all the fullness of God, as we walk in obedience. We can be strong in God's power, giving Him glory in Christ, for He is able to do more than all we ask or imagine, according to his power that is at work within us.

These words are remarkable for the way in which they present the truth of

For this reason I kneel before the Father. . . . I pray that out of his glorious riches he may strengthen you with power through his Spirit in your inner being, so that Christ may dwell in your hearts through faith. And I pray that you, being rooted and established in love, may have power, together with all the saints, to grasp how wide and long and high and deep is the love of Christ, and to know this love that surpasses knowledge—that you may be filled to the measure of all the fullness of God.
EPHESIANS 3:14; 16–19

the Trinity and its bearing on our practical life. Our text reveals the wonderful relationship and the perfect unity that exists in the Trinity. The Spirit is within us as the power of God, and yet He does not work according to our will or His own. It is the Father who, according to the riches of His glory, grants us to be strengthened by His Spirit in the inner person. The presence of the Spirit within us renders us more absolutely and unceasingly dependent on the Father.

The Believer's Daily Renewal

THE SPIRIT AND THE BLOOD

For there are three that testify: the Spirit, the water and the blood; and the three are in agreement.
1 JOHN 5:7–8

WHAT FIRST DEMANDS our attention here is that it is through the Spirit alone that the blood has its efficacy and power. We read in the epistle to the Hebrews (9:14): "How much more, then, will the blood of Christ, who through the eternal Spirit offered himself unblemished to God, cleanse our consciences from acts that lead to death, so that we may serve the living God!" The blood possesses its power to cleanse and to make us fit to serve the living God by the eternal Spirit, who was in our Lord when He shed His blood.

Eternal is one of the words of Scripture that everyone thinks he understands, but there are few who realize its truly deep and glorious meaning. It is supposed that "eternal" is something that always continues, something that has no end. But when Scripture speaks of eternal life, eternal redemption, or eternal joy, it means much more than that these have no end. He who has a share in eternal blessedness possesses something in which the power of an endless life is at work; something in which there can be no change; neither can it suffer any diminution. Scripture's use of the word teaches us that if our faith lays hold of what is *eternal*, it will manifest itself in us as a power superior to all the changeableness of our mind or feelings, with a youth that never grows old and a freshness that does not for a moment wither.

We know that the outpouring of the blood was followed by the outpouring of the Spirit. As long as sin was not atoned for, God by His Spirit could not take up a settled abode in the heart of man.

Children of God, come and let the precious blood prepare you for being filled with His Spirit, so that the Lamb that was slain for you may have the reward of His labor and He and you together may be satisfied in His love.

The Blood of Christ

NO ONE MAY EAT at the Lord's Table without self-examination. The danger of unworthy participation is always present. The possibility of sinning against the body and blood of the Lord is a serious matter. Everyone who truly desires to receive a blessing at the table will be willing to obey the command of our Lord: "Examine yourselves."

A man ought to examine himself before he eats of the bread and drinks of the cup. . . . Examine yourselves to see whether you are in the faith; test yourselves. Do you not realize that Christ Jesus is in you—unless, of course, you fail the test?

1 CORINTHIANS 11:28;
2 CORINTHIANS 13:5

The task of self-examination is simple. According to the apostle there are only two possibilities: either Jesus Christ is in you, or He is not. The manifestation of His life in you may still be less than it could be, but if you are truly born again and a child of God, *Christ is in you*. And as His child you have access to the table of the Father and a share in the children's bread. But if Christ is not in you, nothing you do or are or even desire makes you acceptable to God. The God against whom you have sinned inquires about only one thing: whether you have received His Son. If Christ is in you, you are acceptable to the Father. But if Christ is not in you, you are lost. You have come in to the wedding supper without your wedding garment. You are unworthy. And you eat judgment to yourself.

What will God say of you when He sees you at the table? Will He look upon you as one of His children, who is always welcome, or as an intruder, who has no right to be there? Ask yourself whether you are in the faith. If you know that you do not have Christ, you may receive Him even today. There is still time. Without delay, give yourself to Christ; in Him you have a right to the Lord's Table.

The Lord's Table

Walking by the Spirit

I say then: Walk in the Spirit, and you shall not fulfill the lust of the flesh. . . . And those who are Christ's have crucified the flesh with its passions and desires. If we live in the Spirit, let us also walk in the Spirit.
GALATIANS 5:16, 24–25
(NKJV)

"IF WE LIVE IN the Spirit, let us also walk in the Spirit." These words suggest to us the difference between the sickly and the healthy Christian. In the former, the Christian is content to *live* in the Spirit; he is satisfied, knowing he has new life, but he does not *walk* in the Spirit. The true believer, or healthy follower of Christ, is not content with simply knowing he is born of the Spirit. He daily walks in the Spirit that he might not fulfill the lusts of the flesh.

As we strive to walk worthy of God and well-pleasing to Him in all things, we are often troubled by the power of sin. One of the deepest secrets of the Christian life is to know that the power that keeps the Spirit from ruling our life is the power of the flesh. If you know what the flesh is and how it can be dealt with, you will be a conqueror. As long as the flesh and self-effort and self-will have any influence in your serving God, you will serve sin. The only way to render the flesh powerless to do evil is to render it powerless in its attempts to do good.

"Those who are Christ's have crucified the flesh." We often speak of crucifying the flesh as something that is yet to be done. Scripture speaks of it as something that is already done. Our "old man," or old nature, was crucified with Christ. Through the cross the world has been crucified to me and I to the world (Galatians 6:14). The power of this truth depends upon its being known, accepted, and acted upon. If I only know the cross in its substitution, but not its fellowship, I can never experience its power to sanctify.

The Spirit of Christ

CHRIST THE HIGH PRIEST

IN HIS PARTING ADDRESS, Jesus gives His disciples the full revelation of what the new life was to be when once the kingdom of God had come in power.

"Father, I want those you have given me to be with me where I am."
JOHN 17:24

In the indwelling of the Holy Spirit, in union with Him, the heavenly Vine, in their going forth to witness and to suffer for Him, they were to find their true calling and blessing. While telling of their future new life, the Lord repeatedly gave the most unlimited promises as to the power their prayers would have.

To let His disciples have the joy of knowing what His intercession for them in heaven as their High Priest would be, He gave this precious legacy of His prayer to the Father. He did this at the same time because they as priests were to share in His work of intercession that they and we might know how to perform this holy work. In the teaching of our Lord on this last night, we learn to understand that these astonishing prayer-promises have not been given on our own behalf but in the interest of the Lord and His kingdom. From the Lord alone we learn what the prayer in His name should be and what it should accomplish. We have seen that to pray in His name is to pray in perfect unity with Him. The high-priestly prayer teaches all that prayer in the name of Jesus can ask and expect to receive.

This prayer is divided into three parts. Our Lord first prays for himself (John 17:1–5), then for His disciples (vv. 6–19), and finally for all the believing people through all ages (vv. 20–26). Followers of Jesus who dedicate themselves to the work of intercession and want to pray down blessing upon their circle in the name of Jesus, will submit humbly to the guidance of the Spirit and see this prayer as an important prayer lesson.

Teach Me to Pray

Waiting Only on God

My soul, wait silently for God alone, for my expectation is from Him. He only is my rock and my salvation; He is my defense; I shall not be moved.
Psalm 62:5–6 (NKJV)

THERE IS ONLY ONE GOD, one source of life and happiness for the heart. You desire to be good. "No one *is* good but One, that is, God" (Matthew 19:17 NKJV), and there is no possible goodness except what is received directly from Him. You have tried to be holy. "No one is holy like the LORD, for there is none besides You, nor is there any rock like our God" (1 Samuel 2:2 NKJV), and there is no holiness except what He breathes in you by His Spirit. You would live and work for God and His kingdom, for men and their salvation. "Have you not known? Have you not heard? The everlasting God, the LORD, the Creator of the ends of the earth, neither faints nor is weary. His understanding is unsearchable. He gives power to the weak, and to those who have no might He increases strength. . . . Those who wait on the LORD shall renew their strength" (Isaiah 40:28–29, 31 NKJV).

You will not find many who can help you in this. There will be plenty of fellow Christians who will entice you to put your trust in churches and doctrines, in schemes and plans and human devices, in special men of God, and in special ways of receiving grace. "He removed the high places and broke the sacred pillars, cut down the wooden image and broke in pieces the bronze serpent that Moses had made; for until those days the children of Israel burned incense to it, and called it Nehushtan" (2 Kings 18:4 NKJV). The ark and the temple gave false confidence. Let the living God alone, and none other but Him, be your hope.

No words can tell or heart conceive the riches of the glory of this mystery of the Father and of Christ. Our God, in the infinite tenderness and almighty power of His love, waits to be our life and our joy.

Waiting on God

WE ARE KEPT BY THE POWER OF GOD

THERE ARE TWO WONDERFUL truths about how the believer is kept unto his ultimate salvation. One truth is that he is *kept by the power of God*, and the other is that he is *kept through faith*.

Concerning the first part there is no question. God keeps our inheritance in heaven perfectly and safely. Yet the same God keeps *us* for the inheritance! Picture a man spending his whole life making every sacrifice to leave his children a large inheritance. If the same man took no trouble to educate his children, allowed them to go off in paths of sin and ignorance and folly, what would you think of him? You would say, "How foolish to keep an inheritance for his children but not keep his children for the inheritance." Yet many believers think God is keeping an inheritance for them while they cannot believe God is keeping them for the inheritance. The same God is doing both.

Praise be to the God and Father of our Lord Jesus Christ! In his great mercy he has given us new birth into a living hope through the resurrection of Jesus Christ from the dead, and into an inheritance that can never perish, spoil or fade—kept in heaven for you, who through faith are shielded by God's power until the coming of the salvation that is ready to be revealed in the last time.
1 PETER 1:3–5

Some people think God will keep them in spiritual things but not in temporal things. But when God sends you to work in the world, He does not say, "I must leave now, while you go and earn your own livelihood." Rather, God says, "My child, there is no work you are to do, no business in which you are engaged, but that I, your Father, will not be with you in my keeping power." The greater part of many people's lives is spent amid the temptations and distractions of business; but God will care for you there. The keeping of God includes your whole life.

Absolute Surrender

THE ALL-PREVAILING PRAYER

"I tell you the truth, my Father will give you whatever you ask in my name. Until now you have not asked for anything in my name. Ask and you will receive, and your joy will be complete."
JOHN 16:23–24

UNTIL THIS TIME the disciples had not asked for anything in the name of Christ, nor had He ever used the expression among them. The closest they came to the thought was that they met together *in His name*. Here in His parting words, before He is betrayed, Jesus repeats the word *whatever* in connection with His promises concerning answered prayer to teach them and us that His name is our only and all-sufficient plea. The power of prayer and the answer depend on the right use of His name.

What is it to take action in the name of another? It is to come with the power of attorney for that person as his representative and substitute. Use of another's name supposes a mutual trust.

When the Lord Jesus returned to heaven, He left His work—the management of His kingdom on earth—in the hands of His followers. He gave them His name by which to draw what they needed to conduct His business. They have the spiritual power to avail themselves of the name of Jesus to the extent to which they yield themselves to live for the interests and work of the Master.

There is no one who abandons himself to live by the name of Jesus who does not receive in ever-increasing measure the spiritual capacity to ask and receive in that name whatever he wishes. The bearing of the name of another supposes my having given up my own reputation and with it my own independent life; but then I have also taken possession of all there is in connection with that name.

Believing Prayer

BLESSED WITH ALL SPIRITUAL BLESSINGS

Blessed be the God and Father of our Lord Jesus Christ, who has blessed us with every spiritual blessing in the heavenly places in Christ.
EPHESIANS 1:3

GOD HAS BLESSED US with every spiritual blessing in Christ; He has set Christ at His own right hand; He has made us sit with Christ; the manifold wisdom of God is to be made known through the church to the principalities and powers; we are to be equipped for battling the spiritual hosts of wickedness. The life of the Christian is regarded in this spiritual and heavenly aspect; it can be lived only in the power of the heavenly world.

A believer is to be sealed by the Spirit; taught by the Spirit to know the divine power working in him; kept in the full consciousness of an abiding access to the Father; united with all his fellow saints in the one temple as the dwelling place of God; led into the mystery of Christ among the Gentiles; strengthened with power by the Spirit in the inner man to have Christ dwelling in the heart; and filled with all the fullness of God.

The believer is to walk in all meekness and lowliness; keep the unity of the Spirit; minister in the power of the Spirit for the building up of the body in love; seek to never grieve the Spirit; be filled with the Spirit; fulfill the law of love in all his daily life; be strong in the Lord and the power of His might to fulfill his destiny in wrestling with the powers of darkness by use of the Word and prayer for all the saints.

We all need time, thought, prayer, and quiet waiting on the Spirit of God to see this vision and to maintain it. The Spirit-sealed, Spirit-taught, Spirit-strengthened, Spirit-filled life as described is to be the normal spiritual experience. We need to turn away from self and the world and to allow God to work in us all His purpose according to the counsel of His will.

The Believer's Call to Commitment

THE PRAYER OF FAITH

And the prayer offered in faith will make the sick person well; the Lord will raise him up. If he has sinned, he will be forgiven.
JAMES 5:15

THE PRAYER OFFERED in faith! Only once does this expression occur in the Bible, and it relates to the healing of the sick. The church has adopted this expression, but hardly ever uses it except for the sake of obtaining other graces, while according to the Scriptures it is especially intended for the healing of the sick.

A question arises: "Does the use of remedies exclude the prayer of faith?" To this I would reply no, for the experience of a large number of believers testifies that in answer to their prayers God has often blessed the use of remedies and made them a means of healing.

But we know also that under the power of the Fall and the realm of our senses, our tendency is to attach more importance to the remedies than to the direct intervention of God. This is why the Lord in calling Abraham had not recourse to the laws of nature (Romans 4:17–21). God would form for himself a people of faith, living more in the unseen than in things visible; and in order to lead them into this life, it was necessary to take away their confidence in ordinary means.

God wills to act in a similar way with us. The purpose of God is to lead His children into a more intimate communion with Christ, and this is just what happens when by faith we commit ourselves to Him as our sovereign healer, with or without doctors. Healing becomes far more than deliverance from sickness: it becomes a source of spiritual blessing. It makes real to us what faith can accomplish and establishes a new tie between God and the believer; it launches him on a life of confidence and dependence.

Divine Healing

OUR LORD IN THE seven letters to the churches in Revelation concludes with a promise to each for those who overcome. The phrase "he that over-

In all these things we are more than conquerors through him who loved us.
ROMANS 8:37

comes" is repeated seven times; and with it some glorious promises are given. They were given even to churches like Ephesus that had forsaken its first love, to Sardis, that had a reputation of being alive, but was dead, and Laodicea with her lukewarmness and self-satisfaction—as proof that if they would only repent, they might win the crown of victory. The call comes to every Christian to strive for the crown.

How do we attain victory? The answer is simple. All is in Christ. It all depends on our right relationship to Christ, our complete surrender, perfect faith, and unbroken fellowship with Him. Just as we had no rest until we knew He had received us at our conversion, so now we feel the need of coming to Him to receive from Him the assurance that He has undertaken to keep us by the power of His resurrection life.

Christ, the Victor, is your Lord, who will undertake for you in everything and will enable you to do all that the Father expects of you. Be of good courage. Trust Him to do this great work for you, who has so freely given His life for you and forgiven you your sins. Only be bold to surrender yourself to a life kept from sin by the power of God. Along with the deepest conviction that in you dwells no good thing, confess that you see in the Lord Jesus all the goodness you will ever need for the life of a child of God.

Thank God, a life of victory is certain for those who are aware of their inward ruin and are hopeless in themselves but who have placed their confidence in Jesus. They, by faith in His power to make the act of surrender possible for them, have done it in His strength and now rely on Him alone every day and every hour.

Living a Prayerful Life

THE SPIRIT OF SUPPLICATION

In the same way, the Spirit helps us in our weakness. We do not know what we ought to pray, but the Spirit himself intercedes for us with groans that words cannot express. And he who searches our hearts knows the mind of the Spirit, because the Spirit intercedes for the saints in accordance with God's will.
ROMANS 8:26–27

THE HOLY SPIRIT has been given to every child of God. He dwells in him not as a separate being in one part of his nature but as his very life. He is the divine power by which our life is maintained and strengthened. The Holy Spirit can and will work in a believer all that one is called to be or to do. Of course, the person on his part must yield to the Holy Spirit. Without this, He cannot work, and the person's spiritual life will be less than effective. But as he learns to yield, to wait, and to obey the leading of the Spirit, God will work in him all that is pleasing in His sight.

The Holy Spirit, above all, is a Spirit of prayer. He intercedes for the saints in accordance with God's will. As we pray in the Spirit, our worship is as God desires it to be, in spirit and in truth. Prayer is simply the breathing of the Spirit in us; power in prayer comes from the power of the Spirit in us as we wait on Him. Failure in prayer is the result of a spirit that is not yielded to the Spirit of God. In this sense, prayer is a gauge that measures the work of the Spirit in us. To pray aright, the life of the Spirit must be active in us. For praying the effective, fervent prayer of a righteous man, everything depends on being full of the Spirit.

Each day accept the Holy Spirit as your guide, your life, and your strength, the one who reveals Christ to you. He, unseen but known by faith, gives all the love, faith, and power for obedience that you need.

The Ministry of Intercessory Prayer

THE SPIRIT OF LOVE

LOVE IS NOT ONLY one of the fruits of the Spirit. It *is* the fruit of the Spirit. The other fruits are really by-products of love. The Spirit is nothing less than divine Love come down to dwell in us, and we have only as much of the Spirit as we have love.

God is a Spirit; God is Love. In these two words we have the only attempt

But the fruit of the Spirit is love, joy, peace, longsuffering, kindness, goodness, faithfulness, gentleness, self-control. Against such there is no law.
GALATIANS 5:22–23
(NKJV)

Scripture makes to give us, in human language, what may be called a definition of God. (The third expression, God is Light, is a figurative one.)

Everything owes its life to the Spirit of God. This is so because God is Love. It is through the Spirit that the love of God is revealed and communicated to us. It was the Spirit that led Jesus to the work of love for which He was anointed—to preach good news to the poor and deliverance to the captives. Through that same Spirit He offered himself as a sacrifice for us. The Spirit comes laden with all the love of God.

Complaints or confessions of tempers unconquered, selfishness, harsh judgments, unkind words, a lack of meekness, patience, and gentleness is simply proof that we do not yet understand that to be a Christian is to have the Spirit of Christ, which is the Spirit of Love. We are generally more carnal than spiritual.

In faith that the Spirit of Love is within us, let us look to the Father in earnest prayer and plead for His mighty working in our innermost being, that Christ may dwell in our hearts, that we may be rooted and grounded in love, that our whole life might have its nourishment and strength in love.

The Spirit of Christ

IN CHRIST

"Remain in me, and I will remain in you. No branch can bear fruit by itself; it must remain in the vine. Neither can you bear fruit unless you remain in me."
JOHN 15:4

ALL INSTRUCTION comes first from the outside and then is understood in the mind and heart. When knowledge is obtained of something, whether in word or deed, the mind seeks to uncover the meaning that is not obvious at first. It is the same with the teaching of Scripture concerning Jesus Christ. He is presented as a man among us, before us, above us, doing a work for us here on earth, continuing that work for us in heaven. Many Christians never advance beyond the concept of an eternal, exalted Lord in whom they trust for what He has done and is doing for them and in them. They know and enjoy little of the power of the mystery of Christ in us, of His inward presence as an indwelling Savior.

To all who are preparing to carry the message of Christ to others: Let this abiding in Christ be not only a truth you hold as a doctrine but also a matter of life and experience. Let it energize your faith in Christ and fellowship with the Father. To live in a home means to have all that is in that home at your disposal—comfort, warmth, light, nourishment, shelter. To be in Christ, to abide in Him, is not a matter of intellectual faith but of spiritual reality.

Being in Christ, abiding in Him, means that the soul is placed by God himself in the midst of the wonderful environment of the life of Christ. This life is human and divine, given up to God in obedience and sacrifice, wholly filled with God in resurrection life and glory. The nature and character of Jesus Christ—His disposition and motivation, His power and glory—are the elements by which we live, the air we breathe, our very existence by which we grow and mature in Him.

The Believer's Daily Renewal

VICTORY THROUGH THE BLOOD

FOR THOUSANDS of years there had been a mighty conflict for the possession of mankind between the old Serpent, who led man astray, and "the seed of the woman."

"They overcame him by the blood of the Lamb and by the word of their testimony; they did not love their lives so much as to shrink from death."
REVELATION 12:11

Christ came in order that through death he might destroy him who holds the power of death—that is, the devil. The devil had that power of death *because of the Law of God.* That law had installed him as jailor of its prisoners.

It was through His death and the shedding of His blood that the Lord Jesus fulfilled the law's demands. When the law had been thus perfectly fulfilled, the authority of sin and Satan were brought to an end. Therefore, death could not hold Him. Through the blood of the everlasting covenant God raised Him from the dead. So also He entered heaven by his own blood, to make His reconciliation effective for us.

Even in cases of the most isolated heathen peoples, where the throne of Satan has been undisturbed for thousands of years, this is still the weapon by which its power must be destroyed. The preaching of the blood of the cross as the reconciliation for the sin of the world and the basis for God's free, forgiving love is the power by which the most darkened heart is opened to become a temple of the Most High.

What avails for the church is also available for each believer. In the blood of the Lamb he will always find victory. It is when the soul is convinced of the power that the blood has with God to effect a perfect reconciliation and to rob the devil of his authority over us completely and forever that the temptations of Satan cease to ensnare.

The Blood of Christ

THE HOLY SPIRIT
AND PRAYER

But you, dear friends, build yourselves up in your most holy faith and pray in the Holy Spirit. Keep yourselves in God's love as you wait for the mercy of our Lord Jesus Christ to bring you to eternal life.

JUDE 20–21

TO UNDERSTAND the coming of the Holy Spirit is to open up a new dimension in prayer. We must remember who He is, what His work is, and the significance of His not being given until Jesus was glorified. It is by the Spirit that the Son was begotten of the Father; it is in the fellowship of the Spirit that the Father and the Son are one. It is especially true now, when the Son as our Mediator ever lives to intercede for us.

This gift of the Father was something distinctively new, entirely different from what the Old Testament saints knew. The redemption of our human nature into fellowship with His power and glory, and the union of our humanity in Christ with the triune God were of such inconceivable significance that the Holy Spirit, who came from Christ's exalted humanity to testify in our hearts of what Christ accomplished, was indeed no longer only what He had been in the Old Testament.

The continued efficacy and application of our redemption is maintained in the intercession of Christ. And it is through the Holy Spirit descending from Christ to us that we are drawn up into the great stream of His ever-ascending prayers. The Spirit prays for us without words. In the depths of our hearts, where even our thoughts are at times without form, the Spirit takes us up into the flow of the life of the triune God. Through the Spirit, Christ's prayers become ours, and ours are made His; we ask what we will, and it is given to us. We will then understand from experience that we have not really asked before. Now we can ask.

Believing Prayer

BECAUSE OF UNBELIEF

THE QUESTION MUST be asked: How is it that in the church this mighty power of God working in us is so seldom taught and experienced? Is the whole church in error as it rests content with a far lower standard than what this epistle extends to us? The answer to this question will lead us to discover the root problem.

> *"I say to you, if you have faith as a mustard seed, you will say to this mountain, 'Move from here to there,' and it will move; and nothing will be impossible for you."*
> MATTHEW 17:20

God set Abraham before Israel as the great example of faith in Him, believing that God was able to raise the dead both in his own case and in the proposed sacrifice of Isaac. Yet we know how Israel from the very commencement of God's dealings in Egypt continually grieved Him through unbelief. And through those years, Psalm 78 tells us, "Again and again they put God to the test; they vexed the Holy One of Israel" (v. 41).

Our Lord Jesus continually sought to cultivate in His disciples the habit of faith as the condition for their seeing the power and the glory of God. When He commissioned Paul as the last of the apostles, Paul was used as a witness to the power of faith in all spiritual life and service. And yet just as Israel utterly failed in believing God, so in the church it became evident from the beginning just how little we understand concerning salvation through trust in God alone. We know how utterly the Galatians failed; how sternly the epistle to the Hebrews warns about unbelief; and how quickly the church of the second century was brought into bondage under a system of law. In fact, the entire history of the church is proof of how naturally the human heart turns from grace and faith to law and works.

The Believer's Call to Commitment

THE WAY OF FAITH

*Immediately the boy's
father exclaimed,
"I do believe; help me
overcome my unbelief!"*
MARK 9:24

THESE WORDS HAVE BEEN a help and strength to thousands of souls in their pursuit of salvation and the gifts of God. Notice that it is in relationship to the fight of faith while seeking healing for an afflicted child that they are proclaimed. We see in them the struggle that can arise between faith and unbelief, and that it is not without some effort that we come to believe in Jesus and in His power to heal.

Take note first that without faith no one can be healed. When the father of the afflicted child said to Jesus, "But if you can do anything, take pity on us and help us," Jesus replied, "Everything is possible for him who believes" (vv. 22–23). Jesus had the power to heal, and He was ready to do it, but He put responsibility on the man.

In order to obtain healing from Jesus, it is not enough to pray. Prayer without faith is powerless. "The prayer offered in faith will make the sick person well" (James 5:15). If you have already asked for healing from the Lord, or if others have asked it for you, you must be able to say with faith, "On the authority of God's Word, I have the assurance that He hears me and that I shall be healed." To have faith for healing means to surrender your body absolutely into the Lord's hands and to leave yourself entirely to Him. Faith receives healing as a spiritual grace that proceeds from the Lord, even while there is no conscious change in the body.

How is such faith to be obtained? Say to Him, "Lord, I am still aware of the unbelief that is in me. Nevertheless, I want to conquer this unbelief. I know, Lord, you will give me the victory. I desire to believe; by your grace, I dare to say I can believe." It is when we are in intimate communion with the Lord, and when our heart responds to His, that unbelief is overcome and conquered.

Divine Healing

HUMILITY: THE GLORY OF THE CREATURE

They lay their crowns before the throne and say: "You are worthy, our Lord and God, to receive glory and honor and power, for you created all things, and by your will they were created and have their being."
REVELATION 4:10–11

WHEN GOD CREATED the universe, it was with the objective of making those he created partakers of His perfection and blessedness, thus showing forth the glory of His love and wisdom and power. God desired to reveal himself in and through His creatures by communicating to them as much of His own goodness and glory as they were capable of receiving.

As truly as God by His power once created all things, so by that same power must God every moment maintain all things. Humility, the place of entire dependence upon God, is from the very nature of things the first duty and the highest virtue of His creatures. And so Jesus came to bring humility back to earth, to make us partakers of it, and by it to save us. In heaven He humbled himself to become a man. Here on earth "he humbled himself and became obedient to death" (Philippians 2:8); His humility gave His death its value, and so became our redemption. And now the salvation He imparts is nothing less and nothing else than a communication of His own life and death, His own disposition and spirit, His own humility, as the ground and root of His relationship with God and His redeeming work. Jesus Christ took the place and fulfilled the destiny of man as a creature by His life of perfect humility. His humility became our salvation.

Humility is the only soil in which virtue takes root; a lack of humility is the explanation for every defect and failure. Humility is not so much a virtue along with the others, but is the root of all, because it alone takes the right attitude before God and allows Him, as God, to do all.

Humility

WE ARE CRUCIFIED WITH CHRIST

"I have been crucified with Christ and I no longer live, but Christ lives in me." . . . May I never boast except in the cross of our Lord Jesus Christ, through which the world has been crucified to me, and I to the world.
GALATIANS 2:20; 6:14

PAUL WANTED EVERY believer to live a life that proved they were crucified with Christ. He wanted us to understand that the Christ who comes to dwell in our hearts is the Crucified One, who will impart to us the true mind of the cross. When believers receive by faith the crucified Christ, they in effect give their flesh over to the death sentence that was executed to the full on Calvary. Paul says, "If we have been united with him like this in his death, we will certainly also be united with him in his resurrection" (Romans 6:5).

It is the soul that lives under the shelter and deliverance of the cross that alone can expect to experience the resurrection power of the Lord and His abiding presence. There are many who place their hope of salvation in the redemption of the cross who understand little about the fellowship of the cross. These rely on what the cross purchased for them—the forgiveness of sins and peace with God—but seek to survive for long periods of time without fellowship with the Lord. This is a tragedy.

Many do not know what it means to seek every day after heart communion with the crucified Lord as He is in heaven. In Revelation, John calls Him "the Lamb in the midst of the throne." How wonderful if this vision of Christ could exercise its spiritual power upon us, that we might truly experience His presence with us every day here on earth!

You may ask, "Is it possible?" Without a doubt. Why was the Holy Spirit sent from heaven if it were not to make the presence of the glorified Jesus real to us on earth?

Living a Prayerful Life

THE SCHOOL OF OBEDIENCE

Though He was a son, yet He learned obedience by the things which He suffered. And having been perfected, He became the author of eternal salvation to all who obey Him.
HEBREWS 5:8–9 (NKJV)

FIRST, LET ME WARN against misunderstanding the expression "learning obedience." We are apt to think of absolute obedience as a principle, that obedience unto death is a thing that can only be gradually learned in Christ's school. This is a great mistake. What we have to learn, and do learn gradually, is the *practice* of obedience, to new and ever more difficult commands. But as to the principle, Christ wants us from the very entrance into His school to vow complete obedience.

A child of five can be as implicitly obedient as a youth of eighteen. The difference between the two lies not in the principle but in the nature of the work demanded. Though externally Christ's obedience unto death came at the end of His life, the spirit of His obedience was the same from the beginning. Wholehearted obedience is not the end but the beginning of our school life. A heart yielded to God in unreserved obedience is the one condition of progress in Christ's school and of growth in the spiritual knowledge of God's will. If a man's will is truly set on doing God's will—if his heart is surrendered to do it and as a result he does it as far as he knows it—then he shall know what God has further to teach him.

Study well what gospel obedience is. The Gospel is good tidings. Its obedience is part of that good tidings—*that grace, by the Holy Spirit, will do all in you.* Believe that. Obey in the joyful hope that comes from faith—a faith in the exceeding abundance of grace, in the mighty indwelling of the Holy Spirit, in the blessed love of Jesus, whose abiding presence makes obedience not only possible but certain. Christ, the obedient One, living in you, will ensure your full obedience. That obedience will be to you a life of love and joy in His fellowship.

A Life of Obedience

FAITH

*Then Jesus said to her,
"Your sins are forgiven."
The other guests began to
say among themselves,
"Who is this who even
forgives sins?" Jesus said
to the woman, "Your
faith has saved you;
go in peace."*
Luke 7:48–50

AT THE TABLE of the Lord, Jesus
gathers His friends, and the Father waits
for His children to distribute the children's bread. The table is not the place to
be converted. Salvation is to be sought
beforehand. The table is the place for His
redeemed to confess their Lord, for
believers to have their faith strengthened, for His friends to renew their covenant with Him.

It is through faith in the forgiveness of sins that the soul obtains confidence to draw near to the Lord and thereby also obtain the blessing of
a strengthened faith.

If you are preparing to take the Lord's Supper, do you believe in the
forgiveness of your sins? You know what this means if you are a Christian. Forgiveness does not take away the sinfulness of the heart, nor is it
sanctification, but rather the beginning of the way by which it is reached.
Forgiveness is the declaration by which God acquits you of the sins you
have committed and no longer counts you guilty. Forgiveness comes first,
then sanctification and renewal. For the present, this is the question: Do
you believe your sins have been forgiven?

You know what faith is. You know that it is not trusting in your own
good works but resting in God and in His Word. Consequently faith that
your sins are forgiven is nothing more than the confidence that you, as a
sinner, resting in His Word, have come to Him and that your sins have
been blotted out. You are indeed blessed if you believe this. You have
confidence to draw near to the Lord's Table.

The Lord's Table

THE BLESSING OF A VICTORIOUS PRAYER LIFE

IF WE ARE DELIVERED from the sin of prayerlessness and understand how this deliverance may continue to be experienced, what will be the fruit of our liberty? He who grasps this truth will seek after this freedom with renewed enthusiasm and perseverance. His life will show that he has obtained something of unspeakable worth.

Now to him who is able to do immeasurably more than all we ask or imagine, according to his power that is at work within us, to him be glory in the church and in Christ Jesus throughout all generations.
EPHESIANS 3:20–21

Think of the confidence in the Father that will replace the reproach and self-condemnation that characterized our lives before. Think how the hour of prayer may become the happiest time in our whole day, and how God may use us there to share in carrying out His plans, making us a fountain of blessing to the world around us. We can hardly conceive of the power God will bestow when we are freed from the sin of prayerlessness and pray with the boldness that reaches heaven in the almighty name of Christ to bring down blessing.

Prayer is not merely coming to God to ask something of Him. It is, above all, fellowship with God and being brought under the power of His holiness and love, until He takes possession of us and stamps our entire nature with the lowliness of Christ, which is the secret of all true worship.

This does not come to us all at once. God has great patience with His children. He bears with us in fatherly patience at our slow progress. Let each child of God rejoice in all that God's Word promises. The stronger our faith, the more earnestly will we persevere to the end.

May God strengthen us to believe that there is certain victory prepared for us and that the blessing will be more than the heart of man has conceived! God will do this for those who love Him.

Living a Prayerful Life

WHO SHALL DELIVER US?

What a wretched man I am! Who will rescue me from this body of death? Thanks be to God—through Jesus Christ our Lord!
ROMANS 7:24–25

WHEN WE SPEAK of a lack of prayer and the desire to live a fuller prayer life, there are many difficulties to be faced! We have so often resolved to pray more and better, and have utterly failed. Our prayers, instead of being full of joy and strength, are often a source of self-condemnation and doubt.

It is always important to distinguish between the symptoms of a disease and the disease itself. Weakness and failure in prayer is a sign of weakness in the spiritual life. If a patient were to ask a doctor to give him something to stimulate his weak pulse, he would be told that this is not the issue. The pulse is the index of the state of the heart and the whole system. The doctor strives to have health restored, but he must first determine the cause of the weak pulse.

God has so created us that the exercise of every healthy function causes joy. Prayer is meant to be as simple and natural as breathing or working is to a healthy person. The reluctance we feel and the failure we confess are God's reminders to acknowledge our disease and to come to Him for the healing He has promised.

Your lack of prayer is due to a stagnant state of life. Deliverance is through the Holy Spirit giving the full experience of what the life of Christ can work in us. Do not despair or lose hope, because there is a solution. There is a Physician. There is healing for our sickness. What is impossible with man is possible with God. What you see no possibility of doing, grace will do.

The Ministry of Intercessory Prayer

THE SPRINKLING OF THE BLOOD, AND THE TRINITY

THE TRINITY OF THE Godhead is often considered as merely a matter of doctrine, having no close relationship to the Christian life.

This is not the view of the New Testament when it describes the work of redemption or the idea of the life of God. In the epistles, the three persons are constantly named together, so that in each activity of grace all three together have a share in it. God is triune; but in everything that He does, and at all times, the

Peter . . . to God's elect . . . who have been chosen according to the foreknowledge of God the Father, through the sanctifying work of the Spirit, for obedience to Jesus Christ and sprinkling by his blood: Grace and peace be yours in abundance.
1 PETER 1:1–2

three are one. This is in entire agreement with what we see in nature. A trinity is found in everything. There is the hidden inner nature, the outward form, and the effect. It is not otherwise in the Godhead. The Father is the eternal being—I am—the hidden foundation of all things and fountain of all life. The Son is the outward form, the express image, the revelation of God. The Spirit is the executive power of the Godhead, creating effect or result. The nature of the hidden unity is revealed and made known in the Son, and that is imparted to us and is experienced by us through the agency of the Spirit. In all their activities the three are inseparably one.

The sprinkling of the blood is the full revelation of the Trinity—how wonderful and glorious it is! The Father designed the sprinkling of the blood and elected us to it; the Son shed His blood and bestows it on the obedient; the Spirit of sanctification makes it our own, with abiding power, and imparts to us all the blessings that He has obtained for us. Let this be your joy and your life each day.

The Blood of Christ

THE SPIRIT OF TRUTH

But when he, the Spirit of truth, comes, he will guide you into all truth. He will not speak on his own; he will speak only what he hears, and he will tell you what is yet to come.

JOHN 16:13

GOD CREATED MAN in His image, to become like himself, capable of holding fellowship with Him. In heaven two ways were presented for attaining this likeness to God. These were typified by the two trees: the tree of Life and the tree of the knowledge of good and evil. God's way was the first—through life would come the knowledge and likeness of God; by abiding in God's will and partaking of God's life, humankind would be perfected. By recommending the other way, Satan assured the man and woman that knowledge was the thing to be desired to make them like God. When they chose the light of knowledge over the life of obedience, they entered upon the path that leads to death.

The human race is still led astray by this power of deceit that promises happiness and fulfillment in knowledge. Even when the Word of God is accepted, the wisdom of the world and the flesh still enters in; even spiritual truth is robbed of its power when held not in the life of the Spirit but in the wisdom of man.

When truth enters the heart of man, as God desires it to, it becomes the life of the human spirit. If it only touches the outward life—the intellect and the reason—it becomes nothing more than human argument and wisdom that never really influences the life of the spirit.

The truth in shadow, in form, and in thought, was all the law could provide, and it was in that shell of truth that the religion of the Jews consisted. The truth of substance, the truth as divine life, was what Jesus brought as the only-begotten Son, full of grace and truth. He is the Truth.

Let us embrace the Spirit of Truth.

The Spirit of Christ

It Is As You Came to Him, by Faith

IN THESE WORDS the apostle teaches us an important lesson, that it is not only by faith that we first come to Christ and are united to Him but also by faith that we are to be rooted and established in our union with Christ. Abiding in Jesus can only be by faith.

There are sincere Christians who do not understand this; or, if they admit it

As you therefore have received Christ Jesus the Lord, so walk in Him, rooted and built up in Him and established in the faith, as you have been taught, abounding in it with thanksgiving.
COLOSSIANS 2:6–7 (NKJV)

in theory, they fail to realize its application in practice. They are very zealous for a free gospel in which our first acceptance of Christ and justification is by faith alone. But after this they think everything depends on our diligence and faithfulness. While most firmly grasp the truth that the sinner is justified by faith, they rarely find a place for the larger truth, "The just shall *live* by faith." They have not understood what a perfect Savior Jesus is, and how He will each day do for the sinner just as much as He did the first day he came to Him. They do not know that the life of grace is always and only a life of faith, and that in the relationship to Jesus the one daily and unceasing duty of the disciple is *to believe.*

It is faith that continually closes its eyes to the weakness of the creature—and finds its joy in the sufficiency of an almighty Savior—that makes the soul strong and glad. It gives itself up to be led by the Holy Spirit into an ever-deeper appreciation of that wonderful Savior given to us by God. This faith follows the leading of the Spirit from page to page of the blessed Word with the one desire to take each revelation of what Jesus is and what He promises as its nourishment and its life.

Abiding in Christ

THE SPIRIT THAT GLORIFIES CHRIST

"But I tell you the truth: It is for your good that I am going away. Unless I go away, the Counselor will not come to you; but if I go, I will send him to you. . . . He will bring glory to me by taking from what is mine and making it known to you."
JOHN 16:7, 14

THE SCRIPTURE SPEAKS of the Son being glorified first by the Father, which takes place in heaven, and then by the Spirit, which takes place on earth. By the one He is glorified in God himself and by the other in us.

To glorify someone is to manifest the hidden excellence and worth of that one. Jesus was glorified when He fulfilled all the will of God for His earthly life and death. It is the work of the Holy Spirit to glorify Christ to us and in us. He glorifies Him through us to those who have eyes to see. Of course, before the Spirit could glorify Christ, He needed to go away from His disciples. They could not have Him in the flesh and in the Spirit. Many today know Christ in a measure, but the divine power of His indwelling presence is not yet a reality.

To know Christ after the flesh is to know Him in words and thoughts, efforts and feelings, and as a result of the influence of others. To know Him in this way, we try to learn all we can and believe all there is to be believed of Christ's keeping and indwelling, and yet somehow there is something missing; it is as if faith is not what it should be: the substance of things hoped for. The reason is that faith is still too much the work of the mind, in the power of the flesh and in the wisdom of man.

When the Holy Spirit glorifies Jesus in us, He reveals Him to us in His glory. He takes of the things of Christ and declares them to us with authority. He shows Him to us in personal experience as a personal possession. We partake of Him in our innermost being. All the true, living knowledge we have of Christ is through the Spirit of God.

The Spirit of Christ

WAITING QUIETLY

AS LONG AS WAITING on God is thought of only as a step toward more productive prayer and the obtaining of requests, we will not know the blessing of time with God for the sake of fellow-

It is good that one should hope and wait quietly for the salvation of the LORD.
LAMENTATIONS 3:26
(NKJV)

ship with Him. But when we realize that waiting on God is a blessing in itself, our adoration of Him will humble us, making the way open for God to speak to us and reveal himself. "The lofty looks of man shall be humbled, the haughtiness of men shall be bowed down, and the Lord alone shall be exalted in that day" (Isaiah 2:11 NKJV).

Everyone who wants to learn the art of waiting on God must listen and be quiet. Take time to be away from friends, from duties, from cares and joys; time to be still and quiet before God. Give the Word and prayer high priority; but remember, even these good things may get in the way of simply waiting. The activity of the mind needed to study the Word and to put thoughts into prayer, and the activity of the heart with its desires and hopes and fears, may distract us from waiting on the One who knows our mind and heart. Our whole being is not allowed to become prostrate in silence before Him. Though at first it may be difficult to set aside these activities for a time, every effort to do so will be rewarded. We will find that this kind of waiting gives peace and renewed energy we have not known.

One reason that it is good to learn to wait quietly before the Lord without speaking is that it acknowledges our inability to receive blessing from God on our own. The blessing will not come by our "willing" or "running," or even by our thinking and praying, but by our waiting in His presence. By waiting we confess our trust that God will in His time and in His way come to our aid.

Waiting on God

GOD HAS UNITED YOU TO HIMSELF

Of Him [God] you are in Christ Jesus, who became for us wisdom from God—and righteousness and sanctification and redemption.
1 CORINTHIANS 1:30
(NKJV)

"YOU ARE IN CHRIST JESUS." The believers at Corinth were still weak and carnal, only babes in Christ. And yet Paul wanted them, at the outset of his teaching, to know distinctly that they were in Christ Jesus. The whole Christian life depends on the clear consciousness of our position in Christ.

But the apostle has an additional thought, of almost greater importance: "Of [God] are you in Christ Jesus." He would have us not only remember our union to Christ but also, more particularly, that it is not our own doing, but the work of God himself. As the Holy Spirit teaches us to realize this, we will see what a source of assurance and strength it is to us.

In becoming one with Christ, there is a work God does and a work we have to do. God does His work by moving us to do our work. The work of God is hidden and silent; what we do is something distinct and tangible. As the believer understands the divine side of the work of salvation, he will learn to praise and to worship with new enthusiasm and to rejoice more than ever in his salvation.

What a sure standing-ground it gives him, as he rests his right to Christ and all His fullness on nothing less than the Father's own purpose and work! What confident trust this faith inspires—not only in being kept in safety to the end, but also in being able to fulfill in every point the object for which I have been united to Christ.

The God who has chosen me and planted me in Christ as a branch has ensured (if I will let Him, by yielding myself to Him) that I will in every way be worthy of Jesus Christ. May we fully realize this truth!

Abiding in Christ

A New Spirit, and God's Spirit

IN THE WORDS of Ezekiel we find very strikingly set forth, in the one promise, God's twofold blessing. The first is "I will put a new spirit in you." Our own spirit is renewed and quickened by the work of God's Spirit. The second part is "I will put my Spirit in you." God must have a habitation in which to dwell. He had to create a body for Adam before He could breathe into him the spirit of life. In Israel the tabernacle and the temple had to be built before God could come down and take possession of them. Likewise, a new heart is given and a new spirit put within us as the indispensable condition for God's own Spirit to dwell within us.

"I will give you a new heart and put a new spirit in you; I will remove from you your heart of stone and give you a heart of flesh. And I will put my Spirit in you and move you to follow my decrees and be careful to keep my laws."
EZEKIEL 36:26–27

It is important that we recognize the distinction between the two parts of this promise and blessing. Then we will be able to understand the relationship between regeneration and the indwelling of the Spirit. The first is the work of the Spirit by which He convinces us of sin and then leads us to repentance and faith in Christ, imparting to us a new nature. The second blessing is when the Holy Spirit fills us with himself, setting us apart for holiness and service.

From God's side the twofold gift is simultaneous. The Spirit is not divided: when giving the Spirit, he gives himself and all He is. However, there are indications in Scripture that there may be circumstances in which the two halves of the promise are not so closely linked. The deciding factor is that He is received and possessed only as far as the faith of the believer reaches. Let us believe Him not only for a new spirit but also for the fullness of His Holy Spirit working in us.

The Spirit of Christ

THE PROMISE OF THE SPIRIT THROUGH FAITH

Christ redeemed us from the curse of the law by becoming a curse for us, for it is written: "Cursed is everyone who is hung on a tree." He redeemed us in order that the blessing given to Abraham might come to the Gentiles through Christ Jesus, so that by faith we might receive the promise of the Spirit.
GALATIANS 3:13–14

THE WORD *faith* is used for the first time in Scripture in connection with Abraham. What made him so pleasing to God was that he *believed* God, and so became the father of all those who believe. Just as God proved himself to Abraham as the God who quickens the dead, He revives us by giving us His own Spirit to dwell in us.

Faith is not an independent act by which in our strength we take what God says. Nor is it an entirely passive state in which we allow God to do for us whatever He will. Rather it is that receptivity of soul in which, as God draws near and as His living power speaks to us, we yield ourselves, accepting His word and work in our lives. Faith responds to two avenues of communication: God's presence and His Word. Only when He is present with us does His Word speak to us. It has been said that faith is "taking God at His word." We may have God's Word with all its promises at our disposal and yet fail to receive the blessing we seek. The faith that enters into the inheritance is the attitude of soul that waits for God himself, first to speak His word and then to do what He has spoken. Faith is fellowship with God; it is surrender to God. Such was the faith that enabled Abraham to inherit the promises.

In all our study of the work of the Holy Spirit and of the way in which He comes, from His first sealing us to His full indwelling, let us remember, *We receive the promise of the Spirit by faith.*

The Spirit of Christ

The Father As Intercessor

WHAT A BEAUTIFUL picture of a man in whose heart the fear of God dwells! His greatest concern is that his children not sin against God or forsake Him in their hearts. He is so deeply conscious of the weakness of their nature that even when he does not know of a positive transgression, the very thought of their having been in circumstances of temptation makes him afraid for their souls. He so fully realizes his position and privilege as father that he calls for

When a period of feasting had run its course, Job would send and have them purified. Early in the morning he would sacrifice a burnt offering for each of them, thinking, "Perhaps my children have sinned and cursed God in their hearts." This was Job's regular custom.
JOB 1:5

them to be sanctified and takes upon himself the continual offering of the needed sacrifice. Job is another example among Bible saints of a servant of God in whom faith makes its home and by whose intercession and fear of God his children are redeemed. God could hardly have said of him, "There is no one on earth like him; he is blameless and upright, a man who fears God and shuns evil" (1:8), if this element of true holiness had been lacking. The book might have been complete without it as far as the record of Job's patience and faith is concerned, but we would have missed the much-needed lesson that a man's entire consecration to God implies the consecration of his family life, too.

Through the whole course of God's dealings with parents, from Noah forward, He gives the parent the right and the power to appear and to act on behalf of his child. To grasp hold of the power of this is the very essence of parental faith; to act upon it is the secret of parental authority and blessing. All other influences a parent exerts depend on his being clear on this point: I am the steward of God's grace to my child; I represent my child with God and am heard on his behalf.

Raising Your Child to Love God

The readings in this book have been excerpted and adapted from Bethany House Publishers editions of the Andrew Murray classics with the exception of excerpts from *The Lord's Table*, published by Revell in 1897, and edited by Bethany House for this volume.

The Spirit of Christ, 1979 (newly edited for *The Andrew Murray Daily Reader*)
Teach Me to Pray, 2002
The Believer's Daily Renewal, 2004
Believing Prayer, 2004
Absolute Surrender, 2003
Raising Your Child to Love God, 2001
Humility, 2001
Abiding in Christ, 2003
The Ministry of Intercessory Prayer, 2003
The Blood of Christ, 2001
Living a Prayerful Life, 2002
Waiting on God, 2001
Divine Healing, 2002
A Life of Obedience, 2004
The Path to Holiness, 2001
The Believer's Call to Commitment, 1983 (newly edited for *The Andrew Murray Daily Reader*)
The Fullness of the Spirit, 2004

More Classic Andrew Murray
Edited Especially for *Today's* Readers

Humility: In twelve brief but powerful chapters Andrew Murray takes readers on a journey through Scripture and Christ's life, showing us the utmost need for humility—as opposed to pride—in the Christian life. Demonstrating for us what Christ did when he took the form of a servant, Murray calls humility a distinguishing characteristic of the believer and encourages us to embrace this attitude in our own lives.

The Ministry of Intercessory Prayer: Murray offers practical, biblical instruction in intercessory prayer as well as a 31-day course, "Pray Without Ceasing," at the end of the book. All of this is part of his simple but profound goal to change the world through intercession.

Abiding in Christ: Using the image of the vine and the branches to explain the concept of abiding in Christ, Murray offers a message as timely now as it was a century ago. He urges readers to yield themselves to Jesus in order to know "the full blessedness of abiding in Christ."

BETHANYHOUSE